W9-BKA-667

The Habima—Israel's National Theater
A Study of Cultural Nationalism

THE HABIMA— ISRAEL'S NATIONAL THEATER 1917–1977

A Study of Cultural Nationalism

EMANUEL LEVY

COLUMBIA UNIVERSITY PRESS
1979 NEW YORK

Library of Congress Cataloging in Publication Data

Levy, Emanuel, 1946–
The Habima, Israel's national theater, 1917–1977.

Based on the author's thesis, Columbia University, 1977.
Bibliography: p.
Includes index.
1. Habimah. 2. Jews—Intellectual life. 3. Israel —Intellectual life. I. Title.
PN3035.L4 792′.095694 79-12486
ISBN 0-231-04582-4

Columbia University Press
New York Guildford, Surrey

TO MY MOTHER

Contents

Tables

Acknowledgments

My interest in studying the Habima theater began in 1972, when I wrote a brief research paper for a course entitled "Intellectual Groups in Palestine" given by Dr. Abraham Cordova at Tel-Aviv University. In 1974 this paper was expanded and presented in a research seminar entitled "Historical Dimensions in Social Research" given by Professor Sigmund Diamond at Columbia University. The comments of Professors Diamond and Cordova and those of the students in these seminars helped to clarify the research design of this book.

The study reported here is based on my doctoral dissertation, "The Theater as an Expression of Cultural and Political Nationalism—the Habima Theater, 1917–1968" (Columbia University, 1977). It could not have been undertaken or completed without the support of a number of my teachers. Professor Diamond provided invaluable stimulation and encouragement throughout my work on this study. Professor Gillian Lindt criticized an earlier draft and provided helpful comments. Her encouragement and unfailing interest have accompanied the research from beginning to end. Professor Allan Silver contributed to my early attempts to formulate significant research problems.

Many friends and colleagues have read and commented on earlier drafts of this book. I wish to thank Mr. Harold Clurman, Mrs. Hanna Herzog, Professor Marvin Herzog, Professor Nahma Sandrow, and Professor Yonathan Shapiro, who have all provided helpful comments.

This book gives me the first opportunity to acknowledge my debts to my teachers. My first sociology teachers at Tel-Aviv University included Rina Shapira and Yonathan Shapiro, who introduced me to empirical research. I am especially indebted to the teaching and scholarship of Professors Robert K. Merton and Harriet A. Zuckerman of Columbia University, who in their courses and seminars provided invaluable intellectual and sociological stimuli which a student finds helpful in developing his approach and ideas.

Financial aid from several organizations, which enabled me to spend almost two years, free from other academic duties, studying the Habima theater, is gratefully acknowledged. The Center for Israel and Jewish Studies of Columbia University and the Memorial Foundation for Jewish Culture provided support for an extensive collection of data here and in Israel. I am also indebted to Mrs. Leah Porat, the chairperson of the Council for Culture and Art of the Ministry of Education in Israel, for providing a research grant. Last but not least, I wish to thank Mr. Gabriel Zifroni, director general of the Habima theater, and Mr. Moshe Zanbar, the chairman of the Habima's Board of Trustees, for providing a grant which made it possible for me to devote an entire year to writing. I owe a very special debt to Mr. Zifroni for his permission to examine and to quote from manuscripts and protocols of the Habima that no "outsider" has seen before.

I wish to thank the personnel of the libraries in which this study was researched, particularly Mr. Yaakov Raphael of the Habima Archive who helped me to browse through and use the rich material available there. I also want to thank many of the Habima actors who were interviewed and who disclosed invaluable information. I can only hope that when they read this report, they will feel their time was not wasted.

It gives me a great pleasure to thank Mr. John Dennis Moore, Editor-in-Chief, and Mr. William F. Bernhardt, Associate Executive Editor, of Columbia University Press for the interest they have shown in my book. I also want to thank Mr. William Germano who worked on improving the manuscript. I am indebted to Mrs. Rivka Embon, who helped me to collect some of the data in Israel and who performed with the greatest devotion many other administrative tasks. Finally, thanks to my friends, in particular Natan, who aided and encouraged me at every stage of the research.

December 1978
New York City

EMANUEL LEVY

Introduction

THIS STUDY was prompted by an interest in the artistic and cultural expressions of nationalism—more specifically, in the role of the theater in political and nationalist movements. In the life of a nation, the theater is certainly a social institution which can express the cultural and national aspirations of a people. The theater is not only able to reflect the people's national feelings, but can itself be an effective means of national socialization. Nowhere are language, history, and literature used and interpreted as in the theater. Moreover, unlike many other art forms, the theater is a collective and shared experience and is, therefore, ideal as an expression and instrument of nationalism.

Since Zionism, the Jewish national movement, involved a revival of language and culture, the Hebrew theater would naturally have been a powerful manifestation of this national rebirth. The Habima theater, the first institutionalized Hebrew theater, which later became Israel's National Theater, constitutes the focal point of this study.[1] The Habima was intimately related to Zionism and played a significant role in the revival of modern Jewish nationalism and in the diffusion of the Hebrew language.

The main concern of this work is to account for the political, ideological, and artistic roles of the Habima theater between 1917, when it was founded in Moscow, and the present. The central problem of this study is to identify underlying patterns of change in the roles, structure, and functions of the Habima theater. The major objective is to describe the specific changes in its ideology, mission, repertoire, organization, and audiences between 1917 and 1977 and to analyze the causes and consequences of these changes. The development of the Habima is examined over a time span (sixty years) long enough to permit identification of the major determinants and dimensions of change that the theater underwent.

This study examines five clearly defined periods in the history of the Habima: the formative years in Russia (1917–1926); the period of extensive tours in Europe, the United States, and Palestine (1926–1931); the early years in Palestine[2] (1931–1948); the Habima in the State of Israel (1949–1968); and the Habima as a State Theater (1969–present). An attempt is made to relate the changes that the theater underwent between 1917 and 1977 to changes in the social, historical, and institutional settings within which it operated.

The book's conceptual frame of reference is sociological: it focuses on the social processes of foundation, institutionalization, and secularization with regard to the Habima theater. The Habima is studied with reference to its ideology, functions (political and artistic), social structure, and patterns of relationship between the theater, the drama critics, and its audiences. Systematic comparisons are made with respect to the five periods in the history of the Habima.

The theoretical approach employed is structural-institutional, as exemplified in the writings of Robert K. Merton and Joseph Ben-David.[3] It is the working hypothesis of this study that the various settings of the Habima, in terms of their demographic, age, and political structures, influenced and accounted for the changes in its roles, functions, and repertoire. The institutional approach is fruitful for the explanation of such different issues as the role-definition of the Hebrew actor, the level of theatrical activity, the values attached to the theater by the larger society, theatrical content and style, and the uses made of the theater. In short, the institutional setting shaped not only the activities and organization of the Habima, but also the content that it presented.

The sociological study of art, literature, and drama is a fairly late arrival; unlike other sociological areas, there is no established body of knowledge called the sociology of art. Furthermore, there are scholars who still believe that art is a unique and subjective experience which defies sociological-scientific analysis.

The sociological approach to the study of art departs from other scholarly approaches. Many literary critics, for instance, see literature as a self-enclosed enterprise and approach it in terms of inner structure, plot, delineation of character, and the like. Their work is primarily a textual criticism, focusing on the intrinsic qualities of drama. By contrast, the sociologist employs an extrinsic approach; he analyzes drama in terms of social conditioning factors, such as the demographic, political, and age structures of the society in which it emerges, the ideological and value systems, the social status of the playwright, the significance which a particular play exerts on widely different audiences, and the ways in which it is actually received.[4]

Today, the sociology of art and literature is primarily a European, and particularly French, endeavor. Here, an attempt is made to follow the late Georges Gurvitch's program for research in the sociology of theater. Gurvitch suggested six major issues: the nature and diversity of the public on which the theater depends; the relationship of plays, styles of production, and theatrical tradition to the contemporary social setting; the acting profession, its organization and structure; the relationship between the contents of plays and the social structure in which they were written; the different interpretations that these themes are given at different times and in different societies; and the function of the theater in the social life of its period.[5]

The significance of this study is historical, artistic, and sociological. Historically, the Habima, as a theater intimately related to Zionism, can be seen as a cultural representation of the nationalist revival in twentieth-century Judaism. Moreover, the Habima played a considerable role in the diffusion of the Hebrew language and the Zionist philosophy in the Jewish Diaspora, in Palestine, and in Israel.

Artistically speaking, the Habima was a highly innovative theater which affected and inspired the contemporary modern theater. The Habima grew out of one of the best dramatic schools in the world—the school of Stanislavsky and Vakhtangov. The Habima's 1922 production of

The Dybbuk was one of the most famous productions in the history of the modern theater. It was universally acclaimed as one of Vakhtangov's most remarkable productions. The Habima was one of the first theaters in Russia (and in the world) to use the new artistic style of expressionism on the stage. Indeed, its work has been highly acclaimed by the world's best drama critics.[6] Hence, this study can contribute to the understanding of the social and cultural factors that accounted for the Habima's artistic innovation.

But the study of the Habima theater also has sociological significance. Here the Habima is studied as an example of the political and ideological use of a cultural activity. This study will therefore enable us to throw some light on the general problem of the role of art in political and nationalist movements. This book may thus contribute to the comparative political sociology of art, focusing on the relationship between art and the political arena.

Although this book deals in an intensive way with only one theater, it also has comparative aspects. The Habima is compared in some detail with three other theaters: the old Yiddish theater (until 1918) and the Yiddish theater in the United States in the late twenties; the Ohel theater—the workers' theater (1925–1969)—the Habima's major competitor in Palestine; and the Cameri (Chamber) theater (1944–present), the Habima's current major competitor. The intent of these comparisons is to examine whether the problems that the Habima theater faced—ideological, artistic, and financial—were unique to its operation. Brief comparisons are also made between the Habima and the Russian theater in the late teens and twenties, when the Habima was in Moscow, and between the Habima and the American theater in the late twenties, when the theater visited there.

It is noteworthy that so far no history of the Habima has been written in Hebrew or English, although some paragraphs devoted to this theater can be found in almost every book dealing with the history of the modern theater. Consequently, the history of the Habima has had to be constructed first in order to subject it to sociological analysis. But in the absence of any book which gives the major historical and contemporary details, it was necessary to include much information which might otherwise have been omitted.

The materials on which the research is based are, for the most part, historical, and include primary sources as well as a large number of secondary sources. The primary sources are of five different kinds. First, archives and manuscripts of the Habima's collective and Board of Directors from 1918 to 1968. These archives provided an invaluable information on the artistic policy of the theater in different historical periods; its organizational structure; and its economic and financial practices. They also provided data on the admission of new actors and on every important decision made by the Board and the actors' collective. Second, a large number of files of statistics, which enabled the compilation of the number of performances of each production and the size of the theater's audience in every season. Third, a systematic content analysis, quantitative and qualitative, of the over three hundred productions presented by the Habima. A special emphasis is placed on the Jewish and Israeli plays presented in order to examine the relationship between the content and ideas of these plays and the dominant ideology and social structure prevailing at the time of their presentation. Fourth, a thorough analysis of reviews of all of the theater's productions between 1918 and 1977. This analysis provided information on the yardsticks with which the drama critics approached the Habima's productions in various periods, and on the differences between the artistic taste of the critics and that of the large, lay audiences.[7] Thus, the critical response (as reflected in the critics' reviews) was compared with the audience's response (as reflected in the box-office success). Finally, the primary sources included personal interviews with twelve of the Habima's major actors and actresses (see bibliography). Secondary sources include historical works on Palestinian and Israeli society, works on Zionism and Russian Jewry, books on Russian society and theater, and works on the Hebrew and Yiddish theater.

The sources for this study are located in various libraries and archives: the Habima Archive and the Archive of the Labor Movement, Tel-Aviv; the National Library and the Central Archive of Theater, Jerusalem; the Columbia University Library, the Zionist Archives and Library, and the New York Public Library for the Performing Arts, all in New York City.

The Habima—Israel's National Theater
A Study of Cultural Nationalism

ONE

The Habima in Moscow: 1917–1926

ONE

The Founding Group

THE Habima theater was founded by Nachum Zemach in Moscow in 1917. Zemach was born in 1887 in Rogoshnitzi, a tiny village in Byelorussia, to a lower-middle-class family.[1] He was educated in the *cheder*, the Jewish elementary religious school, and the yeshiva, the religious academy, where he studied the Talmud, the Bible, and the Hebrew language. The ancient language fascinated him and soon became his main interest. He was greatly influenced by Herzl's *The Jewish State*, the first Zionist pamphlet to attract widespread attention, and he was caught by the idea of reviving the Hebrew language. His exposure to a good deal of secular literature created in him the feeling that the small village was limiting his perspective. Determined to make a change in his life, he went to Krinski and after a short time arrived in Bialystok.

Bialystok was then an effervescent center of Jewish cultural life and Zionist associations. Zemach was attracted to a Zionist group called Lovers of the Hebrew Language that strongly urged the revival of the Hebrew tongue. He earned his living as a tutor in Hebrew. Zemach's main concern was to establish a Hebrew art theater, although he had never attended a serious theater before. He spent his free time organizing a number of Hebrew shows with school children, and in 1909 presented a play by Molière. Some of the young players were recruited from the yeshiva and, except for Zemach and a few others, most of the participants did not speak Hebrew. The show, which was presented twice, is considered to be the first play acted in Hebrew in Russia.

Zemach called his amateur group *Habima HaIvrit,* the Hebrew Stage. *Habima* also means the raised stage in the synagogue from which the Torah is read. Since Zemach conceived of the theater as a sacred place, he used this religious symbol as the name of his group.[2] But the governor of Bialystok soon banned theatrical performances in Hebrew and Yiddish, and Zemach was forced to leave the city and move to Vilna. He was already committed to the idea of establishing a Hebrew theater despite the lack of Hebrew plays, actors, or any apparent means of achieving his goal.

In Vilna, Zemach organized a group of adult amateur actors and presented with them a play called *Shema Israel* (*Hear, O Israel*) by Ossip Dymov, the Jewish Russian dramatist. On opening night, May 26, 1912, Zemach delivered a speech in which he said: "I have sown a seed in the ground and it will grow. My aim is Eretz Israel—the Habima in Eretz Israel."[3] The audience consisted of the Jewish intelligentsia, writers, teachers, and students, but Zemach did not get the support he had expected. Besides, in Vilna, as in Bialystok, performances in Hebrew were not permitted by the governor.

Zemach next attempted to gain support for his idea at the Zionist Congress in Vienna in 1913. Here he presented another play by Ossip Dymov—*The Eternal Wanderer,* a historical drama. The director of this play was Yehoshua Bertonov, whom Zemach had discovered in a provincial Russian company. Zemach taught Bertonov Hebrew in a hurry, and the latter taught the amateurs the art of acting and directed the play.[4] The performance in Vienna was not an artistic achievement, but it symbolized Zemach's ambition to present an entire play in Hebrew. As in his previous attempts, Zemach's intent was to demonstrate the use of the Hebrew language on stage rather than to present a high-level artistic performance.

The financial support for which Zemach had hoped did not materialize. Unfortunately, the play was presented only once. According to one source, the Zionists delegates did not attend the performance because it was not scheduled in the program of the meetings.[5] But a delegate who attended the show later wrote that it did not succeed because the creation of a Hebrew theater was not seen as an important issue at that time, and the small audience that did come did not know enough Hebrew to enjoy the performance.[6]

The failure at the Zionist Congress left the troupe penniless, without even the funds to travel back to Bialystok. Exhausted by his labors and disappointed at his failure to gain moral as well as financial backing for his cause, Zemach fell seriously ill.

A few weeks later, the group reorganized itself under Bertonov and Zemach's brother, Shimon. Their intent was to center the dramatic group in Warsaw and from there to tour other Jewish communities. They first appeared in Warsaw, in a one-act play by Sholem Aleichem, *Mazal Tov* (*Good Luck*). Then they went on tour to Minsk, Bobruisk, Vilna, and other cities with *The Eternal Wanderer*. The tour was sponsored by the association of Lovers of the Hebrew Language but was very badly organized and after a few months the group disbanded.[7] Living in Warsaw, Zemach resumed his work as a Hebrew teacher, but soon he met Menachem Gnessin, a Hebrew teacher and actor who had arrived from Palestine. At their meeting, which took place in 1913, the idea of establishing a Hebrew theater called the Habima was reborn.

Gnessin was born in 1882 in Poland.[8] He was a descendant of a rabbinical family and the brother of Uri Nissan Gnessin, a noted Hebrew writer. Gnessin had been attracted to the theater since his early childhood. At the age of eighteen, he went to Gomel—one of the centers of the Zionist movement—and riding the wave of Zionist enthusiasm he emigrated to Palestine, conceiving it his destiny to become the founder of the Hebrew theater there.

In Palestine he worked as a teacher in a Hebrew high school. In 1904, a group of teachers fond of the theater organized themselves at the Secondary School for Girls in Jaffa. They first called their group Lovers of the Dramatic Art; later, Lovers of the Hebrew Stage. The first play to be presented by the group was *Uriel Acosta*, in which Gnessin played the leading role. Their essential goal was "to present shows for the purpose of spreading the Hebrew language,"[9] but they faced a number of difficulties: there were not enough volunteers who knew the language well enough to dare speak it on stage, there were no plays in Hebrew, plays on Jewish topics were scarce, translations were both a technical and financial problem, and audiences were limited. Despite its amateurish character and the lack of supporting conditions for permanent theatrical activity, Lovers of the Hebrew Stage flourished for almost a decade (until 1914). The group's durability is explained not only by its being the only dramatic group in the country, but also in that the group was proving the vitality of the Hebrew language. Gnessin, however, went abroad in 1912; he was the only one in the group of amateurs who thought of the stage as a vocation and therefore felt that he needed further professional training.

The first decision made by Zemach and Gnessin was to draw the attention of rich Jews to their venture; but since well-to-do Jews were not excited by the idea of a Hebrew theater, the two men decided to continue their efforts on their own and, consequently, both resumed their work as Hebrew teachers. One of the main obstacles which they faced was to find theater amateurs who spoke Hebrew. This was especially difficult because they preferred to recruit young and inexperienced amateurs who had not been spoiled by what they felt to be the low-level Yiddish-speaking theaters. Looking for young people who spoke Hebrew, they applied to the director of a Hebrew Seminary for Infant School Teachers in Warsaw who recommended Hanna Rovina, one of the teachers at the Seminary.

Hanna Rovina was born in 1888 in Brazino, Minsk.[10] She received a Hebrew education in a Reformed Yeshiva for girls. Her first teacher was a militant Zionist, and it was he who introduced her to the theater world by giving her parts in the biblical plays that he wrote and presented at school. As she herself later recalled: "I was raised in a small village where a theater troupe never visited. My life would have been completely different had I not had a teacher like Robintchik."[11] She had a strong desire to live in a large city where she could continue her studies, so she moved to Yekaterinoslav, a change which tremendously influenced her spiritual development. But earning a living was difficult there, and six months later she moved to Condsesa, where she worked as a tutor. Two years later she returned to her family but, being restless again, moved to Warsaw. In Warsaw, she attended the Seminary for Infant School Teachers, where she took courses in Hebrew, pedagogy, and

Hanna Rovina as Leah in Anski's *The Dybbuk* (1922), the Habima's best-known production.

education. Teaching was regarded by her as the desirable profession. When she was approached by Zemach and Gnessin about the new venture, she was reluctant to join; after considerable hesitation, she agreed.

The first work presented by the new group was Mark Erenstein's one-act play, *The Eternal Song.* Again, the use of the Hebrew language on stage was the chief element of the production. The second offering was *Marriage,* by the Russian playwright Gogol. The members did not have professional training, nor did they work with an experienced director.

Consequently, the productions lacked artistic merit, and doubts regarding the value of the work spread through the group. In July 1914, with the outbreak of the First World War, the company disbanded, but Zemach, Gnessin, and Rovina decided that no matter what happened, they would not give up the idea of the Habima theater.[12]

Zemach returned to Bialystok where he resumed his teaching. Two years later, in 1916, he moved to Moscow—at that time the center of the theater arts in Eastern Europe. Gnessin and Rovina also resumed their work as teachers, but remained in contact with Zemach. In 1917, both joined Zemach in Moscow.

The Formation of the Theater

There had always been a very small Jewish community in the Moscow of tsarist Russia. In 1890, that community numbered some thirty thousand people who lived there legally or semilegally. An imperial ukase published in 1891 ordered the expulsion of the Jews from the city. It is estimated that in 1894 nearly ten thousand Jews resided in Moscow, this in comparison to over five million Jews in all Russia, most of whom lived within the Pale of Settlement, the poorest part of Russia.[13]

Until 1917, the right to reside wherever one chose and to travel freely throughout Russia belonged only to Jews with university degrees, dentists, pharmacists, and artisans (under certain conditions). It is noteworthy that in 1915 the Minister of Internal Affairs granted permission to Jews to reside in all urban communities, but they were still barred from the capitals, Moscow and St. Petersburg.[14] During the war years, hundreds of thousands of Jews were ruthlessly deported from the border areas to interior provinces. Since it was impossible to resettle them within the Pale of Settlement, Jews were now permitted to reside outside the Pale, and many of them came to Moscow.

The Russian liberals and democrats who assumed power in February 1917 stated that one of the guiding principles of the Provisional Government would be "the abolition of all class, religious and national disabilities."[15] The promulgation of this act ended a long chapter in the history of Russian Jewry. Under the tsars the Jews suffered from constant persecution and frequent pogroms; there were severe limitations on the rights of Jews, including restrictions on residence, military service, participation in elections, and schooling. In tsarist Russia, Zionism had been illegal. The Revolution of February 1917 removed these shackles and led to an unprecedented expansion of the movement. An all-Russian Zionist convention met at Petrograd in May 1917 and was attended by 552 delegates who represented 140,000 shekel-holders in 700 Jewish communities. The Zionist-sponsored educational society, Tarbut (Culture), maintained over 250 Hebrew educational institutions throughout the country. By September 1917, there were thirty-nine Zionist periodicals in Yiddish, ten in Hebrew, and three in Russian. By the end of 1917, there was a strong, well-organized movement with some 1,200 local groups and a membership of 300,000 people.[16]

Zemach arrived in Moscow as a merchant, and this permitted him to stay there. Later, he worked for the sugar industry of Zlatopolsky, the Russian Jewish industrialist, and as a clerk in a bank.[17] From these jobs he was able to save some money. The liberal policy of the Provisional Government and the expansion of the Zionist movement encouraged Zemach to apply for an official permit to establish an association entitled the Hebrew Theater—the Habima. The application was prepared by two famous Jewish lawyers and was signed by Rabbi Joseph Mazeh, the Chief Rabbi of Moscow. The mayor of Moscow approved and signed the permit, which granted Zemach permission to found a Hebrew theater under the name of the Habima.

Soon thereafter a circle of friends of the Habima called Agudat Habima (the Habima Association) was established with Rabbi Mazeh as its head. This association raised twenty thousand rubles from some of the well-to-do Jews in Moscow, with which Zemach leased a theater for one year.[18] Thus, the first financial backing, which was indispensable for the start of the theater, was provided by a group of wealthy Jews, including Zemach's two brothers, Levi and Shimon. However, this support did not last very long; most of the well-to-do Jews left Moscow soon after the October Revolution.

Upon their reunion in Moscow, Zemach and Gnessin began to recruit actors for their theater. At first, they published announcements in *Raszviet*, the Russian-language magazine, and in other magazines, calling for young people to come to Moscow and enter auditions for a Hebrew theater. They received many letters from youths who expressed their wish to come to Moscow but could not afford travel expenses.[19] Since recruitment through magazine announcements proved ineffective, it was decided that Zemach himself would go to various Jewish communities and recruit theater amateurs who spoke Hebrew. This recruitment program was not easy because of Zemach's requirements and high standards: the ideal member was to be young, a master of the Hebrew language, fond of the theater, possessing some acting skill, and, most important of all, ready to devote himself physically as well as spiritually to the theater.

The first group of actors included, in addition to Zemach, Gnessin, and Rovina, six members. This handful of actors began work in the summer of 1917. David Pinski's Yiddish drama *The Eternal Jew* was chosen as the first play, with Mark Erenstein directing. After several weeks of rehearsals the group was dissatisfied with the traditional approach of the director and their own poor training. The members did not want to establish "just another routine theater with the low standards of the Yiddish-speaking theaters."[20] Their newly established theater should be innovative, they believed, a theater that would "justify our performance in Moscow, the center of the theatre-arts."[21] One thing was clear: if they wanted to build a high-level theater, it was necessary to get rid of theatrical stereotypes and to learn, with reverence and devotion, the art of acting. It was decided that Zemach should approach Konstantin Stanislavsky, the director of the Moscow Art Theater, and ask for his advice.

Stanislavsky was then at the height of his fame and influence in the Russian theater world. The Moscow Art Theater, founded in 1897 by him and Nemirovitch-Dantchenko, was one of the world's best theaters by virtue of its extraordinary personnel, notable repertoire, and high standards of production. To approach Stanislavsky was a courageous decision on the part of Zemach, who was not an intellectual or a man of culture and whose theatrical knowledge was quite limited. After all, he was a Hebrew teacher from Bialystok who had hardly seen serious theater until he came to Moscow.

Two major factors motivated Zemach to approach Stanislavsky. The first was the the policy of the government toward national minorities. This policy of national cultural autonomy led to a great revival of cultural life among the small minorities in Russia. Every nationality had the right to use its own language and develop its own culture. In addition, the revolution of February 1917 had abolished tsarist censorship, freeing the theaters from the strict control of censor, police, and clergy. The theaters were also granted much greater autonomy in the choice of plays and in administration.[22]

Second, Stanislavsky, in order to carry out his ideas, had developed several studios consisting of a small number of advanced students from the dramatic school of the theater.[23] Stanislavsky was constantly seeking new forms of expression in the theater, and he was willing to lend his hand to almost any theatrical experiment if he believed that it would help him to improve his artistic approach. He also had a special interest in ethnic matters and dreamed of exhibiting on stage the native drama of all national minorities.[24]

The meeting of Zemach with Stanislavsky was set for Yom Kippur (Day of Atonement), the most sacred day in the Jewish calendar, but Zemach did not dare to postpone the meeting. Years later he recalled this fateful meeting:

> I summoned up all my courage and found an opportunity to tell Stanislavsky about Hebrew culture and our struggle to create an original Hebrew theatre. I went to him in awe, as one goes to a holy man. . . . I spoke to him about the fate of the Jewish people and their longing for Eretz Israel. I explained to him that the Hebrew language, which had for centuries been considered dead, like Latin, in fact never lost its continuity, from the Bible until our modern Hebrew literature. I told him the language is in the heart of the people, that in Hebrew the Jews have expressed and continue to express their longing and desires.[25]

Zemach also told Stanislavsky about the great Jewish actors who had worked in foreign theaters and thus helped to cultivate foreign art. He emphasized that there must be an end to being the guests at foreigners' feasts and that the time had come for the Jews to have a theater of their own.

Zemach was a gifted orator, even in Russian, although he was not fluent in that language. He was a man of extraordinary energy, fanatically—almost insanely—devoted to the passion of his life, the establishment of a Hebrew art theater. He conceived of himself as a prophet with a sublime mission.

Zemach must have impressed Stanislavsky, because the latter replied that the cause was close to his heart, and immediately went on to discuss practical matters. Stanislavsky appointed his best pupil and protégé, Eugene Vakhtangov, the director of the First Studio of the Moscow Art Theater, to serve as director. Although he was a very busy man, he offered to teach the Habima players (and he later did), and he promised to take the theater under the wing of the Moscow Art Theater. Indeed, Stanislavsky remained the Habima's mentor, counselor, and supporter till the troupe left Russia in 1926.

At his first meeting with the actors, the new director, Vakhtangov, ordered the group to stop the rehearsals for *The Eternal Jew* and leave the big theater hall that Zemach had leased. They were to sit down and learn the art of acting from the beginning; this process would last a year or two. The opening performance of the Habima theater, *Neshef Bereshit* (*Evening of Beginning*), took place on October 8, 1918, almost a year after their meeting with Vakhtangov.

Recruitment

In the spring of 1917, there were only three members: Zemach, Gnessin, and Rovina. All three had met and performed in Warsaw in 1914. For all three, the theater was a calling rather than an occupation, and each had been committed to the Zionist cause and the Hebrew language prior to the establishment of the Habima in Moscow. Zemach, Gnessin, and Rovina represented the spirit of the group and highlighted its purpose. They were the core of the founding group and played central roles in the organization of the theater and in the formation of its ideology.

Recruitment to the theater was determined to a large extent by turning points in the artistic work of the troupe. The twelve players who participated in the first public performance on October 8, 1918 belonged to the first recruitment wave. The second wave occurred between opening night and the premiere of the second production, *The Eternal Jew*, in December 1919. In the years 1920–1921 there arose the need for additional actors because of the large number of parts in Anski's play *The Dybbuk*, which the theater was then rehearsing. This was the third and largest recruitment wave, in which more than ten actors joined the theater. From the opening night of *The Dybbuk*, on January 31, 1922, until

The three founders of the Habima theater: Gnessin, Zemach, and Rovina.

the company left Russia in January 1926, only four additional players were admitted.

Most players were recruited in the years 1918–1920. This means that most actors studied with and were trained by Stanislavsky and Vakhtangov. Stanislavsky's lessons were given at the Habima in the winter of 1921, and Vakhtangov worked with the group on *The Dybbuk* between 1919 and 1922. The exact point at which each member joined the Habima was of great importance, because the earlier he joined, the better and longer he was trained. And the longer he trained and worked with Vakhtangov, the higher his social position and prestige within the group. Long after the Habima left Russia, members still ranked each other in terms of the duration of their membership in Moscow.

There were three main patterns of recruiting actors to the group: recruitment through announcements in various magazines and in the street, informal recruitment through personal contacts and acquaintances, and recruitment done or supported by nonmembers. Recruitment through magazines was used by Zemach in the beginning, but on the whole was ineffective. In later years, instead of announcements in magazines they posted announcements, in Hebrew and Russian, in the streets; still, only a few candidates showed up.

Informal recruitment based on personal contacts was the dominant method. The evidence suggests that at one time or another the players met each other, and these meetings—usually accidental—resulted in their joining the theater. For instance, Starobinitz and Grober were recruited by Zemach in Moscow, but they had first met in Bialystok. In the case of Grober, Zemach had attended a concert in Bialystok in which Grober sang in Russian. Impressed by her singing, he later sent his brother to Kharkov, where Grober lived, to influence her to join the Habima. Until then, Grober's wish had been to become an actress on the Yiddish stage; but as she later wrote, "I joined the Hebrew theater due to an accidental meeting with Zemach."[26]

Recruitment was also supported by Chaim Nachman Bialik, the famous Hebrew poet, and Vakhtangov. Bialik had heard Shoshana Avivit reading the Bible in Russian and impressed by her talent recommended her to Zemach, who a few months later called unannounced at her home in Odessa. Zemach affected her by his powers of persuasion and his "holy madness." Zemach, as if in a trance, said to her: "We will appear in all countries, before all nations, we will sail the seven seas, we will carry out what is extremely difficult, we will cross a bridge over an abyss . . . we will eventually arrive in our safe harbor—Jerusalem."[27] Vakhtangov influenced several Jewish members of two dramatic studios—one in Hebrew, the other in Russian—in Kharkov (when he visited there with the First Studio of the Moscow Art Theater) to move to Moscow and join the Habima.

Recruitment to the theater was in many cases accidental and unplanned. A case in point is the recruitment of Aaron Meskin—all the more interesting because Meskin was to become the greatest actor of the Habima and the Hebrew stage. Born in 1898, he was educated at the *cheder* and later studied at a Russian high school. Zionism and Hebrew were far removed from him during his adolescence. In 1918, he came to Moscow as an officer of the Red Army. On one of his first evenings he saw a production of Stanislavsky's at the Moscow Art Theater. It was the first time he had ever visited a theater, and the impact was so great that he began attending performances almost every night. At that time he met two men from his home town who were members of the Habima. They visited him quite often for the simple reason that as a government employee he enjoyed the luxury of a room of his own and plenty of coal to heat the stove. Until then Meskin had not thought of becoming an actor, and certainly not in Hebrew, which he did not speak. However, when he heard that the great Stanislavsky himself would teach at the Habima, he could not resist joining.[28]

It should be pointed out that apart from Zemach, Gnessin, and Rovina, all other members passed auditions before they were accepted into the theater. However, it is difficult to estimate the significance of the auditions for admission. It is plausible to assume that there was some screening. But one gets the impression that at times the auditions were not so much a weeding-out process as an initiation rite for all new members. This is likely to have been true in the case of Yehoshua Bertonov. Bertonov's theatrical career began as early as 1905. He was an experienced actor who had performed extensively in many Yiddish and Russian theaters. However, Bertonov's wide experience and the fact that he had performed with Zemach in 1913 did not exempt him from the requirement of auditioning at the Habima.[29]

At the auditions, most candidates chose to declaim a song or poem by Bialik; usually it was his poem *The City of Slaughter.* This poem was a dirge on the Kishinev pogrom of 1903, written with the indignation and moral fury of an outraged prophet. The choice of Bialik's most violent poem was not an accident. No one before or after Bialik has expressed the Jewish will to live in words of such beauty and poetic force. Indeed, Bialik's *Poems of Wrath* had a tremendous impact upon Jewish youth.[30]

Recruitment and admission into the theater were ideally based on three criteria: knowledge of the Hebrew language; possession of talent and acting skill; and willingness to devote time, energy, and other resources to the cause. In practice, only a few members met all these demands. Knowledge of Hebrew, though only one of the requirements for acceptance into the Habima, was at times more important than acting skill. On the other hand, the evidence suggests that youngsters who were fond of the theater and displayed some acting talent, but nonetheless did not speak Hebrew and were far removed from Hebrew culture and Zionism, were also accepted. Zemach was not happy with the situation but he had to compromise and accept those youngsters who had some acting skill and, more importantly, were willing to join such an odd venture as a Hebrew theater in Moscow.

Indeed, the founders attached great importance to the motivation and readiness of the candidates to devote themselves wholeheartedly to the theater. Miriam Goldina (later Zemach's wife) recalled that in her first meeting with Zemach he told her: "If your wish is to become just an ordinary actress and no more, the Habima is not the place for you. But if you wish to devote your life and talent to the establishment of a theater which might enrich the Hebrew culture and raise the prestige of the dramatic arts with a new style and form . . . then the gates of the Habima are open to you."[31]

The recruitment of almost every member showed evidence of self-selection and self-screening. Many left their families and home towns despite the resistance of their parents. In some cases, even Zionist parents were reluctant to approve their children's decision to leave home and move to Moscow. After all, to join a Hebrew theater that had just begun to operate, and in Moscow, was indeed a strange thing to do. Thus, when Rovina's family emigrated to America, as many other Russian-Jewish families did at that time, they wanted Rovina to join them; but she said, "My family is the Habima and I shall follow the theater wherever it goes."[32] And, indeed, she did stay in Moscow.

The coming together of these performers in Moscow was a miracle in itself. The formation of the Habima occurred during the years of the Revolution and Civil War, in a time of tumult, when all Russia was in chaos. For the ordinary man, railway travel was almost impossible; most passengers were either speculators or soldiers. In these circumstances, the vow of the group of Odessa actors "to arrive in Moscow or to die" was not far from reality. The journey from Odessa to Moscow was extremely dangerous due to the frequent changes of the regime. The Odessa group managed to take the last train to Moscow because one of the military officers fell in love with Tamar Robins, and, consequently, was ready to help the whole group.[33] It is plausible to assume that a sense of high adventure also played a role in the decision of the members to join the Habima. It was so dangerous to come to Moscow that an intense thirst for adventure must have supplemented the motives of idealism, selflessness, and commitment to the cause.[34]

Social Characteristics of the Habima Group

The Habima members had diverse class origins. Gnessin and Chemerinsky, for instance, came from educated families; Gnessin's father was a rabbi and his brother a noted writer, Chemerinsky's father was a writer and teacher. Meskin and Bertonov came from poor and large families; Meskin's father was a shoemaker and Bertonov's a bookbinder. The diversity of class origins suggests that the variable of class did not account for the recruitment and formation of the theater. Furthermore, the cognitive orientation of the Habima was never based on or related to any class orientation. The troupe never regarded itself as a class-oriented theater. Rather, it always aimed at being a national theater, appealing to all strata of the Jewish people.

The Moscow group constituted an age group: the majority of the members were born in the last decade of the nineteenth century and were in their late teens or early twenties when they joined the theater (see Appendix 1). Furthermore, the Moscow members constituted a generation unit, i.e., a social unit bound together by a common structural and historical location, a common cultural system, self-consciousness as a social unit, and social interaction and solidarity among its members. The members "participated in the characteristic social and intellectual currents of their society and period," and were exposed to the symptoms of a "process of dynamic de-stabilization."[35]

The Habima members came of age in a dynamic period in which an intense surge of nationalism was sweeping Russia. They lived in a period which witnessed the awakening of Zionism and the revival of the Hebrew language, and these factors affected their education and socialization. In the first decade of the twentieth century, intellectual and spiritual turmoil characterized the Jewish community of Eastern Europe. "It was a period of extreme restlessness, feverish collective dreaming, pretentious ideological effort. The sufferings of an oppressed people rub against and contributed to utopian expectation and secularized messianic fervor." In this period, "the life of east European Jewry boils over with movements, parties, associations, many of them feeble and short-lived, but others—like socialism, Zionism, Yiddishism—soon to become major forces in Jewish public life."[36]

Since most of the Habima members were in their late teens and early twenties when they joined the theater, the commitment to the cause was highly functional for their personality and identity formation. Ideologies offer to youths "overly simplified and yet determined answers to exactly those vague inner states and those urgent questions which arise in consequence of identity conflict. Ideologies serve to channel youth's forceful earnestness and sincere asceticism as well as its search for excitement."[37]

Apart from the common problems of identity formation that all youth face, one must bear in mind the period in which the Habima members came of age. It was a time of awakening, of excitement, and of political aspirations for both the Jewish and the Russian peoples. Pogroms, repression, and persecution of the Jews, the First World War, the October Revolution and Civil War, to mention only the most significant political events, all took place during the coming of age of the Habima members. This dynamic and unstable social, political, and intellectual climate of Russia undoubtedly affected all youth, Jewish and non-Jewish. An awareness of it is indispensable to the comprehension of the rationale for the formation of the Habima.

Many members were exposed to the Zionist cause and Hebrew language during their adolescence. Some actors were even involved in Zionist study circles and clandestine clubs which sprouted up all over Russia at that time. It was a period in which youth were extremely sensitive to literary influences, especially Zionist poems and pamphlets. Poems of Bialik, for instance, written after the Kishinev riot in 1903, passed from hand to hand. Young people would suddenly change their entire way of life after reading a single poem or pamphlet.[38] The participation of the members in various Zionist clubs strengthened their commitment to the Hebrew culture and language.

Mention has been made of a considerable group of players who were far removed from Zionism and Hebrew before they joined the Habima. However, the dominant orientation of the theater as a whole was a strong commitment to Zionism and Hebrew. All members who had not known Hebrew learned or improved their knowledge of it with Zeev Gordon, the distinguished pedagogue and Hebraist. Regular Hebrew lessons were held until 1924.[39]

Perhaps more importantly, Zemach and all those members who held central positions not only spoke Hebrew but were committed to Hebrew prior to the formation of the Habima in Moscow. They were Hebrew teachers whose attraction to the theater was inseparable from their love and commitment to Hebrew. In many ways, their approach to the theater was mediated through the Hebrew language. As early as 1909,

Zemach refused to join the dramatic group of Pessach Kaplan, the Yiddish writer, because it performed in Yiddish.[40] Rovina's ideal was to be a Hebrew educator and it was the Hebrew language more than any other factor that attracted her to the Habima. And Vardi and Gnessin had both lived in Palestine, where they taught Hebrew and performed in amateur Hebrew dramatic groups.

The motivation of the founding group to establish a Hebrew theater derived by no means from their wish to become actors. They did not consciously choose that career. Rovina, for instance, agreed to join Zemach only "until the real actors arrive."[41] It was the commitment to the Hebrew language which provided the psychological and pragmatic motivations to establish a Hebrew theater, a profession strongly linked to language.

The high rate of mobility of the Habima players before they arrived in Moscow is also noteworthy. Indeed, urbanization and, consequently, a profound dislocation and breakup of traditional society occurred in the late nineteenth century. The large movement of Jewish youth out of the shtetl and into the Russian and Polish cities showed this wish "to flee the economic and cultural stagnation of the shtetl," where one "felt himself stifled and without hope."[42] Most members had been born and raised in small villages, in shtetls. Some were born to Orthodox parents and, therefore, received a traditional Jewish education. However, at one time or another in their lives they all moved to big-city Jewish cultural centers in which they were exposed to and affected by universal (non-Jewish) cultural influences as well as Hebrew and Zionist ideas. Mobility from small villages to big cities was cultural as well as geographical. It was a result of the restlessness which motivated them to change their lives and enlarge their intellectual horizons. Their small villages could not satisfy their intellectual and cultural ambitions, and they felt a strong need to leave their home towns in order to achieve self-realization.

The big cities through which many of them passed were Bialystok, Vilna, Odessa, Warsaw, and Kharkov—all centers of Zionist and Jewish cultural activity. It was also in these cities that most members saw high-level art theaters for the first time.

TWO

Ideology and Repertoire: 1917–1926

THE Habima was not merely an art theater but also a theater that had ideological and political missions. The ideology of the Habima reflected its raison d'être. It consisted of five major elements that were interdependent: the Habima as a Hebrew theater; biblical-historical theater; moral-educational purposes; national theater in Palestine; and high-level art theater. Indeed, the theater's political and ideological components were as important as its artistic components.

The Habima as a Hebrew Theater

The Habima as a distinctively Hebrew theater was the central value in the ideology of the theater and the chief motivation in its founding. Hebrew was the first language to have been used by the Jews as a people. As a result of their dispersion, Jews created new Jewish languages and dialects based upon the languages of the countries in which they resided. Especially noteworthy were Judezmo—used by Sephardic

Jews, descendants of the Jews who were exiled from Spain and Portugal—and Yiddish, the most important of the Diaspora languages. As time went on, the circle of the Hebrew-speaking population grew smaller until Hebrew became exclusively the language of literature and prayer.

Yiddish was a fusion language spoken by Ashkenazic Jews since the Middle Ages. It was the mother tongue of all East European Jewish communities. But in the East European milieu, Yiddish had been regarded as mere jargon, a street tongue: "it had been loved for its pithiness and folk strength yet regarded as unworthy when compared with the sacred tongue of Hebrew." Decades of struggle were required before the learned, modernized Jews could be convinced that "Yiddish could become the vehicle of literature through which Jewish life would regain its bearing."[1] Indeed, toward the end of the nineteenth century there was a change in attitude toward Yiddish. The awakening of the Jewish consciousness, social as well as cultural, led to a flowering of Yiddish literature in Russia, and the Jewish populists and socialists assigned a new role to Yiddish as an instrument for educating and uplifting the people.

Hebrew was revived by the Haskala (Enlightenment) movement in the nineteenth century. And with the revival of Zionism at the end of the nineteenth century, Hebrew became the main symbol of the movement. Hebrew was regarded as a means of reawakening and regenerating the national consciousness of the Jewish people. The Habima, strongly influenced by Zionism, decided to perform only in Hebrew. To Zemach, Hebrew was more than a language; it reflected a program, an attitude to life and history. The Habima's decision to perform exclusively in Hebrew was therefore ideological; the founders regarded their theater as an outgrowth and integral part of Zionist ideas.

But Moscow did not have a large potential Jewish audience. And of the audience it did have, only few spoke Hebrew; on the whole, Hebrew was considered an ancient scholarly language, used by a small minority of religious scholars, intellectuals, and militant Zionists. Furthermore, it was not the mother tongue of many of the actors. Zemach was aware of these difficulties, but he conceived of the revival and dissemination of the Hebrew language among the Jewish people as one of the most important missions of the Habima.

A theater that would perform only in Hebrew was a continuation of

Zemach's earlier efforts in Bialystok, Vilna, and Warsaw. When Zemach prepared the application for a permit to establish a theater in Moscow, he insisted that it would specify explicitly that the goal was to establish a *Hebrew* theater and not just a Jewish theater. He wanted to make sure that the new theater would be legally permitted to perform in Hebrew.

The founders also decided that the Hebrew spoken by the Habima would be in the Sephardic rather than the Ashkenazic pronunciation—a decision based on the speech of the small minority of Jews in Palestine at that time.[2] It is noteworthy, however, that Bialik suggested the use of the Ashkenazic tradition in the beginning so that the audience would get used to the sound of Hebrew, and then gradually to shift to the Sephardic tradition. But the founders were determined not to use the Ashkenazic. They also insisted that the players speak Hebrew in the Sephardic manner off-stage as well as on.[3]

The commitment to perform exclusively in Hebrew was deeply rooted in the theater and was never to change. In later years, when the Habima was persecuted by the Yevsektsia (the Jewish Section of the Bolshevik party) and the theater had practically no audience, some members who had come from the Yiddish theater believed that the Habima should switch to playing in Yiddish, or at least should perform in both languages. These members argued that performing in Yiddish, the language spoken by the Jewish masses, would give the Habima a broad popular base.[4] However, the proposition to switch to Yiddish, or to perform in both languages, was heresy to Zemach and the others who believed that the Habima was specifically created for the purpose of playing in Hebrew. Zemach always insisted that the theater was performing in Hebrew not out of stubbornness, but because its mission was to revive the Hebrew language and to express in it the national struggles of the Jews.

The commitment to perform in Hebrew raised an important question: in which way should the language be spoken? The Habima had no model for a spoken language, no language mannerisms or intonations of living expressions. Thus, as Leah Goldberg, the Hebrew poet, described it: "The punctuation of the Hebrew word on the stage had to be invented. . . . Not to attach the language to reality and not to detach it from reality—but to create a stylized form of speech. And so a stage Hebrew came into being. It was not a realistic use of the language. But since the theater's concept and style at that time were nonrealistic, that stylized Hebrew fitted perfectly the action that took place on the stage."[5]

The Habima as a Biblical and Moral Theater

Zemach saw in the Bible a collection of themes, events, and heroes eminently suited to dramatic adaptation. He wanted the Habima to bring to the world not only the ideas, the thoughts, and the feelings of the prophets, but also the beauty of the language that they had used.[6] Indeed, the group knew that if the Habima was to be a distinctively Hebrew theater, it plainly had to borrow its stock from the historical past of the Jewish people, from the biblical period. To this basic source, dramatic material from later periods in Jewish history could be added, and depictions of the nation's life down through the generations would follow. The Habima was therefore meant to be a theater which would also express the national revival and cultural tradition of the Jewish people. As such, it should not only praise and glorify the past, but should stress the continuous relationship of the heroic past of the Jews and their contemporary present, and in so doing it should have a vision of the future of the Jewish people.[7]

Zemach conceived of the Habima players as contemporary prophets. He considered a deep knowledge of the Bible and Jewish history important prerequisites for being a true Hebrew actor. As Bialik wrote, "The Habima members considered themselves priestlings in preparation for the Service of the Lord in the Temple." Bialik strongly supported the role-definition and images of the Habima: "The Hebrew theater should be in particular the theater of prophetic pathos, one of holy pathos and sacred attitude. . . . Just as the prophets have made use of theatrical means, in like manner should the theater aim toward prophetic and visionary ends."[8]

The Habima was to reach and educate the Jewish people, to communicate with them as preacher and educator. But the theater was by no means to cater to the low artistic and educational standards of the masses. Quite the contrary, it was "to raise the artistic level and enlarge the horizons of the people."[9] The theater was to express as well as to solve the human, social, and national problems of the Jewish people. The founders denounced concepts like "theater for theater's sake," contending: "The theater does not exist for the entertainment of the masses. . . . The goal of the Habima is to improve and refine the Jewish soul."[10]

The Habima was therefore regarded as a socially and nationally aware theater, a didactic weapon. It was to present socially and historically significant plays. Again, Zemach wanted each Habima member to become a "Bialik, a modern prophet who would travel the world over . . . and bring comfort and solace to the poor, the down-trodden Jewish masses everywhere."[11]

The Habima as a National Theater

As early as 1913, Zemach suggested the establishment of a foundation devoted to the creation of a Hebrew theater in Eretz Israel. He believed that only there "will our national language find its natural expression and the Hebrew art its suitable form and natural conditions for development."[12] At its very inception, Zemach had a vision of the theater in Eretz Israel: "And now we are in Jerusalem, the Habima edifice rising in splendor on Mount Scopus. Our actors are the modern Levites. We have our choir, painters, directors, dancers—all our own. And all the people living in Zion come to us, pilgrims from all corners of the land come to see the spectacle presented for them by the Habima."[13]

Zemach created a hymn for the theater which, perhaps, symbolized his ideological vision best of all. The hymn was called "Hikkonu, Hikkonu Labima Birushalyim" ("Prepare ye, Prepare ye for the Habima in Jerusalem") and was enthusiastically sung by all members after special performances, on Holy Days, and whenever the group was in low spirits. The hymn was an evocation:

Prepare ye, prepare ye for the Habima in Jerusalem
We will build the Habima in Jerusalem
Our home will be the Habima in Jerusalem
Purify and sanctify for the Habima in Jerusalem.[14]

The Habima was, therefore, a Zionist theater in the full sense of the term since it involved not only the determination to perform in Hebrew those Jewish plays compatible with the Zionist cause, but also the decision to migrate to Palestine and establish a permanent home there. The theater adhered to the heroic image of the *chalutz,* the young Jewish pioneer who goes off to Palestine to till the soil. The group rebelled against the culture and life of the shtetl; it wanted to establish something new and innovative that would be totally different from traditional Jewish culture.

The Habima as a High-Level Art Theater

Apart from the historical, national, and moral mission of the theater, there was another component in its ideology, one that referred to the Habima as an artistic institution. When Zemach and Gnessin met again in Moscow in 1917, they decided that a Hebrew theater was worth establishing only if it were innovative from the artistic point of view.[15] This decision was a crucial factor in determining the location of the Habima. Zemach resolved that the Habima should be founded in Moscow, the world center of the theater arts. He thought that the credibility of a Hebrew theater born in Moscow would be greater.[16] The dramatic groups that Zemach had established prior to the Habima no longer satisfied his artistic ambitions; these groups were amateur endeavors as far as the training and the artistic work of the actors were concerned.

The emphasis on serious and systematic training set the Habima off from most of the Yiddish-speaking theaters. The members talked with scorn about the vulgar Jewish theaters which presented cheap melodramas and operettas with stock characters. It was decided that all this must be discarded. The Habima players wanted to establish "an honorable and dignified theater, a theater in harmony with the dignity of Jewish traditions and aspirations."[17] The group's wish to attain high standards of excellence in performance and production was one of the main innovative components of its ideology. Dramatic groups which performed in Hebrew had existed before the Habima came into being, but all had had a short life and none attained a high professional or artistic level.

The slogan of the Habima's ideology was: *Emet* (Truth), *Emuna* (Belief), and *Omanut* (Art). The inner connection between the ideological and artistic components of the theater's belief system was best expressed by Bialik:

> I dare not say that the theatre should be one of tendencies from the very start, and that its goal should be moral from its inception. It must remain artistic. But art takes its root in truth and the truth is always both beautiful and moral. It is useful too. Art must give expression to the truth of life. . . . It should be nationalistic and serve the national interests in the same measure and with the same end as the prophets have. This general theatre, the theatre of art, should be filled with a Hebrew, national content, in the highest sense of these words.[18]

The Habima's artistic ideology was, to a large extent, a product of the impact of the Moscow Art Theater. This troupe conceived of the theater as a group of sincere artists who work together closely over a long period of time in one organization. Instead of stressing the individual star, the Moscow Art Theater emphasized collective work and ensemble acting.

The impact of the Moscow Art Theater on the Habima can be summed up on terms of the following features: producing in repertory; long and intensive periods of rehearsals; thorough study of each play and each part, including minor parts; ensemble acting rather than the star system; rotation of parts among the actors in successive performances; and the belief that all theater arts (directing, acting, lighting, and designing) must complement each other so that the style of the production is unified.[19] Like the Moscow Art Theater, the Habima held that a true art theater should be a collective, developing its special art form. Hence, the Habima was established as a cooperative, collective organization. Organizationally as well as artistically, it was a democratic venture.

It should be pointed out that all the features that characterized the artistic ideology of the Habima—acquired from the Moscow Theater with which it was affiliated—were missing from most of the Yiddish theaters, and especially from the Yiddish wandering troupes. Most of the old Yiddish theaters (those established before 1918) were characterized by cheap, tawdry, *shund* (trash) productions: poor plays with stock characters; a lack of rehearsal time; lack of a unified concept of an artistic whole; and, most importantly, either amateur or semiprofessional actors. Indeed, the old Yiddish stage was "sans script, sans director, and sans intellect." Everything in these theaters revolved around and deferred to the star actor, who used the whole troupe and production to his personal advantage.[20]

The attitude of the Habima toward the Yiddish theater was rather complex. On the one hand, the players did not condemn the traditional old Jewish theater that, wandering from place to place, very often had "to appear almost daily in a new play, and to rely entirely upon the prompter." Dependent upon the audience, the wandering troupes "catered too much to the taste of the public."[21] On the other hand, the Habima, striving to achieve high standards, denounced the methods of the old Yiddish stage and rejected its slogan, namely, "entertainment for entertainment's sake." It believed that the actor had a moral obligation and mission and that these went far beyond mere entertainment.

Hence, the Moscow Art Theater functioned as the Habima's positive reference group because it involved "motivated assimilation of the norms of the group or the standards of the group as a basis for self-appraisal." By contrast, the old Yiddish stage operated as a negative reference group because it involved "motivated rejection, i.e., not merely non-acceptance of norms but the formation of counter-norms."[22] It should also be stressed that most of the idea-elements in the Habima ideology, artistic and nonartistic, were based primarily on moral and ethical rather than on esthetic considerations.

The Moscow Repertoire

Since the Habima was founded before there existed any native drama in Hebrew, it was forced to translate all the plays it performed into Hebrew. The question, therefore, arose of which plays to translate.

In the beginning, in keeping with their political and ideological convictions, the founders thought that the theater should confine itself to biblical and historical plays with heroic characters. They wanted to give voice to the awakening of Zionism and the renaissance of the Jewish national consciousness. However, the first production of the Habima, which took place on October 8, 1918, neither was a biblical play nor did it contain "prophetic pathos." It consisted of four one-act plays that concerned Jewish life in Eastern Europe. Since it was the first public performance of the Habima, it was called *Neshef Bereshit* (*Evening of Beginning*) and consisted of short plays by Sholem Asch, I. Katzenelson, I. L. Peretz, and I. D. Berkowitz. These plays were chosen for purposes of learning; since the members had little experience, they wanted plays that would be suitable for beginners.

The production, prepared by Vakhtangov, proved to be an artistic achievement and made a great impression on the cultural elite of Moscow—most of all on Stanislavsky, who attended the opening night. Stanislavsky was impressed by the group's seriousness, sincerity, and devotion. At the party given after the premiere, he said that long before the Revolution he had dreamed of exhibiting on stage native drama of all the national minorities and that he was happy because the Habima had helped him realize his dream. He expressed his satisfaction with the Habima's artistic work and contended that, although he did not understand the language in which they performed, he felt that the special artistic language of the Habima was stronger and richer than spoken language. In short, Stanislavsky publicly praised the group and gave it his blessing to continue its work.

Despite the artistic success of *Neshef Bereshit*, it was clear to the group that if the Habima intended to become a moral and national theater "it could not confine itself to an existence of art for art's sake."[23] The players could not be satisfied with short plays based on Jewish folklore in the Pale of Settlement. Zemach strongly advocated plays that "should light the Jewish path," and decided that the next play should express the national problem of the Jews.[24] Accordingly, David Pinski's

The Habima's audience at its first public performance in Moscow, October 8, 1918.

Yiddish play *The Eternal Jew* was chosen. It was a biblical and historical drama that underlined the unique problem of the Jewish people.

The Eternal Jew was a one-act drama written in 1906. It was based on the ancient Jewish legend that on the day of the Temple's destruction by the Romans, the Messiah was born. At the end of the play, a violent storm breaks out and the Messiah disappears in the wind, taking with him all chances of redemption. Since then the Jews have been forced to wander through the world seeking the Messiah, with no hope of rest or peace until the Redeemer is found. The Messianic tragedy described the lamentation of the Jewish people over their lost country and destroyed Temple, but its stress was nevertheless on the prophetic revelation—that a child born during the catastrophe would be the Savior and would restore the departed glory of the Jews.

The Eternal Jew was the ideal play for the Habima; all the social and national feelings of the Jews could be read into Pinski's play. The drama portrayed Jewish national death but it also held out the promise of Jewish national rebirth. Furthermore, the content and message of the play were most appropriate to the political events and aspirations of Russian Jewry in 1919, when the Habima presented it. It was two years after the Balfour Declaration of 1917, which favored the establishment of a National Jewish Home in Palestine, and two years after the overthrow of the tsarist regime. In 1919, both events seemed to herald the fulfillment of Jewish national rebirth and liberation from foreign oppression.

The Eternal Jew was presented in two versions: the first in December 1919, the second in 1923. Both versions were directed by Vsevold Mchedelov, another pupil of Stanislavsky. The success of the production was based on its national message rather than merely on its artistic elements. Most critics pronounced it a compelling work and praised the production. Maxim Gorky was moved to tears at the first performance and went to see it a second and a third time, after which he wrote an enthusiastic review:

> I have seen three performances of Pinski's *The Eternal Jew*. . . . Without understanding the language, and only by the pleasure of listening to the sound and rhythm did I feel all the anguish of the prophet who was not understood by his people he loved so dearly. . . . But it was not the play that made the deep impression. No, the impression was created by the harmony of performance, by the

Zvi Friedland as the prophet and Hanna Rovina as the young woman in David Pinski's *The Eternal Jew* (1919).

musical unity of the performance at large and each individual in and for himself. . . . Logic then asks: What, O Russian atheist, do you want with Jerusalem and Zion, with the destruction of the Temple? But the heart trembles in anguish at the sight of the prophet who foretells the misfortune of his people, who foresees the imminent exile of his people. . . . The strange and the distant become close to you and part of your very life, as it were, for on the stage you see young and gifted people. . . . This performance which is enchanting in its beauty and harmony, brings back to me the good years of the Art Theatre well known in Moscow. . . .[25]

Other critics, like Akim Lvovich Valinsky, the Jewish intellectual and noted critic of Petrograd, were most impressed with the weeping in *The Eternal Jew*, which was "something monumental, psalm-like."[26] In his review, Valinsky defined the Habima as "the theater of national expression," and contended that the destiny of the troupe was to wander from city to city and to convey its message to all the dispersed Jews of the world.[27]

The next production of the Habima was *The Dybbuk* by S. Anski.[28] Stimulated by the Dreyfus Affair, Anski began to explore Jewish folklore, and was struck by the legend of the dybbuk, the spirit of a dead person which enters another's body. In a first version of *The Dybbuk*, which he entitled *Between Two Worlds* (1914), he contrasted the otherworld of love with this world. Originally Anski wrote his play in Russian. He then submitted it to Stanislavsky, who studied it for his theater. But Stanislavsky soon reached the conclusion that it would be much better if a Jewish group produced the play because the characters would then be portrayed much more effectively.[29] Stanislavsky also brought the play to Zemach's attention. Soon thereafter Bialik translated it into Hebrew for the Hebrew literary quarterly *Hatkufa* (The Period).[30]

The Dybbuk tells a love story.[31] It takes place in a small Jewish village in southern Russia in the middle of the nineteenth century. In an old synagogue, Channan, a young student, realizes that the girl whom he loves, Leah, is going to be married off by her father, Sender, a rich merchant, to a wealthy man. Channan is a mystic scholar: he studies the forbidden, the Kabbalah, which deals with the interpretation of the supernatural. In his despair, he tries to win Leah with the help of the Evil Power, but suddenly he is stricken dead.

At the wedding celebration, beggars are included among the guests, according to the Jewish custom of inviting the poor. As Leah is about to take her marital vows, she rejects the bridegroom in a voice not her own. She is possessed by the spirit of Channan, and the wedding stops. Sender hurries Leah to the Court of the Zaddik, a righteous and sage man, who, failing to persuade the dybbuk to dispossess Leah, decides to excommunicate him. But excommunication needs the approval of the Rabbinical Court, so Rabbi Shimshon and his jurors are called in. Rabbi Shimshon dreams about Channan's dead father, Nissan, who claimed that years ago Sender had made a promise to him: were he, Sender, to have a daughter, she would be married to Nissan's son. In breaking the promise, Sender caused Channan's death. The Zaddik calls Sender to judgment and finds him guilty. The punishment is to share half of his wealth with the poor and to pray daily for the elevation of the spirits of Channan and Nissan.

The dybbuk departs from Leah's body and the wedding is to proceed. Channan's spirit returns but, unable to enter Leah's body, he enters her soul. Leah's soul is fused with the soul of Channan in eternal love.

It is of interest to mention that in the beginning, Zemach did not want to produce *The Dybbuk* because the play depicted customs of the Jewish ghetto and did not deal with a national problem. He agreed to present the play because there was no better alternative. Zemach decided that *The Dybbuk* would be a temporary production until an original biblical play could be written.[32] And Bialiḳ translated the play without much excitement; he thought that although *The Dybbuk* was a treasure trove of Jewish folklore, it did not have any significant national values.[33]

The Dybbuk was the kind of play that demanded an imaginative director who would be able to transform the folkloristic drama into a monument of Jewish tradition. In this regard, Vakhtangov was the right director. Vakhtangov's imagination was boundless. His originality lay in the fact that for each play he sought the most expressive form for its idea, its style, and its genre. Of Armenian origin, Vakhtangov was attentive to the problem of national minorities, and especially of oppressed minorities. For him, the actual establishment of a Jewish theater in Hebrew, the original language of the Jews, was proof of freedom for minorities.

In *The Dybbuk,* Vakhtangov exemplified his doctrine of theatricality, according to which every play must be given a special form and must be viewed from a contemporary standpoint. Vakhtangov reedited the play and succeeded in imbuing *The Dybbuk* with the revolutionary spirit of contemporary Russia. Thus, the sense of the contemporary was reflected in the interpretation and new artistic forms which he applied to the old content of the play. The struggle in *The Dybbuk,* which according to Anski was the struggle of a soul between two worlds (the earthly and the heavenly) within the religious order, was interpreted by Vakhtangov as a revolutionary social drama. Vakhtangov saw in the play the struggle for freedom from the old religious order and the erection of a tombstone for the old Jewish life. He criticized the old Hassidic customs and way of life and interpreted *The Dybbuk* as a rebellion against the Jewish re-

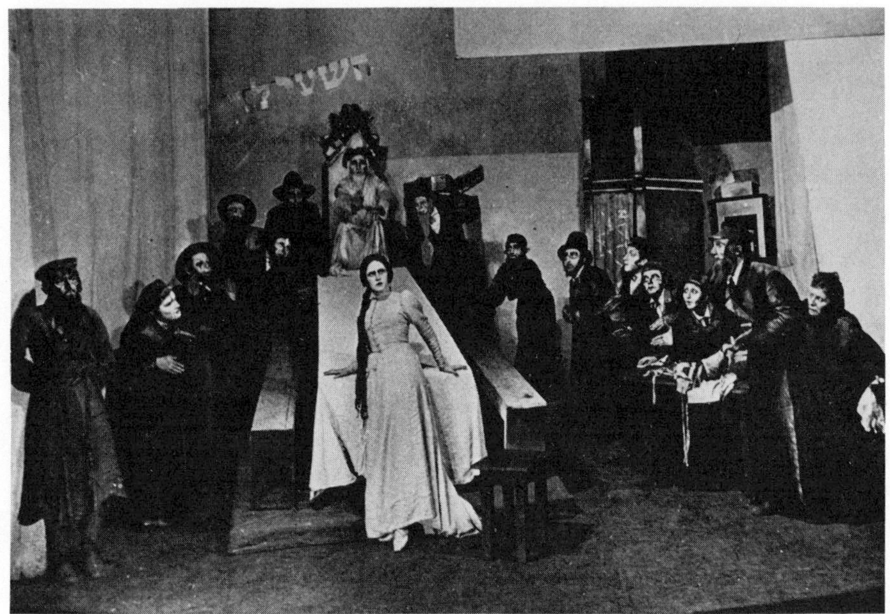

Act III of *The Dybbuk* (1922). At the center, Hanna Rovina as Leah.

ligious establishment. For him, the struggle of Channan and Leah was a social and cultural revolution against the old order.[34]

Furthermore, in the second act of the play, Vakhtangov shifted the accent from Anski's folkloristic elements to a specific class struggle between the beggars and Sender, who was made to represent the materialistic establishment. In the dance of the beggars, he sought to express the spirit of the Revolution by transforming the beggars from a background element traditional at Jewish weddings to a central element of his interpretation: the suffering inflicted upon the beggars by the rich establishment.[35]

Since Vakhtangov did not speak Hebrew, he used a Russian version of *The Dybbuk*. He also read many books on Jewish religion, folklore, and the Hassidic movement. Vakhtangov wanted the audience to be able to enjoy the production of *The Dybbuk* without understanding a word of Hebrew; he believed that the sound should render the meaning.[36]

Since the Habima worked on *The Dybbuk* for more than two years, different theatrical styles are found in the play. Each of the three acts

The Beggars' Dance in Act II of *The Dybbuk* (1922).

was directed differently and reflected the theatrical approach of Vakhtangov in three different periods. A rare combination of talents also contributed to the success of *The Dybbuk:* the talents of playwright Anski, composer Yoel Angel, designer Nathan Altman, and, above all, the genius of Vakhtangov. Seldom do so many gifted people work so long in such complete harmony to produce a work of art.

The Dybbuk was a play that could be interpreted in different ways. Indeed, the play appealed in different ways to different audiences. This is clear from the reviews of the production. Nikolai Evreinov, a playwright and critic, wrote:

> The play? According to the usual criteria, there is nothing special about it; a fine, symbolic play, with much folklore beautifully executed. . . . Anski's "dramatic legend" . . . contains nothing that would give it a place in the history of literature as a "dramatic creation." But there is something else to the Habima production. If I may speak thus, the entire performance is lit by a theatrical light. To take this folklore, all this humor of Jewish life, and make of it an integral, deeply moving, organic part of a mystery play, calls not for

> ability, but—and I say this without hesitation—genius. For me the ultimate demonstration of Vakhtangov's genius lies in the fact that, though I do not understand Hebrew, I was constantly excited, and my excitement rose and fell with the rhythm of the plot. . . .[37]

To Evreinov, *The Dybbuk* was a revelation of a life that had been going on in Russia for centuries without many Russians being aware of it. He and others saw the significance of the production in its attempt to capture the quintessence of Jewish ghetto life, just when modernization was driving this life out of existence.

The play meant something else to A. L. Valinsky, the Jewish intellectual who moved away from Judaism: "On the stage of the Habima I saw a picture of a way of life which greatly differs—in its quality, color, and manner—from the way of life of other peoples. This is a Semitic-Hamitic way of life that is part of the ethnic essence of the Jewish people."[38]

Another critic, M. Zagorsky, found an entirely different meaning in *The Dybbuk:*

> What would you say, please, if you found the mythos of the Soviet Revolution revealed in ancient folk legend created by the genius of a people? Wouldn't your heart be moved to see the spirit of the Revolution revealed in its internal, essential meaning as the victory of a great love? On the surface of it, there is nothing in common between the Russian Revolution and *The Dybbuk.* So . . . why is that thanks to *The Dybbuk* I recognized the deep meaning of the mythos now being created? Because this production reveals the meaning of destruction, of abandoning a historic tradition for the sake of victory of love. . . . In a sea of powerful human emotions—of a love stronger than death—a centuries-old social system disintegrates.[39]

But Homo Novus (A. Kugel), the noted critic of Leningrad, expressed disappointment with the Habima productions of *The Eternal Jew* and *The Dybbuk:*

> With all his talent and profoundity, Vakhtangov deviates from the Jewish spirit. Let us take the highly successful second act of *The Dybbuk.* With all its theatrical inventiveness, it is made of fabric which does not belong here. The beggars and cripples and monsters belong to the world of Hoffman, Poe, Andreyev. . . . The accent on the grotesque folklore is not in keeping with the spirit of Judaism.

Known for his conservative views, he opposed the expressionistic manner in which both productions were presented: "This slow tempo, all those pauses, represent a Russian truth. . . . But when you present a Jewish play as a succession of tableaux, you are guilty of pouring strange wine into Jewish bottles."[40] It is noteworthy that Homo Novus was the first to express dissent from the general chorus of enthusiasm which greeted *The Dybbuk*.

The Habima production of *The Dybbuk* was not merely a milestone of the Hebrew stage but also one of the most famous productions in the history of the modern theater. It was universally acclaimed as one of Vakhtangov's most remarkable productions. Though Stanislavsky's pupil, Vakhtangov discarded Stanislavsky's naturalism and the psychological methods of the Moscow Art Theater and evolved instead the doctrine of theatricality or "Fantastic Realism."[41] *The Dybbuk* announced the end of naturalism and exemplified a method of production and a style of acting which for originality, expressiveness, and general power are among the most effective features of the modern theater. Thus, the Habima was one of the first theaters in Russia to launch expressionism, the new artistic form.

The Dybbuk opened on January 31, 1922, four months before the untimely death of Vakhtangov. Although one of the first productions of the theater (actually the third), it became the emblem of the Habima, in the same way that Chekhov's *Seagull* was for the Moscow Art Theater. Since its premiere, *The Dybbuk* has been presented more than a thousand times; and despite the fact that since then the Habima has produced more than three hundred plays, the theater and the play are still synonymous. Moreover, although the Habima achieved many subsequent successes, it was hard to rival the triumph of *The Dybbuk*. Without Vakhtangov's genius, the general enthusiasm and the conspicuous talents of many of its actors were not fully exploited. The Vakhtangov production remains by far the most important production in the history of the Habima; all subsequent attempts to produce plays in the spirit of *The Dybbuk* were doomed to superficiality. *The Dybbuk* remained in the theater's repertoire for forty-three years and was generally admired by the troupe and audiences, but this very adoration itself became an obstacle to future development.

After the production and immense success of *The Dybbuk* there was a

A scene from the original production of *The Dybbuk* (1922).

desperate need for a new play. This need was resolved in the decision to present again, but with higher standards, *The Eternal Jew*. Consequently, the play's one act was stretched into two; new dialogue and characters were created and new costumes and sets were devised. The group was so happy to get back to work that no one questioned the wisdom of producing the same play again. Mchedelov, the director of the first version, was invited back. The opening night took place on June 5, 1923. The new production, like the first, was a success. What made it successful was the harmony of color, costumes, decorations, and especially the music by Krein, which gave the production the quality of biblical lamentation.

The repertoire of the Habima thus consisted of two plays. Its first production, *Neshef Bereshit*, was considered by the group as an artistic exercise and was rarely performed after the opening of *The Dybbuk*. So, for almost two years, the Habima alternated performances of *The Eternal Jew* and *The Dybbuk*.

The repertory problems created doubts concerning the ideology of the

Habima and the possibility of realizing it. According to its original mission the Habima had to confine itself to the presentation of specifically Jewish, preferably biblical, plays. Ideally, the theater was to present plays that were Jewish and national in content, and modern and revolutionary in artistic form. But the question was: where was one to find such plays? And there was also the question of the wisdom of performing in Hebrew when no plays were written in that language.

Zemach, seeking appropriate plays for the Habima, went to Berlin in 1923. There he met with a group of players who had come from Palestine to study their craft and had made contact with some Zionist leaders, among them Zeev Jabotinsky and Nachum Goldman.[42]

A meeting was arranged between Zemach, Jabotinsky, and the group during which they held a long and passionate debate concerning the mission of the Hebrew theater. Zemach advocated fervently a Hebrew theater that would present only biblical and national plays; he also contended that the Hebrew actor should study thoroughly the Bible, the Talmud, and the Jewish tradition. Jabotinsky, on the other hand, thought that the Hebrew theater should not confine itself to Jewish plays alone. Rather, it should also present classical and historical plays based on the experience of other nations. Furthermore, he thought that the messianism which the Habima presented in its plays was too static and limited in scope. Jabotinsky believed that heroic plays, Jewish as well as non-Jewish, should be presented by the Hebrew theater, and was therefore a proponent of a repertoire that would draw from the world's classical drama.[43] As a result of his meeting with Jabotinsky, Zemach realized that others did not share the Habima ideology as widely as he had thought or wanted to believe.

The Habima's next production was *The Golem* by H. Leivik, a Russian-born Yiddish-speaking poet. This play deals the the legend of Rabbi Judah Loeb (known as the Maharal) of Prague (1513–1609), who became famous for his good deeds and scholarship. He was a student of the Kabbalah and, according to the legend, learned the ineffable Name which enabled him to perform miracles. One day he fashioned a Golem, a human figure made of clay, breathed into it the spirit of life, and gave his creation monstrous strength. He then used the Golem to act as a protector of the Jews against their oppressors and enemies. But after killing all those who persecuted the Jews, the Golem turned upon its own people, and so had to be destroyed.

Aaron Meskin as the Golem (with axe) and Baruch Chemerinsky as the Maharal in Leivik's *The Golem* (1925).

In Leivik's hands the legend became an expression of the eternal Jewish quest for the Messiah. The Maharal, representing the sufferings of his people and impatient with God's promise of Redemption, decides to take matters into his own hands. In the end he fails, and Redemption remains as remote as ever. Two figures—the Messiah in the guise of a young beggar, and the prophet Elijah in the guise of an old beggar—appear in the play; both disapprove of the Maharal's attempt to use physical force in the fight against the enemies of the Jews. *The Golem* was a play in which the Jews became the symbol of a mankind suffering innocently and yearning for Redemption. Opposed to the Maharal (and the Jews) stands Thaddeus, the antagonist (the world). Thaddeus hates the Jews because he cannot stand the moral principles they represent—because they are a constant reproof to the principles of the fist, by which the world is governed. The play stressed the tragedy of the Maharal who learns that force cannot really solve problems, and that suffering is the lot of man.

The Golem was a most appropriate choice for the Habima. Leivik used the historical legend to cast light upon the contemporary world. More than a philosophical morality play, *The Golem* was a political parable about the relationship of ends and means. Leivik was disgusted by the bloody deeds of the revolutionary years (he worked on *The Golem* from 1917 to 1920) and by the degradation of socialist ideals through Bolshevik brutality. The Golem could be—and was—interpreted as a symbol of the Revolution; like the Revolution, the Golem was created with good intentions, but, having found a way of its own, turned away from the intentions of its creator.[44] Indeed, in 1925, when the Habima produced *The Golem,* the violence and destruction of Jewish cultural life in Russia were such that the production became all the more significant.

Apparently the Moscow official authorities did not understand the allegory of the play for they raised no objection when the play was submitted for approval. They asked only for the deletion of one scene—one with ghosts—which the censor thought fostered superstition. The audiences sensed, however, what the censors did not. There was a scene in the play when Tanchum, the town simpleton, cries out in despair: "Who will save us?" At one performance when the cry came, voices from the audiences shouted back "We will!" and a number of people stood up and sang the "International."[45]

The Golem was directed by Boris Illich Vershilov, a pupil of Stanislavsky and Vakhtangov. Its decorations were done by Yignat Nivinsky, who excelled in his decorations for Vakhtangov's masterpiece and swan song, *Princess Turandot;* the music was the work of Moshe Milnar, a well-known composer from Leningrad. The Habima troupe itself reached a new standard of acting with *The Golem.* The production became one of the Habima's greatest successes (second only to *The Dybbuk*) and remained in the repertory for more than three decades.

At the end of 1925, a few months after the opening of *The Golem,* the Habima mounted a new production: *Jacob's Dream,* a biblical legend by the Austrian Jewish poet Richard Beer-Hoffman. With the addition of this play to the repertoire, some members became concerned that the Habima would be stamped as a theater which limited itself to past history and legends. But Zemach remained committed to the biblical and national repertoire. *Jacob's Dream* reconstructed a story from Genesis. The play dramatized Jacob's dream, his wrestling with the angel of the Lord, the change of his name from Jacob to Israel ("prince prevailing with God"), and the prophecy of eternal woe but eternal life. Beer-Hoffman's poetic tragedy dealt with the constant trials and missions of the Jewish people: the privilege, penalty, glory, and tragedy of being a chosen people, the light of the world, and the suffering involved in the high religious mission of the Jews.

It is noteworthy that Stanislavsky himself was willing to supervise the production of *Jacob's Dream.* He did begin preparatory work on the play, but became ill, and the direction was taken over by Suchkevitch, the director of the Second Moscow Art Theater. Suchkevitch was a good technician but lacked imagination and, therefore, his production did not bring out the beauty of the playwright's poetic dialogue. *Jacob's Dream* was a highly stylized production, but it was not an artistic success; its only advantage was that it helped the actors try another type of theater, the operatic form of dramatic representation.

The scene of the angels in Richard Beer-Hoffman's *Jacob's Dream* (1925).

While working on *Jacob's Dream,* the Habima rehearsed another play, *The Flood* (or *The Deluge*). This was an American tragicomedy written in 1906 by Hennig Berger. The group decided to present the play because the theater could not find plays based on Jewish historical and national themes. It also believed that *The Flood* could be produced without too much difficulty and in a short time. Moreover, *The Flood* had been successfully produced by Vakhtangov in 1915, and had achieved success in Russia, Germany, and other countries, so the Habima decided to include it in its repertoire.

The subject of *The Flood* is universal. The drama deals with a group of people caught by a torrential rain in a cellar bar of a small town along the Mississippi. Under the shadow of death all social barriers are knocked down and all make vows of loyalty and promises to help each other if they are rescued. However, as soon as the telegraph reports that the flood is slackening and they learn that there is no more danger, their own characters emerge again, revealing all their vices, greed, meanness, and hatred.

To present a foreign, non-Jewish play from the world repertoire was a departure from the Habima ideology. It was also the first time that the theater presented a contemporary play with actors appearing in contemporary costumes. Zemach and other players were not very happy with this deviation from the theater's original ideological commitment. Consequently, they decided to adapt the play and give it a more specifically Jewish content. They soon discovered, however, that Jewish characters and music did not do justice to the play, so they returned to the original version but retained the music—Hassidic melodies. The effect was indeed strange and audiences wondered why American farmers on the shores of the Mississippi sang Hassidic chants.[46]

The Flood was the Habima's last production in Moscow. A couple of weeks after it opened, the troupe left the Soviet Union. Of all its productions, this was the least noteworthy and the least successful. However, *The Flood* was unlike the group's other productions in that it was a modern play written as a tragicomedy, and as such offered great possibilities for the actors.

THREE

The Social Context: Jewish and Russian

THE Habima group created and institutionalized in Moscow a new role with new status images—the role of the Hebrew actor. The new role-definition was based on the ideology of the group, which conceived of the Habima as a Hebrew, biblical, national, moral, and artistic theater. The Habima player was conceived of as a modern prophet, a missionary who employed artistic means in the revival of the Jewish nation and the Hebrew language.

Prior to the work of the Habima, there had been naive and abortive attempts in Palestine and Eastern Europe to establish a Hebrew theater. All these groups performed exclusively in Hebrew. Nonetheless, unlike the Habima, they were not guided by a clear ideology; the repertoire that they presented was not consistent and included Jewish (though not biblical or messianic) as well as non-Jewish plays. Furthermore, these ventures were amateur as far as the training and the artistic work of the actors were concerned and were short-lived; none lasted for more than several weeks or months. Indeed, the importance of the Habima is to be ascribed not to its distinctive artistic or acting style, but rather to its success in a venture in which its predecessors failed, namely, to create a permanent Hebrew art theater.

The success of the Habima in establishing a permanent Hebrew art theater was made possible by the political, social, and cultural setting of Russia within which the group operated from 1917 to 1926. In order to understand the existence and institutionalization of the Habima in Moscow, the following factors should be examined: the attitude of the Soviet regime toward Hebrew and Zionism; the state of the Russian theater in the first decade after the Revolution; and the formal and informal attitude of the regime and cultural elite toward the Habima.

Zionism and the Hebrew Language in Russia: 1917–1927

In its early stages, the new rulers did not affect Zionist activities. On November 15, 1917, the government issued a formal "Declaration of Rights of Peoples" that proclaimed the "free development of national minorities and ethnic groups inhabiting Russian territory."[1] Indeed, in the spring of 1918 a "Palestine Week" was proclaimed and celebrated in hundreds of Jewish communities. Palestinian emigration offices functioned freely.

In January 1918, a commissariat for Jewish National Affairs (Yevkom) was established as a subdivision of the Commissariat for Nationality Affairs headed by Joseph Stalin. Distinct from the state apparatus, the Communist party also created within its own structure a Jewish Section, the Yevsektsia, which was assigned the task of carrying out Party policy among Jewish workers and conducting propaganda in the Yiddish language.[2] The main organ of the Yevsektsia was the Yiddish-language daily newspaper, *Der Emes* (The Truth), which was published in Moscow and was attached to the Department of Propaganda of the Communist party's Central Committee.

By the summer of 1918, the Yevsektsia began to denounce the "counterrevolutionary" essence of Zionism. In 1919, it condemned the government's failure to act vigorously and speedily against Zionism. The Yevsektsia was anxious to prove to the Communist regime that it had purged itself of all vestiges of Jewish nationalism. Indeed, the second conference of the Yevkom and the Yevsektsia in Moscow, during June 1919, urged the dissolution of the "counter revolutionary, clerical and nationalistic Zionist organization."[3]

But 1919 was the most critical year for the new regime because of the fight against the White armies. Soviet authorities were, therefore, not inclined to pay attention to such a relatively innocuous movement as Zionism. Indeed, in July 1919, the All-Russian Central Executive Committee of Soviets resolved that since neither its decrees nor the Council of People's Commissars had declared the Zionist party to be counterrevolutionary and since the cultural activities of the Zionist organization did not contradict the decisions of the Party, all Soviet organizations were instructed not to hamper the Zionists. The resolution was therefore a negatively phrased expression of official tolerance.[4]

However, in September 1919, several Zionist leaders were arrested by the Cheka (Soviet Secret Police), and the Hebrew Zionist periodical *Haam* (*The People*) was suspended. In the following months, the Russian-language Zionist weekly, *Raszviet* (*The Dawn*), was suppressed. This ban on the publication of Zionist periodicals remained in force, although the actions did not assume the character of a massive and consistent anti-Zionist drive. The Yevsektsia was dismayed by the apparent semitolerance of the regime and in its third conference, in July 1920, urged the total proscription and liquidation of Zionism. Furthermore, *Der Emes* called in 1922 for a campaign to exterminate Zionism in the USSR forever.

Yet the Soviet regime repeatedly asserted that the government was actually not against Zionism and that all the harassment was the work of the Yevsektsia only. True, the regime saw no real danger in the existence of a Zionist movement which was in no way a challenge to its power. But if Zionism was not outlawed, neither was it legalized. It was only in the late twenties that a consistently anti-Zionist program aiming at total destruction of the Zionist cause became the declared policy of the Party and the government.[5]

The position of the Hebrew language was similar to that of Zionism. No formal decree outlawed Hebrew, "but without a legal endorsement, the illegality of Hebrew had been firmly established in practice." Hebrew was regarded as the language of rabbis and clerical reaction, and as a vehicle of Zionism. Hebrew literary works were banned, not necessarily because of their contents but because the language itself was viewed as defective and dangerous: it was described as reactionary and bourgeois. Indeed, even Communist and explicitly pro-Soviet publications in Hebrew, or Hebrew translations of Russian and Soviet literature, were prohibited.[6] Again, the authorities denied that Hebrew was being persecuted; but, on the other hand, they argued that it was a dead language. The official line in regard to Hebrew remained undefined in the twenties; it was more convenient to suppress Hebrew in practice without actually decreeing a formal ban on it.

Of all the areas of Jewish culture, only Yiddish and its secular literature received the seal of legitimacy and the right to exist under the new regime. The non-Zionist sections of the Jewish labor movement, and particularly the Bund, gave full recognition to Yiddish. The Bund was basically atheistic—it repudiated the Jewish religion on principle—and identified Hebrew with clericalism on the one hand and with "chauvinistic" Zionism on the other. The claim of the Jewish labor movement leaders after the Revolution was that only by using Yiddish was it possible to bring about the sovietization of the Jewish masses. They stressed the importance of Yiddish as a weapon of propaganda; propaganda in Hebrew would have no significant influence because it was not spoken by the masses. This argument was accepted by the regime and, accordingly, schools with Yiddish as the language of instruction, Yiddish theaters, and Yiddish publishing houses and press were established. At the same time, there was a deliberate and merciless suppression of all Hebrew education and culture.[7]

Anti-Zionism did not help the Habima in its struggle for existence in Russia. But there was an even more important problem, the lack of a Jewish and a Hebrew audience in Moscow, which made the founding of the Habima there a minor miracle. Until the mid-twenties, the largest Jewish towns in Russia were Kiev and Odessa. The Jewish population in the capitals—Moscow and Petrograd—grew rapidly between 1923 and 1926. When the Habima left the Soviet Union in 1926, 131,000 Jews resided in Moscow, and 84,000 lived in Leningrad.[8] But the vast majority of Jews in the Soviet Union—including Moscow, of course—did not speak Hebrew. According to the 1926 census, 90.7 percent of the Jews in the Byelorussian Republic and 70.4 percent of all those considered to be of "Jewish nationality" in the Soviet Union declared Yiddish to be their mother tongue.[9]

Consequently, the appeal of the Habima was restricted to a "spiritual aristocracy" the members of which spoke Hebrew. In its early years various Zionist groups attended the theater, but they constituted a small minority of the Jewish community. Nonetheless, because the Habima was the only place in Russia where one could publicly hear or speak Hebrew without risking arrest, Jews visiting Moscow from other cities would rush to the theater to see "the wonder of the Revolution."[10]

Moreover, except for a short tour in Petrograd in 1923, the Habima performed only in Moscow during its seven years in Russia, making it all the more difficult to find an audience. People outside the theater could not understand what prevented the Habima from touring other cities of Russia, especially after the artistic acclaim of *The Dybbuk*. But, in fact, the Habima was not allowed by the authorities to tour Russia, and the members themselves "did not dare take the risk of bringing our particular type of repertoire—in a language which few could understand—to audiences caught in the ferment of Soviet Russia's new way of life."[11]

Despite its achievements, the Habima's constant and major problem in Russia was the lack of an audience. The theater hall, which seated only 126 people, was rarely full. At times, there were no more than five or six people; and even then, the performance went on. Many performances had to be canceled according to the rule, "no less than six people in the audience."[12] Sometimes, the actors would not know if there would be a performance until the last moment. To keep the performance going, students of other dramatic studios were admitted free of charge.[13]

Under these circumstances, the Habima's existence in Moscow was indeed a miracle. The theater performed in Hebrew while there was an actual ban on its language, regarded as clerical and counterrevolutionary. The Habima operated in Moscow where there was a small Jewish community, the vast majority of which did not speak Hebrew. The Habima remained committed to the Zionist cause while around it Zionists were arrested and Zionists periodicals were suspended. Long after the Bible had become taboo and teaching it had been banned, critics referred to the Habima as the biblical studio. The theater continued to present Jewish (biblical and national) plays while many Jewish schools and synagogues were liquidated. It is no wonder that the Yevsektsia, which rejected Zionism, Hebrew, and the Bible, was the Habima's major political opponent.

The Russian Theater: 1917–1927

In October 1917, Lenin, the president of the Council of People's Commissars (Sovnarkom), appointed Anatoly Vasilyevich Lunacharsky as the People's Commissar of Enlightenment, a position which he held until 1929. A decree issued by Lunacharsky in November 1917 put all theaters, including the former imperial theaters, under the jurisdiction of Narkompros, the People's Commissariat of Enlightenment.[14] In January 1918, a Theater Section, TEO, was established as part of Narkompros. It was headed by Olga Kameneva, Trotsky's sister, with the aim of establishing new theaters and experimental workshops.

Two organizational issues confronted Narkompros with regard to the theater: the administration of the state (formerly imperial) theaters, and the status of the private theaters like the Moscow Art Theater.[15] Lunacharsky believed that both theaters had traditions worth preserving. To assure their continuation he created a special department of state theaters, separate from TEO.

One of Lunacharsky's great personal successes was to win the confidence of the old theatrical establishment. To the left, his association with the old establishment was highly suspect; it thought that the traditional theaters used Lunacharsky as a "tortoise-shell" to protect themselves from the Revolution, both in a political and artistic sense. In some respects they were right; the confidence of the traditional theaters was given to Lunacharsky personally rather than to the government he represented.

In March 1918, Lunacharsky drafted a decree according to which the state undertook to finance the state theaters, retaining some rights of financial control. The decree entrusted their administration and artistic direction to a "Soviet of state theaters" consisting of representatives of the artists and Narkompros. The debate over the nationalization of the theaters continued during 1919, when leading figures of the theater, including Stanislavsky, opposed nationalization on the grounds that it was impracticable and irreconcilable with the principle of the freedom of creative work. Consequently, Lenin rejected TEO's project for the nationalization of the theaters. As a result, Kameneva resigned as the head of TEO and Lunacharsky succeeded her.

The spontaneous municipalization of theaters by soviets all over the country—due to the economic conditions of the time, coupled with political pressures from the left—required a reorganization of theatrical administration. In August 1919, Lunacharsky created a central organ of theatrical administration, Tsentroteatr. Accordingly, theatrical property became the property of the state and was put, on conditions, at the disposal of theater companies. Theaters under reliable direction and whose cultural value was incontrovertible were recognized as autonomous, although Tsentroteatr reserved the right to make certain demands in respect to their repertoire in the direction of "bringing the theatres closer to the popular masses [and] to the socialist ideal."[16] Tsentroteatr's jurisdiction included state and municipal as well as private theaters. Lunacharsky's project maintained the status quo in theater administration, and put Tsentroteatr, TEO, and the department of state theaters under his personal control. Private entrepreneurship in the theater was not excluded, however, and the regulations imposed on the private theaters were often less burdensome than the practices of many local soviets had been. At the end of 1919, the state theaters and the Moscow Art Theater were given the title of academic theaters, an acknowledgment of their role as repositories of theatrical art.

Thus, the administration of the theater remained in the hands of traditionalists. Lunacharsky's problem was that, apart from himself, there was no prominent Party member of moderate views to take charge of the theater. At the end of 1920, he appointed Vsevolod Meyerhold as head of TEO. He hoped that Meyerhold's work in the imperial theaters before the Revolution had made him tolerant of theatrical tradition. But Meyerhold became a strong proponent of the theatrical left and proclaimed a "Theatrical October"—a revolution in the theater, which meant the full nationalization of theaters, the introduction of revolutionary plays, and the development of revolutionary theatrical techniques. Assuming the editorship of the department's organ, *Vestnik Teatra* (The Theater Herald), he conducted a violent polemic on behalf of proletarian, provincial, and Red Army theaters, and demanded a redeployment of the manpower and financial resources then concentrated in the small group of state and academic theaters.[17]

Meyerhold's slogans, however, were unacceptable to Lunacharsky because they were directed against tradition and against toleration of any group except the avant-garde. In November 1920, Lunacharsky announced that the state theaters, the Kamerny, and the Moscow Art Theater with its studios were and would remain outside the jurisdiction of TEO. He wanted to limit the sphere of the "Theatrical October" movement to those theaters that were already revolutionary and to the smaller and less successful of the traditional private theaters. As a result, Meyerhold resigned as head of TEO.

In 1921, Narkompros underwent a radical reorganization. All the theaters that received a state subsidy, including the Moscow Art Theater with its studios, were put under the new Academic Center of Narkompros. TEO was left with very few theaters of importance and no financial control over any theater at all. And in 1922, because of the critical position of the state theaters, Lunacharsky took over the administration of the state and academic theaters and put them under his personal control.

Thus, the principles of creative freedom and mutual tolerance were strongly defended by Lunacharsky. His opponents on the artistic left found no support. Furthermore, in the absence of any government or Party statement to the contrary, Lunacharsky remained the official spokesman on the arts, and through him the principle of individual creative freedom continued to receive government sanction. Therefore, in the first years after the Revolution, the liberal approach of the Bolsheviks toward the theater stemmed, at least in part, from a lack of clear policy in artistic matters. Lenin's artistic taste was conservative, and he was too busy with political affairs to formulate a clear Soviet policy that would impose new revolutionary paths on the theaters. Because of Lunacharsky's efforts, the official Soviet policy was conservative: it maintained the old and most valuable theaters and aimed at the continuing existence of various artistic groups. The old theaters were granted a new lease on life by the new government, and a great deal of autonomy in their artistic and administrative management.

The theatrical world was further enriched in the first decade after the Revolution by a tremendous mushrooming of new theaters and studios. A theater psychosis possessed the country: actors were called upon to teach the nation; they became something like Salvation Army soldiers; pay, food, and comforts lost all value when compared to bringing theater to the people. Many actors believed that the Revolution was a chance to realize their mission, i.e., to educate and uplift the people. The Revolution brought to the theater a new audience: peasants, workers, and soldiers. The theater, which had previously been restricted to the upper classes and the bourgeoisie, was opened now to all the people.

In fact, the theater became the center of cultural and educational work in Russia. There was no plant or factory in the country that did not have its own dramatic circle. More than three thousand theatrical organizations operated in Russia during the years 1918–1922. New types of theaters were created: the Proletcult (The Proletarian Cultural Movement) to foster proletarian art, theaters of trade unions, and peasant theaters. In 1920, for example, the Red Army alone had 1,210 theaters, 1,800 theatrical clubs, and 911 theatrical groups. In the decade 1917–1927, seven million workers saw over 33,000 performances of the Proletcult. And by 1927, there were 24,000 theatrical circles all over Russia.[18]

In seeking a revolution of its own, the theater in many ways followed the example of the political revolution. The greatest effect of the Revolution on the theater was giving it freedom and subsidy. Censorship was abolished and artists were encouraged—both morally and financially—to explore new forms of expression. The subsidies which were given by the state freed the theaters from depending on box office receipts. In the first decade after the Revolution, almost any theatrical theory or attempt at innovation found enthusiastic followers and material opportunities.[19]

The Habima's Struggle to Survive

With the support of Stanislavsky and Vakhtangov, the Habima was recognized as a state theater in November 1919, one year after its first public performance. The official recognition by the Tsentroteatr meant a yearly subsidy of 100,000 rubles.[20] In addition to the financial support—which was extremely important to the Habima—its official status meant that the Tsentroteatr thought that artistically it merited state sponsorship and subsidy.

A month after the Habima's official recognition, the theater presented its second production, *The Eternal Jew*. Opening night was attended by members of the Russian theatrical elite. This production was a greater artistic achievement than the first and was highly acclaimed by the critics. It proved to those who still regarded the theater as a studio on trial that the Habima's work had high artistic merit.

But the greater the Habima's reputation as an artistic theater of the first rank became, the stronger it was persecuted by its opponent—the Yevsektsia. Including the Habima as a target of its campaign to proscribe and liquidate the Zionist movement, the Hebrew language, and the Jewish religion, the Yevsektsia's main accusation against the Habima was that it was counterrevolutionary because it performed in a dead and counterrevolutionary language. Consequently, the Yevsektsia opposed the government subsidy given to the Habima and tried to abolish the theater's official status.

On February 16, 1920, Dimanstein, one of the Yevsektsia Commissars, who had been a Bolshevik and anti-Zionist even prior to the Revolution, called a meeting of the Tsentroteatr. At this meeting, he said:

> There is no Jewish organization . . . which does not complain about the Habima. Its existence is a cinder in the eyes of not only Communists but all Jewish democrats because the Habima is a caprice of the Jewish bourgeoisie. It should not be allowed that the funds of the revolutionary regime, public funds in a democracy of workers and peasants, should support a theater which is not needed by the workers and peasants. Even if we admit that the theater is of high artistic merit, this is an enterprise needed by no one except a handful of nationalistic bourgeoisie who want to revive forcibly a dead language, to thrust the Jews back into religious superstitions, to separate them from the masses, to prevent their class progress. Supporting such a theater means helping the development of Jewish chauvinism, helping a bourgeois group par excellence. . . . In fact, Hebrew is a dead language; like an unburied corpse, it stinks. If the bourgeoisie is determined (to keep this corpse) let them do it with their own money. They should be thankful to the Cheka for not closing their institution.[21]

Dimanstein's speech must have been effective, for two weeks later, on March 2, 1920, the Council of the Tsentroteatr decided to discontinue the subsidy to the Habima.

Zemach, as a last attempt, appealed directly to the highest authority—the Executive Committee of the Bolshevik party. In his letter, he tried to prove that there were no contradictions between the Habima and the Revolution. First, he wrote, the repertoire of the Habima reflected the revolutionary aspirations of the Jewish people. Second, since every nationality was free to choose its language, the Soviet government had to be neutral in this matter. And third, the Habima was accepted by other theaters as a worthy institution of culture; thus, it was the Habima's artistic merit and not its political ideas which led to its high acclaim.[22]

Zemach's fight was supported by all those familiar with the theater's work. Prominent artists wrote a memorandum and addressed it personally to Lenin. In their memorandum, they expressed their discontent with the artistic damage inflicted upon the Habima and with the abuse of the Soviet principle of national self-determination. Moreover, they stated that "Russian art is a debtor to Hebrew art," and demanded freedom for the work of the Habima. The manifesto was signed by Stanislavsky, Nemirovitch-Dantchenko (the codirector of the Moscow Art Theater), Fyodor Chaliapin (the famous singer), Alexander Tairov (the founder and director of the Kamerny theater), K. Mordzhanov (the stage director), Nicolai Efros (the well-known drama critic), and others.[23]

As a result of Zemach's efforts and the memorandum of the Russian artists, Stalin, then head of the Commissariat for Nationality Affairs, decided to resume the yearly subsidy to the Habima. He wrote: "The protest of the Jewish Section (Yevsektsia) in the Commissariat for Nationality Affairs is cancelled and I do not oppose the continuation of the subsidy." On July 8, 1920, Kamenev, the head of the Moscow Soviet (and Trotsky's brother-in-law) notified the Tsentroteatr that the decision to discontinue the subsidy was cancelled and, consequently, the yearly subsidy of 100,000 rubles was continued.[24]

However, the Habima's persecution by the Yevsektsia also continued. Failing to dissolve the theater on political grounds, it spread the rumor that the Habima operated as a center of the black market and was the meeting place of brokers and speculators.[25] The fight against the Habima was conducted by major figures of the Yevsektsia—Shimon Dimanstein; Moshe Litvakov, the chief editor of *Der Emes;* and Chaim Gildin, the editor of the Kharkov Yiddish monthly, *Riotvelt.*

Many people outside the theater could not understand "what prevented the Habima from abandoning the stubborn insistence on performing in a strange language, from giving up our legendary unreal repertoire and starting to perform for the masses."[26] These people failed to realize that the Habima performing in any other language than Hebrew would perhaps be a popular theater among the Jewish people, but it would most definitely not be the national-historical theater that Zemach had intended it to be.

The Habima remained an official Soviet theater up until it left the country in January 1926.[27] The Habima had the status of an academic state theater as did the Maly, the Bolshoi, the Moscow Art Theater with its studios, and several other theaters. As an academic theater, the Habima was granted a union affiliation and its members were given subsistence cards enabling them to procure rations and theater supplies otherwise unobtainable. Thus, before the opening of *The Dybbuk* the Habima got from TEO all the necessary equipment, including prayer-shawls.[28] But official status and union affiliation had their peculiarities, as well. The Habima was required to issue free tickets for its performances to all unions; thus, "for a time we played to audiences [workers, peasants] that were completely strange to us."[29]

Official status permitted the Habima to exist and to perform in Hebrew. But how was the Habima permitted to present specifically Jewish—national and biblical—plays at such revolutionary times? Why was its work not censored? Moreover, what was the impact of the historical and political context on the repertoire of the Russian theaters in general and the Habima in particular?

Subsidies from the state combined with low-priced tickets or free admission democratized the theater and made possible a completely new audience. The theater, which had previously been restricted to the upper classes, now performed for soldiers, workers, and peasants, who had never been to the theater before. The theater was expected to express the social changes that the Revolution had brought about. The proletarian revolution demanded the creation of new forms of expression that would project the new ideas of the time. Yet, the number of new Russian plays of any dramatic merit was small. Furthermore, good contemporary drama was impossible during the first years following the Revolution because events happened so fast that it was impossible to depict them—artistically—on stage. In addition, most major Russian playwrights were neither enthusiastic about nor prepared to hail the new regime. Note that Gorky, for example, never wrote a play with a Soviet theme.

Vakhtangov, for instance, was convinced that a basic reform was needed in the theater. But since this depended completely on texts and there were no texts that met the new demands, he thought that there were two possible ways to meet the new challenge. He could read the classics with a new eye and endeavor to find in them some consonance with the Revolution. Or, he could prepare the way for new plays by developing new artistic forms. Indeed, not a single one of the plays Vakhtangov directed from the time of the Revolution to his death (in May 1922) was a contemporary play dealing with a contemporary topic, and only one play was Russian—Chekhov's *Wedding.* His productions in this period included: Ibsen's *Rosmersholm,* Maeterlinck's *The Miracle of Saint Anthony,* Strindberg's *Eric XIV,* Anski's *The Dybbuk,* and Gozzi's *Princess Turandot.*[30]

Indeed, the main concern of the Russian theater in the first decade after the Revolution was the interplay between content and form. The history of two prominent artists, Stanislavsky and Meyerhold, who represented completely different political and artistic lines, perhaps best illuminates this topic.[31]

During the October Revolution, the Moscow Theater was closed.[32] In 1919, a large part of the troupe touring in southern Russia was cut off from Moscow by the White Army. Many performers returned to Moscow, but others defected to Prague. Stanislavsky refused to present a propagandist play and to have anything to do with the new Soviet plays. Indeed, by 1920–1921, the Revolution seemed to make no difference for the theater, which continued to present its old plays, such as Maeterlinck's *The Blue Bird,* Chekhov's *The Three Sisters,* and Gogol's *The Inspector-General.*

The Moscow Art Theater soon reached an impasse. At a time when tendentiousness was rampant on the stage, Stanislavsky was helpless. He could not find the right solution to the problem of adjusting the theater to the new revolutionary conditions, nor could he give a convincing answer to the accusations hurled at him by the revolutionary theaters. The best thing he could do was to take his theater for a tour abroad—

both to escape and to keep the actors away from the people who, in his opinion, were destroying dramatic art in Russia. The theater left for its tour in September 1922. In August 1924, Stanislavsky returned to Russia; he felt that the Moscow Art Theater was a Russian national theater and therefore should stay and perform there.

Only in the 1925–1926 season did the Moscow Theater produce a contemporary play, *The Days of the Turbins,* by Bulgakov, although the play's message was counterrevolutionary: it depicted sympathetically the human side of a White Guard's family. In the same season, the theater presented a historical drama by Trenëv about Pugachev, the hero of the peasant uprising in the eighteenth century. This play brought the theater into closer touch with contemporary life in Soviet Russia. However, not until 1927, a whole decade after the Revolution, did the Moscow Theater hail bolshevism with the presentation of Ivanov's *Armored Train 14–69,* which presented a false picture of the Whites and was a "party" presentation. This was the first strictly Soviet play to be presented by the theater. Despite the fact that this and other productions showed an acceptance of Soviet ideas, there was no definite answer to the question of whether Stanislavsky was really sincere in presenting Soviet plays.

In comparison to Stanislavsky, Meyerhold was a committed Bolshevik and belonged to the Artistic Left.[33] In 1918, upon joining the Bolshevik party, he staged Mayakovsky's decidedly Soviet play, *Mystery Bouffe,* in Petrograd. However, the theaters in Petrograd were still maintaining a position of cautious neutrality and the production was boycotted by most of the professional actors. *Mystery Bouffe* attracted violent criticism and it closed after three performances. After this failure, no serious attempt was made to use the professional theater for propaganda purposes.

In 1922 even Meyerhold himself presented Ibsen's *A Doll's House* and Sukhov-Kobylin's *Iarelkin's Death,* a Russian satire on tsarist police methods written in 1869. In his search for revolutionary drama, Meyerhold turned to the German Expressionists and staged Toller's *Machine Wreckers* in 1922 and *Mass-Man* in 1923. Both plays portrayed the inhuman oppression of the individual and the world revolution soon to come. But the repertoire crisis was such that he staged no new work to mark the tenth anniversary of the October Revolution.

Even Meyerhold believed in the artistic freedom of the theater: "The only theatre which can become exemplary in this age of mighty Revolution is a Revolutionary theatre. However, it is wrong to imagine that the repertoire of such a theatre must consist exclusively of Verhaeren's *Dawn* and Vermishev's *The Truth*. It could just as easily include Wilde's *Salome* and Shakespeare's *Hamlet*, everything depends on the interpretation."[34]

In conclusion, in the late teens and early twenties, the revolution in the Russian theater was one of form rather than content. The serious theaters, and especially the academic state theaters, denounced the new propagandistic and political plays. The revolution in the theater, therefore, involved experiments with staging, acting, designing, and lighting—not with playwriting. The masterpieces of this period had nothing in common with contemporary Soviet themes. Rather, classical, western, and old Russian drama were chosen for the theatrical experiments. The new form and style, it was hoped, would give new meaning to the old content. Thus, one of the paradoxes was that non-Soviet plays were staged with Soviet money. Furthermore, the search for new forms of expression was for the most part carried on by people who had nothing to do with bolshevism.[35] Under this tolerant administration the theater flourished:

> The Great Period of Innovation and creativity in Soviet theater began approximately in 1921 and lasted until 1929 or 1930. It was unparalleled in the history of the international stage. Its lavishness and luxury were almost fabulous, and its schools and techniques not only enriched the Soviet theater alone but benefited the theaters of many other people as well. It was almost a miracle that such activity could take place amidst hunger, typhus, poverty, and total destruction, and right after a fratricidal civil war.[36]

The Habima, like other theatrical experiments, benefited from Lunacharsky's benevolent and enlightened supervision of the theater and from the fact that the other academic state theaters also did not present Soviet revolutionary plays. The Habima was therefore able to present Jewish plays that had nothing in common with the political spirit of the Russian Revolution. Just as the Russian theater had attained through the Revolution freedom of content and form, the Habima had attained through the Revolution the right to present a distinctively Jewish content.

But the factor that was most responsibile for the existence and institutionalization of the Habima in Moscow was the strong support of the Russian cultural and theatrical elite.

Support of the Russian Cultural Elite

Stanislavsky, who had adopted the theater as early as 1917, remained the Habima's mentor and faithful counselor until the company left Russia in 1926. He was fascinated with the group's sincerity and devotion, and his relationship with the theater was always warm. He often said he was happy to have been able to pay at least a small part of the debt humanity owed to the Jewish people, a people that had been cruelly persecuted. Upon the troupe's departure from Russia, he sent it a letter in which he wrote: "I consider myself fortunate that in this work of mine I realized the greatest of the artist's missions. . . ."[37]

In addition to Stanislavsky and Vakhtangov, the theater gained the support of other intellectuals and theater people. Especially noteworthy in this regard is Maxim Gorky, who was well-read in Yiddish and Hebrew literature (in Russian translation). In an enthusiastic review, written after he had seen *The Eternal Jew* for the third time, Gorky wrote:

> I know the obstacles and hindrances that the Habima had to overcome. I also know how much energy they spent combatting folly, jealousy and cruelty. But when there is a chance to speak of the great victory of the spirit I have no desire to talk of these sufferings. . . . There is a great piece of work in this little theatre, which is additional evidence of the magic charm of art and the super spirit of the Jewish people. The Habima is a theatre which the Jews can be proud of. This tender and pretty child promises to be great in days to come.[38]

Gorky was a close friend of both Lenin and Stalin, and he used his influential position to defend and speak on behalf of the theater.[39] Gorky did not regard the Habima as just another ordinary studio, but rather as an artistic achievement in itself and a major contribution to the Russian theater.

This view of the group was also shared by other Russian intellectuals and artists—especially after the production of *The Dybbuk*, a production which was for them a landmark in the history of the Russian theater.

The Habima was seen as a cultural innovation, and it was its artistic merit which, in their opinion, justified the existence of the theater in Moscow and its right to be subsidized by the state.

Support for the theater came from various groups with different political and artistic views. Stanislavsky, Nemirovitch-Dantchenko, and Tairov represented the old theatrical establishment—the academic theaters. But Meyerhold, who, as we have already seen, was the leader of the "Theatrical October," was also a friend of the theater. Meyerhold was even invited to direct a play at the Habima after Vakhtangov's death. He did come and talk with the group, but his commitments to other theaters were so pressing that he could not take on any new work.[40]

The Habima was also supported by artists and intellectuals who were not theater people. Thus, Vyacheslav Ivanov, the symbolist poet, was a member of the Moscow Theater Section and defended the Habima at the 1920 meeting of the Tsentroteatr during which the Yevsektsia convinced this unit to discontinue the subsidy.

The moral and artistic support that the Habima gained among the Russian cultural elite was both formal and informal, organized as well as personal. An example of informal and personal support occurred while the troupe was working on the second act of *The Dybbuk*. The actors suddenly realized that they did not have funds for necessities like lighting, costumes, etc. Vakhtangov proposed having a party and inviting those wealthy Jews who had remained in Moscow as well as actors from the other theaters. At the party, Vakhtangov and Mikhail Chekhov (the playwright's nephew and an actor and director of the First Studio of the Moscow Theater) dressed like waiters, served tea—and asked for donations. As a result of the party, the Habima was able to buy the materials it needed for the production.[41]

As a result of its affiliation with the Moscow Art Theater, the Habima worked with the best people of this theater and its studios. Consequently, students and artists attended the Habima's productions. This Russian audience was highly important to the troupe for several reasons. Numerically, it constituted a substantial part of the Habima's audience, which was very limited. Furthermore, the Habima aimed at establishing a Hebrew theater with high artistic standards, and it was the Russian theater which shaped these standards. Despite the importance that the theater ascribed to its mission and to Jewish audiences, it was the Russian theater which was the group's artistic frame of reference, and, therefore, it was extremely important that it approve the new theater's artistic work. Finally, the Russian audience—which at times included not merely artists but also officials—strengthened the Habima's legitimate existence, always threatened by the persecution by the Yevsektsia.

Yet, despite the opposition of the Yevsektsia and the lack of a Jewish audience in Moscow, the Habima survived. It was the enlightened and tolerant policy of the regime toward the theater, the official recognition of the Habima as a state theater, and the support which it gained from the Russian cultural elite that permitted the Habima to exist in Moscow in the first decade after the Revolution. These favorable conditions on the one hand, and the devotion of the members to the theater on the other, were indispensable to the Habima's legitimate existence in Russia.

It is of interest to mention that the Habima was fortunate to operate in Russia in the most liberal and creative decade in its history, 1917–1927. In 1927, a year after the Habima left Russia, a new period began. A conference on the theater, called by the Central Committee of the Communist party in 1927, marked the beginning of the end for this period of comparative freedom. Here, Stanislavsky, later revered as a forerunner of socialist realism, was denounced for "petty-bourgeois liberalism." Lunacharsky, who rose to Stanislavsky's defense, was himself under attack.

The following years saw the introduction of the five-year plans, the collectivization of agriculture, and an increasing reliance on totalitarian methods to achieve these goals. The changing atmosphere was quickly reflected in the theater. Lunacharsky's liberal influence was weakened and, by 1929, removed altogether, and Party control became even more stringent and stultifying. In 1929, Lunacharsky was replaced as Commissar of Enlightenment and Education. Four years later, he was appointed Soviet Ambassador to Spain, but died on his way there.[42]

A resolution of the Central Committee of the Party in 1932 announced the suppression of all literary organizations and their replacement by a single unit of Soviet writers. An analogous change was ordered in all other areas of the arts. This organizational centralization made it easy to control Russian artists and writers and to impose on them an ideological unity. Indeed, in 1934 this unity was fixed in the formula of "socialist realism," which was proclaimed a "historically superior and qualitatively new step in the development of the arts." This aesthetic commandment required "truthful historically concrete representation of reality in its revolutionary development," combined with the task of "ideological transformation of the working man in the spirit of socialism."[43] Theatrically, the formula of socialist realism was contradictory and vague because it confused such concepts as aesthetic methods, artistic goals, and political propaganda.

The impact of socialist realism on dramatic repertory and on acting and production was tremendous; it demanded that all plays reflect contemporary reality and topical themes and that production style conform to the strictures of representational art, ranging from sheer naturalism to psychological realism in the old-fashioned manner. Stalin expressed the new doctrine succinctly: "Literature should be national in form and socialist in content."[44]

In the thirties, the Party's call for "national art" resulted in the decline of theatrical activity and creativity. Meyerhold assessed this decline at a theater conference in 1939:

> Go visiting the theatres of Moscow. Look at their drab and boring presentations that resemble one another and are each worse than the others. . . . Recently creative ideas poured from them. People in the arts searched, erred, and frequently stumbled and turned aside. But they really created—sometimes badly and sometimes splendidly. Where once there were the best theatres of the world, now—by your leave—everything is gloomily well regulated, averagely arithmetical, stupifying, and murderous in its lack of talent. Is that your aim? If it is—oh! you have done something monstrous![45]

Predictably, after that speech the Meyerhold Theater was dissolved and he was arrested. He is believed to have died in a concentration camp.

FOUR

The Social Structure of the Habima

THE Habima's founders were single men and women in their early twenties, ready to devote their life to the establishment of a Hebrew theater. The fact that most of them were young, single, and cut off from their families intensified their commitment to the theater. Indeed, as their estrangement from their families and home towns grew, the Habima became a second or substitute home. Mention has been made of the self-selection of the theater's members. Zemach strengthened this self-selection; he talked at length with each prospective member to make sure that he knew that "he was not entering just another dramatic studio." Zemach thought of the Habima as a new type of yeshiva and told the new members that they must devote themselves entirely to study as if they were at the yeshiva. He made every member feel that "by joining the Habima, he assumed a great responsibility toward the Jewish people."[1]

The Habima's members adhered to the ascetic, puritanical, and idealistic tradition of all Russian Populists. The influence of the Russian intellectual style, its moral gravity and self-conscious idealism, was extremely strong. Indeed, the members lived under an obsessive urge to conquer themselves, to fashion their personalities after some great ideal. They believed that "there was no art without sacrifice, without ecstasy."[2] The whole group became so devoted to the cause that it was even ready to perform without an audience—the most important requirement for a regular functioning theater. Its motivation went far beyond pragmatic considerations, and the group set upon its task with an energy that was made possible by a sense of righteousness and an awareness of a higher purpose.

The members' readiness to devote themselves wholeheartedly to the theater was further reflected in the resolution of the founders not to get married until the Habima became well established.[3] This vow of celibacy, adopted by all members, was to assure only one attachment and commitment, for Zemach wanted all personal interests and resources channeled into the realization of his vision.

In the kind of involvement that it demanded from its members, the Habima displayed many characteristics of ideological groups. Members

The first twelve actors who participated in *Neshef Bereshit* (*Evening of Beginning*) (1918), the Habima's first production.

of ideological groups "forego willingly all familial attachment and personal ties for the sake of some . . . central symbols and collectivities." Ideological groups demand that their members obliterate completely the sphere of privacy and lay bare all their innermost feelings and desires. Moreover, the Habima, like other ideological groups, became "country, family, everything."[4]

Indeed, the members' involvement in the theater was intense. Looking for a suitable place for rehearsals and performances, they found an empty house that had belonged to a wealthy Muscovite who had fled when the Revolution broke out. The authorities requisitioned the house and Lunacharsky gave it to the Habima. The members themselves put their new quarters in order. They covered the walls with gray linen which gave the studio the feeling of a sanctuary, of a holy place. The studio was equipped with a small stage and an amphitheater with benches seating 126 people. It was very important to the members that the studio have an intimate atmosphere. Indeed, the closeness of the auditorium to the stage—it was a direct continuation without any physical barrier—afforded a face-to-face encounter between the audience and the actors and provided the intimacy they were seeking. In addition to the auditorium, the studio had an office, dressing rooms, and several rooms for the students who lived at the studio. There was also a small storehouse and a kitchen, and members who lived there took turns cooking.[5] Thus, the studio served not only for performances but also as a residence; it was physically as well as symbolically the home of many members.

Because the Habima's members valued group experiences and group living, they often held meetings of the collective. All problems and nagging questions, artistic as well as nonartistic, were discussed in a typically Russian manner—at emotional and unending nocturnal debates. The members took social as well as theatrical problems extremely seriously, and debated thoroughly, passionately, and with intensity. Whenever a new play was selected, for instance, there was a great deal of what the group referred to as "soul-searching," whether for the correct interpretation of a specific part, for the correct make-up, or for the solution to some other problem. But all meetings, including those dedicated to pragmatic matters, had a religious nature and were conceived as having moral implications.[6]

There were also informal social gatherings and formal holiday celebrations. On Friday evenings they never performed; instead they gave social parties to a small and select Jewish audience or for themselves. On these occasions, the artistic program usually consisted of reciting Hebrew poems, singing and dancing, and all these were performed with intense emotionality. On Passover, the holiday that commemorates the Exodus from Egypt, the group had a formal celebration with matzoth and wine, exactly like a large family. Such social gatherings, formal and informal, refreshed the spirit of the group and promoted its social solidarity.

During the years in which the Habima operated in Moscow, it worked under conditions of near starvation. Both food and coal were a rare luxury. Vardi, one of the first members, who kept a diary during these years, made the following entry on September 9, 1918: "We held a general meeting of Habima today and discussed the food question. It was decided to send two members to the countryside around Moscow to buy flour and potatoes. Otherwise we shall simply die of hunger."[7] The hunger and cold were so severe that many players fell seriously ill and suffered from typhus and tuberculosis. Rovina, for example, had consumption and was sent to a sanitarium to recover, but as soon as she heard that the work at the studio and resumed, she returned to Moscow—despite the doctors' disapproval.

At the end of 1919, when the Habima was recognized as an official state theater, it received both a subsidy and a union affiliation. As employees of the government, they received lumber, electricity, and food. The food was brought to the studio's storehouse, and a kitchen was set up in the basement. Bread was carefully divided so that each member got his fair share. Indeed, there was little to eat, but the members were committed to a modest, even ascetic, way of life. These conditions helped to unify the group by creating a sense of intimacy, fraternity, and comraderie. Despite—or, perhaps, because of—the hunger, cold, and fatigue, there was wild exhilaration and the passion of creation.

In many respects, the Habima's artistic creed and its organizational embodiment were an outgrowth of the Bolshevik Revolution's egalitarian spirit. Most Russian revolutionists were collectivists, their chief belief being that "man fulfills himself only by serving society." Members were taught that they were responsible not only for themselves, but also for the entire collective and each of its members. They believed in the sovereignty of the collective over its individual members, and in its exclusive right to define the social norms and behavior of the individual member.[8]

The Habima was deeply affected by these ideas. The group believed that only one type of theater would correspond to their ideological and artistic convictions: a collective, group theater. As Ben-Ari wrote: "A collective theatre gives to all its players the chance to share in creative work. There is a common ideal, to which all members strive."[9] Indeed, the Habima was regarded as an organic, artistic commune and every individual as a commune member. Equality and fraternity—in theory as well as in practice—were the group's chief moral principles.

When the officials of Sovkino (the Soviet Film Department) produced Sholem Aleichem's *The Deluge,* parts were offered to some of the Habima's players, but the Habima as a group was now involved. Nonetheless, the right of the troupe's actors to participate in the film had to be purchased from the collective, and "the money we received went to the group, not to the individual players, and was divided among all of us, whether or not we had taken part in the filming."[10]

The members also believed that the collective had the right to define norms for the individual players off stage as well as on. The group's norms and symbols were internalized by the members and affected their conduct. One of the first dominant symbols was simplicity: "We wanted to avoid anything that was noisily vulgar, anything that was tinselly and tawdry." This simplicity was expressed in the members' clothing as well as in the studio's style. Another important group value was dignity: "The conduct of rehearsals, the relationships with colleagues—all should be characterized by dignity and modesty. The women in the group, for example, did not smoke, although smoking was the fashion."[11]

In the early years, there was no need to exert pressure on the members to conform to the group's norms. The whole group felt that "if each of us did not assume our responsibilities, exercise our old self-discipline, improve the relationships between us, dispel all our prejudices and grievances, then we might as well say goodbye to everything we had been working toward." The group's norms were "unwritten laws which governed the group, and they were quite apparent to all."[12] Indeed, before the theater's Leningrad tour in 1923, there was a discussion at the general meeting "concerning the discipline we should impose on ourselves, what our behavior should be, what we should tell the newspaper people . . . and what things we should not do."[13]

The members believed that the theater, as a group, should get publicity, but they strongly opposed any personal publicity or hint of stardom:

> On the rare occasion that one of us seemed dissatisfied, we will let him know quickly that we were not interested in breeding stars. If any of us ever got the notion that he was something special and apart, we would simply lose confidence in him and quickly put him in his place. . . . The whole idea of specialness had to be uprooted; it was dangerous, especially for the young actors who were just beginning.[14]

Players who had already tasted fame and applause now had to forget about personal fame and success.

Material rewards had apparently not motivated the members before they joined the Habima, and such incentives continued to be unimportant afterwards. Rather, the members aimed at a collective goal, and their chief reward was the great honor of being a Hebrew actor on a Hebrew stage. Indeed, the rewards for their work were intrinsic: self-realization and self-actualization. But not all members were satisfied with these nonmaterial rewards and extremely difficult working conditions. As a result, a further process of self-screening took place.

Only a few players left the Habima; motivated by pragmatic and personal considerations, these actors wanted a greater career and success as actors. They went to big theatrical centers, New York and Paris, where they performed for a time, but none of them developed artistically. These actors had failed to realize that the power of the Habima at that time stemmed from its collective power and not from the acting skill of some individual players. Those who left did not take into account that most of the Habima players (including themselves) benefited from the great challenge of a Hebrew theater, and that under other circumstances they might have never become actors or attained such artistic standards. However, the desertion of these members ultimately benefited the group; it was now left with those who were really willing to devote their life to the theater. The defections, therefore, helped to integrate the group and strengthen its esprit de corps.

The Habima's collectivism not only reflected the revolutionary spirit and collectivist ideas of the time; it was also appropriate to the group's idealism and the conditions under which it operated. The Revolution brought about a shift in theater ownership. A 1923 survey of ownership of theaters, cinemas, and other artistic enterprises (excluding Moscow and Petrograd) showed that the extent of private proprietorship in the legitimate theater was small. Only 9 percent of the theaters were privately owned, but 34 percent were owned by actors' collectives, 21 percent by unions, the Red Army, and other public organizations, and 36 percent by the state. The percentage of collectively owned theaters was high because state and public funds were not sufficient to support all the theaters. Furthermore, because of economic conditions, at least one out of every three theaters that existed in 1922 had disbanded by the end of the year.[15]

The state theaters were in better condition than the others because in addition to their state subsidy they charged admission for the majority of seats. The Habima, as a state theater, received a yearly subsidy. But the subisdy was extremely small and became irregular toward the end of the theater's stay in Moscow. Furthermore, unlike the other academic state theaters, the Habima did not receive money from ticket sales because it did not have an audience. Thus, the theater had serious financial problems and these problems strengthened its collectivist structure.

It is noteworthy that the members did not refer to the Habima as a "theater," but rather as a "studio." They thought that the notion of a theater was too confining to describe their work and their relationship to the group. The notion of a dramatic studio was very popular in Russia in those years; it even implied special social and psychological attributes in the members who took part in it and in the venture itself:

> In the evening, after a hard day's work at the factories and elsewhere, the young people would gather. . . . They were all ardent and enthusiastic about the "new theatre." They would rehearse from evening to late at night, and they searched for "new forms" with a fanatic passion. . . . They constructed the decor with their own hands gluing the props together and sewing the costumes and curtains often until dawn. . . . The studios were almost like hermitages or monasteries, and the devotees who worked in them were a mendicant order of the militant faithful to the theatres . . . they performed a great service in maintaining the burning flame of pure love for the pure art of the theatre—especially among the

young. The studios also retained much else that could not be found in the orthodox theatres.[16]

During the Civil War, hunger and devastation caused people to flee into an illusory life; the theater provided a refuge from the terrible reality outside, as the following observation indicates:

> Was it escape from reality, a glance into a new world of fiction, a discovery of an artificial paradise by people who for centuries had not been admitted to the entertainments of the upper classes, or a kind of collective curiosity, that inextinguishable Russian desire to learn and experience new things. Whatever the explanation, from 1918 to 1924, the collective psychosis assumed striking proportion, creative inventiveness rose in a fountain-like jet.[17]

The conditions and circumstances which brought into existence hundreds of dramatic studios in Russia also shaped the Habima, which soon became an integral part of the setting within which it operated. The members attributed sacred qualities to their studio; they saw it as a cloister, where the players—like priests—were dedicated to the mastery of their art. For them, the work at the studio came close to being a religious rite.

The Habima troupe in Moscow.

Stanislavsky and Vakhtangov had a tremendous impact on the theater's code of ethics, artistic style, and social structure. From their own teachers the actors learned that ethics were just as important as the work on a play and that each individual actor was a participator in the spiritual as well as physical building of the theater. The group felt strongly that to build a theater one must be concerned with every facet of its operation. Therefore, besides performing on stage, they had responsibilities backstage, in the hall, and in wardrobe. Before the opening of *Neshef Bereshit,* the women in the group sewed curtains and made lampshades, and the men put together benches, tables, and whatever else was needed.[18]

Stanislavsky taught the group to be proud of being students of the theater. For him, to be a student meant a perpetual seeking of new forms of expression, and in this he saw the greatest happiness a true artist could achieve. And Vakhtangov preached to the group: "Do not be professional; first the soul, and then the profession."[19] Vakhtangov considered a narrow professional attitude inadmissible in the theater. He thought that "one of the sicknesses of contemporary acting is 'professionalism.' " He severely criticized those students who entered the theater merely to show off, and he spared neither time nor himself to straighten out a student who had lost the high aim of true art.[20]

In light of their youth, their commitment to the notion of a creative dramatic studio, and their opposition to viewing acting as a career, the members' strong opposition to admitting Yehoshua Bertonov into the group is understandable. Bertonov was born in 1879 and was older than most of the members by almost two decades. Moreover, he was a professional actor; he came to the Habima with almost twenty years' acting experience in both the Yiddish and the Russian theater. He had an already established theatrical "baggage" and mannerisms. Under the tsarist regime, Bertonov had not been allowed to appear in big cities and had therefore acted in several provincial wandering troupes. But provincial players were looked down on by the serious actors of Moscow; the commonly held view in the established theaters was that provincial actors were unqualified because they employed vulgar acting methods.

Since the Habima was dedicated to "casting aside everything that was cheap or ordinary from the theatrical point of view, getting rid of theatrical stereotypes, and creating something new and innovative," Bertonov's provincial acting experience gave the troupe even more reason to object to him. The ideal member was an amateur (in the positive sense of the term) who was open-minded and ready for experimentation. The metaphor was a "virgin soil that could be sown anew with new theatrical seeds."[21] Bertonov, who, according to his biological and theatrical age, could have been the group's teacher, had to pass auditions given by the young amateurs. Without Zemach's insistence, Bertonov would probably not have been admitted.[22] Yet even at that, the group grudgingly accepted Bertonov only for a trial period. It is of interest to mention that Bertonov, in order to join the Habima, renounced a spectacularly successful career on the Yiddish and Russian stages. He was willing to start anew as a beginner, and for several years he was content to perform small parts.

In order to establish a theater based on firm artistic foundations, thorough and professional training were required, especially since most members were amateurs when they first joined the theater. The Habima's years in Moscow had therefore been a period of study and apprenticeship. In these years, the troupe had received superior instruction and had learned a great deal about the art of acting, and it was this training that had transformed amateur members into serious actors. This contributed to the establishment of high artistic standards for the Habima, and, consequently, to its artistic merit.

The production methods of Stanislavsky and Vakhtangov meant that plays were in rehearsal for long periods. Accordingly, every play followed carefully the following procedures: it was read to the group; the spirit of the play was analyzed in great detail; every single part was analyzed and built up carefully; and only after each single part became a unity in itself were all the parts tied together by the predominant spirit of the play. Following strictly these production methods, the group worked nearly nine months on the first production, *Neshef Bereshit*, and almost the same length of time on the second production, *The Eternal Jew*. Before the premiere of *The Dybbuk* in 1922, they performed only twice a week; the rest of the time, day and night, they rehearsed *The Dybbuk*. The work on *The Dybbuk* lasted, with long interruptions due to the state of Vakhtangov's health, more than two years. The rehearsals for each of the other productions in Moscow—*The Golem*, *Jacob's Dream* and *The Flood*—lasted several months, as well.

Stanislavsky himself gave a series of lessons at the Habima studio in the winter of 1921. The sessions were attended by the Habima, the Chekhovs, the Vakhtangovs, and the Armenian studio. Stanislavsky's lectures had the character of informal talks, and had "an elevating ethical and moral influence" on the actors. His talks "wandered beyond the theatre; they encompassed the deepest and most fundamental feelings."[23] In order to apply his method of acting and to prove the universality of art, Stanislavsky planned a production of Shakespeare's *The Merchant of Venice* in which the Habima members would play the Jewish parts, the Armenians the parts of the Prince of Morocco and the Prince of Aragon, and the members of the two Russian studios the rest of the parts. He began the work, but the plan was never realized.[24]

The Habima regarded Stanislavsky's lessons as sacred. For these lessons the members put on their best clothes, clothes appropriate to the festiveness of a Jewish holiday. The players wrote down every word that Stanislavsky uttered and late at night carefully memorized their notes.[25] And they kept their notes, and continued to use them for decades.

The Habima's work with Vakhtangov was definitely the group's most significant experience. After the Revolution, Vakhtangov was at the peak of his career and, therefore, very busy. In addition to the Habima he worked with other groups, especially the studios of the Moscow Art Theater, and also worked as an actor. Consequently, it was not uncommon for rehearsals on *The Dybbuk* to begin after midnight and to last long after dawn. Because of Vakhtangov's many obligations, a regular schedule of rehearsals was impossible; nor was it desired, since a schedule symbolized for the group an ordinary, orthodox, and strictly professional theater, which they opposed.

The all-night sessions with Vakhtangov were usually a most inspiring and uplifting experience. He used to say to the group: "Remember that your task is to inspire, teach, render judgement. The stage must be holy for you." With such a dictum as their guide, it is hardly surprising that "every student considered himself chosen above all his fellows when he was permitted to stand on the stage . . . or to carry some property on or off."[26] Vakhtangov's aim was to create a Jewish actor well qualified for the role, whose feeling toward the theater would liken it to a "temple and himself as a priest ordained to transmit its message and perform its rites."[27] He not only taught the Habima the art of acting, he also educated the actors and contributed to their outlook on life.

Vakhtangov often inspired those with whom he worked: "Every hour of a rehearsal with Vakhtangov was an inspiration; always a new discovery, never anything routine. He guarded us from all that was tasteless and conventional," as one of the actresses recalled.[28] During the work on *The Dybbuk,* he often interrupted the rehearsals to share with the members his thinking on art. Every meeting with Vakhtangov became "an academy of theatrical questions."[29] Vakhtangov was for the Habima much more than a director, guide, and coach. He was "a big brother, a loving mother, and a preaching father."[30]

Mention has been made of the fact that *The Dybbuk* remained in the Habima's repertoire for four decades. When the production was presented, every actor remembered to the last small detail what Vakhtangov had told him to do at every moment of the play. The group was very strict, insisting that every player do exactly—no more and no less—what he had done in the original 1922 production. When some of the players could no longer perform their original parts, they instructed the young actors on where to stand, at which moment to move, and which gesture to use. These veteran members always complained that the young actors did not perform their parts with the same sacred and serious attitude with which they had performed them. And the young actors were amazed by the clarity and detail with which the veterans remembered their work with Vakhtangov.[31]

The serious and intimate atmosphere that existed at the Habima studio was immensely inspiring. On one occasion, Vakhtangov said to Bialik, "I work in other studios and with other groups, but when I enter this place I am obsessed, I become a different person." Gorky held a similar opinion of the unique atmosphere at the Habima: "How great is the charm of this small house. When one craves rest and wishes to afford himself of the peace of the soul in getting away from the turmoil of life, he is only to enter this house and he soon finds himself in a different world."[32] And on another occasion, Gorky said: "I believe that the Habima actors have one advantage over those of the Moscow Art Theatre of those days, for in addition to their artistic abilities which they possess in no lesser quality than do the former, they have the element of ecstasy. The theatre for them is a rite, a worship, and this can be sensed immediately."[33] The Habima intoxicated everyone who visited the studio. This was at least part of the reason why Stanislavsky chose to teach at the Habima's studio. He hoped that the ecstasy and fire of the Habima would inflame and intoxicate the members of the other studios.

In summary, in Moscow there was no distinction between theatrical and nontheatrical activities, there was no distinction between life on stage and off. In the kind of participation that it demanded from its members, the Habima displayed many characteristics of ideological and totalitarian groups, groups which are "homogeneous, exclusive, and sacrosanct."[34] The Habima, like other totalitarian groups, encompassed the members' whole life: work, family life, and leisure. It organized all the members' outside activities and gave them a philosophy and a way of thinking and living. The theater, like the totalitarian group, was sacred, surrounded by special respect and reverence. Work at the studio was the object of a real cult, and participation was religious in nature.

The total loyalty and commitment of the individual players to the theater was also made possible by another characteristic that the Habima displayed: intragroup marriage and intimate social relationships. Although the first members had adopted a resolution to remain unmarried until the Habima was firmly established, most did not live up to that promise. But many of them—almost one-half of the group—married within the Habima itself. In addition to intermarriages, there were also kinship relationships, and a group of singles, some of whom never married. Furthermore, none of the married couples, except for Bertonov, had children while in Moscow.

The intragroup marriages, kinship relationships, singleness, and lack of children permitted a greater devotion and commitment to the theater, a devotion that under different conditions would have been difficult or impossible to achieve. The players could dedicate themselves entirely to their work because they had no important obligations or attachments outside the theater. For most members, life and work at the theater were more important than their private lives.

The devotion to the theater was neither motivated by nor based upon any consideration of strict "careerism," a term which meant the egotistical pursuit of self-interest.[35] The Russian revolutionary milieu in which the Habima had grown up had generated a deep contempt for "careerism." To be a "careerist" meant to be outside the framework of the collective, to be pursuing self-aggrandizing rather than communal goals.

The anticareerism of the Habima can be seen in the conduct of the group's two greatest players, Hanna Rovina and Aaron Meskin. During the troupe's tours in Europe in the late twenties, both of them achieved world success and fame—Rovina in *The Dybbuk* and Meskin in *The Golem.* But they were never tempted by the great offers and opportunities offered them during the tours. Rovina and Meskin were offered tempting contracts to appear on the German and Yiddish stages in America, but they refused to perform in theaters other than the Habima.[36] Their reaction to these offers proved not only that they were loyal to the theater as a whole, but that they were faithful to its self-appointed national mission.

The group's lack of interest in pursuing personal careers and their opposition to rewards common in other theaters—material benefits, fame, publicity, and better working conditions—were among the distinctive characteristics of the theater in its formative years.

TWO

The Habima in Transition: 1926–1931

FIVE

The Habima in Europe and the United States

THE Habima left Russia on January 26, 1926, never to return. From 1926 to February 1931, the theater toured Europe, the United States, and Palestine. These five years were a transitional and extremely important period in the history of the theater. Significant changes occurred in its composition, ideological mission, repertoire, organization, and audience.

The First Tour of Europe

Zemach always contended that the Habima should stay in Russia until it acquired the necessary training and established itself on firm artistic foundations. With the production of *The Flood* in 1925, the theater reached an impasse, and despair overcame the group. The illegality of Zionism and Hebrew in Russia in the mid-twenties, the financial situation and, most important of all, the lack of an audience resulted in uncertainty about the fate of the theater.

Fortunately for the troupe, M. A. Gefen, an entrepreneur whom Zemach had met in his visit to Riga, suggested that the Habima tour Europe. A European tour seemed to be the best way to raise the morale of the troupe and improve its financial situation. The three hundredth performance of *The Dybbuk* was given as a farewell-to-Russia performance on January 18, 1926. Zemach delivered a message to the audience, which erupted with cries of farewell in Russian, Yiddish, and Hebrew. Stanislavsky sent his farewell in a letter, in which he wrote: "Now upon our departure I send the Habima my most heartfelt greetings, the greetings of a friend. May the Habima abroad seek and support that which we, together with my pupil, Vakhtangov, loved, sought for, and created."[1]

The Habima was granted permission to leave the Soviet Union by Maxim Litvinov, the Deputy People's Commissar for Foreign Affairs, who was a Jew. The Soviet government believed that the theater was

Poster of the Habima's farewell performance in Russia, *The Dybbuk*, January 18, 1926.

going on tour to demonstrate Russian theatrical culture throughout the world. Permission was given for a one-year tour with the possibility of extension, and the government provided the troupe with special papers that would give the actors back their living quarters upon their return to Russia.[2] The Habima, therefore, left as an official state theater. At the time of the departure, the actors believed that "we are merely leaving on a tour" and that "we will be back in half a year, or a year at most."[3] Only Zemach and a few others realized that the Habima was never to return.

Actually, the Habima left the Soviet Union at the last moment, so to speak. It is quite probable that had the theater stayed longer, it would have been dissolved. In the late twenties, a consistently anti-Zionist course, aimed at total destruction of the "Zionist hydra," had been the declared policy of the government. By the end of the decade there had been the total destruction of many Jewish—not only Zionist—institutions. Furthermore, even the Yevsektsia, the Habima's major opponent, was abolished in 1930; it had outlived its usefulness for the regime.[4]

During the tour, the Habima's official status as a Soviet state theater created many difficulties. In almost every city that the troupe visited, the local Soviet Embassy greeted and gave parties for the Habima because they regarded the theater as a representative of Russian culture. But banquets for the theater were also given by local Jewish and Zionist organizations. In Riga, for instance, when the Soviet ambassador sent a bouquet of flowers to the stage at the end of the performance, the result was both pro and con yells from the audience.[5] And when the Habima performed in Berlin, the Soviet Embassy prohibited the troupe from participating in a Zionist banquet.[6] The Soviet regime continued to view the Habima players as Soviet citizens touring Europe as official emissaries of the Soviet theater and as "another achievement of the new Russia."[7]

The European tour had two separate missions: national and artistic. Warsaw, which had the largest Jewish community in Europe, and Berlin, the world theater center in the twenties, were the most important challenges for the Habima. Warsaw was a national challenge; Berlin an artistic one. As in Russia, the Habima aimed its appeal at two distinct audiences: a Jewish audience for which the appeal was intended to be political as well as artistic, and a non-Jewish audience for which the appeal was meant to be merely, or mainly, artistic.

But the Habima's tour was an event transcending artistic importance. It became a national holiday for the Jewish communities all over Europe, especially in Eastern Europe. The large Jewish communities in Latvia and Poland were then vibrant with an intense cultural life dominated by the Zionist idea, while suffering at the same time from active anti-Semitism. To them, the Habima, as the first Hebrew-language theater, was proof of the revival of their ancient language and a symbol of Jewish national unity. Indeed, the tour enabled the Habima to attain some of its original missions, ones that could not be realized in Moscow. From its inception, the Habima wanted to reach the Jewish masses in the Diaspora and uplift them morally, nationally, and artistically. As Bialik once described the theater: "From the very beginning the Habima has had functions other than the purely dramatic. It serves us as an artistic ambassador to the outside world. The living truth of a Habima performance is far more effective Zionist propaganda than any number of speeches and articles and pleas."[8]

The success of the tour was enormous; in every city, thousands of people met them at the railway station. In Bialystok, a city where Zemach and several actors had lived, the Jewish inhabitants closed their stores and put on their best clothes. And in Kovno, the theater found a unique situation: the audience consisted predominantly of young people who knew Hebrew and understood every word that was uttered on stage.[9] Mass enthusiasm and glorious receptions repeated themselves in the other cities of Latvia and Lithuania.

In Poland, the anti-Semitic government raised many obstacles, but the Habima finally got permission to perform. However, the Warsaw audiences did not receive the theater with the same enthusiasm that had greeted them before. Reviews of *The Dybbuk* in the Warsaw Yiddish press were full of praise, but the other productions did not fare so well. In addition, the Habima's visit there led to a not very friendly debate within the Jewish community, between partisans of Yiddish and Hebrew, and between Zionists and non-Zionists. The anti-Zionist Bund, the socialist party, used the visit to attack Zionism in general and the theater in particular as agents of clerical obscurantism. The Bund even organized a "public trial" at which party leaders accused the Habima of betraying the Jewish people by performing in Hebrew, a language understood by very few. Other anti-Hebraists did not think of the Habima as a distinctive expression of Jewish art and stressed that the theater was a part of Russian culture.[10] Fortunately for the theater, the reception in other cities in Poland was much warmer and more enthusiastic than in Warsaw.

The next stop was Vienna, one of the greatest artistic challenges of the tour, for Vienna was a great world cultural center. Thus, in Vienna, artistic rather than political considerations would attract the public to the Habima. The Vienna visit turned out to be a big success. Their stay, originally scheduled for one week, was extended to three, and during the entire run the Habima performed to packed houses.

The drama critics praised the productions, even though none of them spoke Hebrew. The performances were attended by the cultural and political elite of Vienna, luminaries like Arthur Schnitzler, the Austrian dramatist, Max Reinhardt, the noted state director, Richard Beer-Hoffman, the playwright (he wrote *Jacob's Dream*), and Alexander Moissi, the noted German actor. Moissi, for instance, praised the Habima thus: "When the players of the Moscow Habima Theater perform, I do understand Hebrew."[11] He proved—like many others before and after him—that "the Habima stirred even those who do not understand a word of Hebrew."[12] Reinhardt, who saw the Habima's productions of *The Dybbuk* and *Jacob's Dream*, said:

> I do not have to search for words. The shows of the Habima made a tremendous impression on me; the acting, the discipline deserve the highest praise. *The Dybbuk* carried me away. The acting is perfect. In the first act of *Jacob's Dream* I thought that *The Dybbuk* is the Habima's greatest asset, but after the third act I came to the conclusion that here too the theatre reached an unusual height.[13]

The Habima's tour was an international artistic event. Western Europe had not seen the achievements of the new Russian theater, and especially the work of Vakhtangov, who had already become legend. In Berlin, *The Dybbuk*, with its innovative use of expressionism and theatricality, caused a sensation. The Habima was identified as an official Soviet state theater and as an offspring of the Moscow Art Theater. Consequently, its performances were theatrical events of the first order, gaining world fame during the European tour. Even the anti-Semitic critics praised its productions, and Yiddishists ignored the national significance of the performances and attended the productions solely because of their high artistic merit. Indeed, the theater's audience was very varied; it included Hebraists as well as Yiddishists, Zionists as well as non-Zionists, and Jews as well as non-Jews. When it came to appreciating the production, "these various elements forgot their political differences and applauded us heartily."[14]

The success of the European tour, however, was overshadowed by the actors' concerns about the future of the Habima. "Where is our home?" "What is the end to be?" Questions which plagued the troupe during the Moscow period remained unanswered.[15] According to its original ideology, the Habima was to be the Hebrew national theater in Jerusalem. Indeed, in Moscow, it had been the group's hope of establishing the Habima in Palestine that enabled them to overcome obstacles—poverty, hunger, and a hostile environment—that would otherwise have been insurmountable. The group believed that the Habima would eventually settle in Palestine, but it remained uncertain just when and how this dream would be realized.

Another major question faced by the Habima was whether the theater should settle permanently in Palestine and serve only the Jewish community there, or serve the entire world Jewish community. Zemach thought that "the Habima must wander like the prophets, from town to town and from country to country throughout the Diaspora, and then meet again each year in Jerusalem, where the 'mother' theatre would be established."[16] He maintained that the Habima should be "a stimulant for Jewish art, the center of the entire Jewish theatrical life."[17] Zemach thought that this arrangement was also desirable from the financial point of view because Palestine would presumably not be able to sustain the whole troupe.[18]

In the meantime, the Habima continued its European tour. Paris was the last city on the schedule. Unlike the cities visited before, Paris did not have a large Jewish community, and a non-Jewish audience was not attracted to the theater, despite favorable reviews. The morale of the troupe was low; it found itself with no more bookings to continue the tour—and it was out of money. Fortunately, the American impresario Sol Hurok had seen the troupe perform in Paris and he decided to bring the company to the United States. The contract with Hurok permitted the Habima to show its artistic achievements to American Jews—then the largest Jewish community in the world.

In November 1926, the theater left for New York without knowing how long the American tour would last or when they would realize the vision of a permanent home in Jerusalem. Now all future plans seemed to depend upon the success of the tour in the United States.

The Habima in the United States

The Habima arrived in New York on December 6, 1926. The theater originally planned to perform in New York for several months and then tour other cities. It also hoped to raise funds and prepare new plays. However, the company soon realized that from the Jewish point of view New York was no Riga, nor from the artistic point of view was it Berlin or Vienna. Although the press covered their visit and there were the usual reception committees, on the whole they were not received as warmly and enthusiastically as in Europe.

In artistic terms, most of the productions were highly acclaimed. Brooks Atkinson, the drama critic of the *New York Times,* wrote that "the spoken words obviously did not matter . . . for the attention was naturally focused upon a highly stylized type of acting developed to a state of plastic perfection." He also wrote that "no other performance in the city has been so bold in its stylization, so daring in its treatment of details and so skillful in evoking the latent moods of a production."[19] Stark Young, America's greatest drama critic at that time, saw in *The Dybbuk* the most perfect production since the *Cherry Orchard* of the Moscow Art Theater had been presented in New York in 1923. Like all the other critics, he was particularly impressed by the blending of the various elements of the production—the acting, music, make-up, and costumes.[20]

Other productions of the Habima were also critically acclaimed. Following the premiere of *The Golem,* the *New York Times* wrote: "No one who has seen the acting of the Habima troupe can be in two minds as to the quality of their performance. Action, word and gesture are welded into a unity."[21] *The Eternal Jew* and *Jacob's Dream* did not fare as well, although Atkinson wrote of *The Eternal Jew* that it was "a very interesting exhibition of the Habima's methods and a demonstration of their courage."[22]

Despite favorable reviews, the Habima did not enjoy a box office success in the United States. It is noteworthy that *The Dybbuk* was not new to the American public. In 1922, it had been produced in Yiddish by Maurice Schwartz, and in 1925, the Neighborhood Playhouse presented *The Dybbuk* in English. Furthermore, Atkinson, Young, and other critics who wrote enthusiastic reviews of *The Dybbuk* expressed the opinion of an enlightened minority. Other critics, like Abe Cahan, the influential leader and editor of the Yiddish *Jewish Daily Forward*, disagreed with the theater's interpretation and staging of the play.[23]

The Jewish population of New York preferred the Yiddish theater which was then very popular. The Yiddish stage usually presented original Yiddish drama. During the Habima's visit, the Yiddish Art Theatre of Maurice Schwartz—one of the best Yiddish theaters—presented Goldfaden's *Tenth Commandment;* Yushkewitz's *Mendele Spivak,* Asch's *Reverend Doctor Silver,* and two plays by Ossip Dymov, *Yoshke Musicant* and *Menschen Shtoib*—all original Yiddish plays. Another major theater, the New Yiddish Art Theatre founded by the actor Jacob Ben-Ami, presented original Yiddish plays as well as foreign plays in Yiddish translations, like Galsworthy's *Justice* and an adaptation of Dostoevsky's *The Idiot.*[24]

In the late twenties the composition of the Yiddish theater's audience had changed considerably and, consequently, the repertoire also underwent a change. Until then, the Yiddish theater had catered to the first-generation immigrants who had arrived in the late nineteenth century. These immigrants were seeking the familiar culture of the homeland during a painful period of adjustment, and therefore the Yiddish theater presented plays that consisted for the most part of either classics of their homeland or dramatizations of Jewish legends. But by the late twenties, the Yiddish theater had become the theater of the second and third generations, persons who desired to be assimilated into American society. Thus, the newer plays strove to express contemporary attitudes of the audience "here and now."[25] The type of plays—not only the language—that the Habima presented was very different from the repertoire of the Yiddish theater. The Habima's plays catered neither to the first generation of immigrants nor to the second and third generations. Once again, the Habima realized that from the point of view of both language and repertoire it was a theater of a select few.

Because the Habima was a Zionist theater, it was antipathetic to the whole idea of Jewish migration and settlement in America. In addition, Zionism was the slowest and the last of the major Jewish movements to take root in the Jewish immigrant community. In the first two decades of this century, Zionist organizations remained marginal, seldom rivaling Jewish socialism. And even in later years, when Zionism became a powerful force among American Jews, they were still reluctant to accept migration to Palestine as an objective for themselves. Furthermore, the Jewish socialists regarded Zionism as a troublesome competitor, and the Yiddishists—who advocated the preservation of Yiddish culture and saw in the *galut* (Diaspora) a rich historical epoch—"were enraged by the Zionists' [and the Habima's] depreciation of the Diaspora experience."[26]

Indeed, on the whole, the Habima appealed to a small minority composed of serious theatergoers, a few Hebraists, and some progressive workers who were imbued with the Jewish national idea. The American Zionists honored the theater at many banquets and lauded it on many occasions as "our national theater," but nothing was done to secure the future of the troupe.[27]

The Habima's audience in New York became smaller and smaller. The theater left the city and went on tour, but things were even worse in other cities. Sol Hurok gave up the company and a new impresario took charge. The new manager's advice showed how alien the Habima was on the American scene: he attempted to change the scripts of the plays by attaching happy endings. He could not understand why the actors had to lament the destruction of the Temple in *The Eternal Jew*, an event which had taken place two thousands years ago.[28]

The Habima was not merely alien to the Jewish-Yiddish scene, but also to the American theatrical scene in general. In the twenties, the American theater was highly commercialized and there were no permanent theater troupes, let alone a cooperative theater group like the Habima. Most American companies were formed by producers who invested their money in the production, and the actors were paid on the basis of their part in the production and according to their fame. Most American plays dealt primarily with everyday life, without a definite message of the kind the Habima plays had. In the absence of permanent theater groups, most plays on Broadway—the heart of the American theater—differed little from one another in terms of direction or acting style. No theater had its own style or particular form of expression. Most theatergoers expected to be entertained; they conceived of the theater as an amusement.

A brief examination of the plays presented in New York during the 1926–1927 season (during the Habima's visit) reveals that of the 257 plays, 98 were serious drama, 93 were comedies and farces, 42 were musical comedies and revues, and the others were operettas, melodramas, etc. Of importance is the fact that most of the popular productions were either comedies or musical comedies.[29]

Hence, the Habima differed from the American theaters in the language in which it performed, the types of plays it presented, its organizational structure (a cooperative theater), its artistic style and school of acting (expressionism and ensemble acting) and, most important of all, its conception of the theater's mission and the actor's role.

The Habima stayed in the United States for six months. Although most of its performances were given in New York, the theater performed in other major cities, such as Boston and Chicago, as well. When box office receipts fell off, the second manager abandoned the troupe. The players had to interrupt their tour and return to New York, with no home to go back to.

The financial failure of the Habima's visit disappointed the members who had been sure that the troupe would attract large audiences, especially in New York. They had also hoped that the East European origins of most American Jews, and the fact that the theater arrived in New York after it had earned world fame on its European tour, were factors that favored a successful tour. The failure of the tour also intensified already existing conflicts within the company. In June 1927, the theater split into two groups: the minority, headed by Zemach, stayed on in New York; the majority left for Berlin and from there for Palestine.

The Split in the Habima

The main conflict was between Zemach and most of the group, and concerned the Habima's artistic and administrative direction. In Moscow, so long as Vakhtangov was alive, it was he who assumed the role of guide and artistic director, and his authority was accepted by all members. Zemach had been the General Director and in charge of the theater's ideology and administration.

The first serious crisis in the group's work occurred after the untimely death of Vakhtangov in May 1922. The Habima still conceived of itself as a studio and, as such, needed a guiding spirit, but it seemed impossible to find a successor of Vakhtangov's stature. It was then that Zemach aspired to the position; he was determined to have absolute authority in all matters—artistic and nonartistic. But the group could not see him as its artistic leader.

The members soon demanded the election of a small committee to work with Zemach; they felt that he should take counsel with the members. But Zemach took this decision as a proof of the group's distrust in his work and as an attempt to lessen his authority.[30] He ignored the fact that with *The Dybbuk* the theater had developed artistically and was no longer a studio on trial. Furthermore, several actors had excelled and established themselves as gifted players. The members did not regard Zemach as one of the greatest talents of the theater. Nor was he the most knowledgeable where artistic affairs were concerned. Consequently, the group could not see him as its sole artistic director. Zemach finally relented and agreed to the election of a council with which he was to work; but he did not accept the decision wholeheartedly and, in practice, continued to act on his own authority. It is noteworthy that two of the first and leading members, Gnessin and Halevi, deserted the theater and Moscow primarily because of Zemach's autocratic nature and dictatorial rule.

The chief source of the split in New York was no different from the problems in Moscow: disagreement over the type of management the Habima theater should have. The crucial question was: who is to decide artistic matters? Should it be one man, Zemach, or a council, elected by the troupe in a majority vote? Zemach contended that there were some issues that could be discussed by the group collectively, but artistic decisions should be made only by him. He even maintained that he should have the right to veto decisions that were reached by a majority vote of the collective. Zemach was an individualist who, in matters that concerned the theater, behaved autocratically. It is small wonder, then, that the feelings of the members of Zemach were a mixture of adoration, respect, and hatred.

During the tour, the relationships between Zemach and the troupe worsened. While the theater was in Berlin, Zemach was ousted from his position as General Director by a majority vote, although he was still the head of the council.[31] Zemach could not stand the insult of being just one member of the council. He protested, but without result. He therefore saw no choice but to resign.[32] But despite his resignation, Zemach continued to act as the theater's General Director. It was a strange situation; people outside the theater did not know about the conflict within the group, so they continued to refer to and approach Zemach as the Habima Director. At one time, the council had to ask Zemach to stop interfering with its work.[33] Nonetheless, Zemach continued to represent the Habima and make speeches on its goals at all parties given for the theater.

The failure of the American tour intensified the conflict between Zemach and the group. Zemach ascribed the failure and the confusion concerning the future to the members' loss of faith in his leadership and to the rule of the collective and the council, which was based on a majority vote. In June 1927, the Habima split into two groups. One, the majority, consisted of the senior members and the Hebraists and included most of the gifted actors.[34] The other faction, the minority, was headed by Zemach and included his family and close friends. The majority group was in favor of a council, with Zemach as its head, while Zemach and the minority group insisted that all authority must be vested in Zemach alone.

The last meeting of the whole collective was held at the Ansonia Hotel in New York. The single issue on the agenda was whether a council headed by Zemach should conduct the Habima's affairs or whether Zemach should have full powers. The evidence suggests that it was Zemach who proposed splitting the theater into two groups—one in New York, the other in Europe—with the vision of a permanent home in Jerusalem to guide and unite them.[35] Zemach went on to propose that he stay on in New York while the other group depart for Europe. He was determined to split the Habima; he was sure that the theater would not survive without his direction.[36] It is reasonable to assume that

Zemach's resolution to stay on in New York and found a Hebrew theater there was also supported by some Jewish leaders who promised to assist him financially as well as morally.

Zemach stayed on in New York with a group of ten actors which included his wife, Goldina, his brother and sister, Binyamin and Shifra, and his close friends. Most of these actors had come to the Habima from either the Russian or the Yiddish culture. Some were motivated from the start by professional rather than ideological considerations, and were never fully committed to Hebrew and Zionism. Moreover, some of the players, such as Yitzhak Golland and Chayele Grober, did not at all intend to continue their collaboration with Zemach; they decided to stay on in New York because it provided better opportunities for their acting careers. Indeed, Golland left New York for Berlin, where he pursued a spectacular career as an opera singer. Grober pursued her career as a Yiddish actress and singer in Canada and South America.

In New York, Zemach attempted to establish a second Habima theater. The group's first production, *Jacob's Dream*, opened on November 12, 1927, at the Neighborhood Playhouse.[37] However, again the Jewish audience did not come, and the play closed after several performances. It had not been a good idea to reopen with *Jacob's Dream*, a production that had already been presented by the original Habima and even then had not fared very well.

After the failure of *Jacob's Dream*, the group scattered. The players who stayed on in New York wanted to present Shakespeare's *The Merchant of Venice*, but the undertaking did not go beyond a few rehearsals.[38] Since they were unemployed, the actors decided to perform in Yiddish. With encouragement and finances from Leon Pruzhansky, a supporter of the theater, the remnant of the troupe produced a Yiddish version of Gozzi's *Princess Turandot*, directed by the newly arrived Russian director Boris Glagolin. This play was chosen to prove that the actors' talent and ability were not confined to biblical plays and to one artistic style.

Princess Turandot opened at the Metropolitan Opera House in January 1929, but since the adaptation was poor and the staging uninteresting, the play ran only one week. However, the actors learned how "important it was to have the audience understand the language of the performance."[39] The failure of *Princess Turandot*, and the oncoming economic depression, shattered the final effort of the American Habima to have an organized group under this name in the United States.

Zemach did not take part in this production. He left New York for San Francisco where he produced with great success an English version of *The Dybbuk*. In 1930, he settled in Hollywood, hoping to produce a movie version of *The Dybbuk*, but this did not materialize. He then organized some dramatic youth clubs and, to make his living, appeared in concerts and at parties. In 1933, Zemach returned to New York and directed Leivik's social drama, *Hirsh Leckert*, retitled *Heroic Years*, in Yiddish, with a nonprofessional group of the Workmen's Circle. In the following year, he and his wife Goldina took part in a crime drama, *Nowhere Bound*, on Broadway at the Imperial Theater. In 1936, Zemach visited Palestine, where the Habima had already been settled. An attempt at reconciliation was made, but it failed because the group refused to readmit him into the theater. He returned to New York and in 1939 died of cancer at the age of fifty-two.

The American Habima did not succeed as an organized group, but, apart from Zemach, most members succeeded as individual artists. Since the Habima had been affiliated with the Moscow Art Theater and had learned from Stanislavsky himself, most became teachers of Stanislavsky's method and pursued careers in the Yiddish and the American theaters. Benno Schneider, for instance, was the stage director of the Artef Theater, a major Yiddish theater in New York, from 1929 to 1940, and also worked in the American theater. David Itkin, another member who stayed with Zemach, worked at the Goodman Theater in Chicago.

The split of 1927 reflected the tragedy of Zemach who had dreamed for decades of establishing a Hebrew art theater that would settle in Jerusalem. Of all the members, Zemach was the most committed to the vision of a Hebrew biblical and national theater, and without his efforts the Habima would never have been created or have reached the artistic level that it did. Ironically, Zemach, who was the most committed to the Hebrew language, had to compromise after the split and had to stage performances in Yiddish and in English in order to earn his living.

The failures of both the visit to the United States and Zemach's later attempt to establish a Hebrew theater there convinced the group that there was no permanent and natural home for the Habima other than

Palestine. The social and artistic milieu in Europe and New York was alien to the Habima; the company realized that this was not the setting of which it had dreamed for such a long time. Yet, seen in a historical perspective, it was the failure of the visit and the split that saved the Habima from demise. The split accelerated the decision to leave for Europe and from there to Palestine and made the members all the more determined to think of Palestine as their home. Until then, Palestine was a dream; no one knew when and how it would be realized.

SIX

The Search for a Permanent Home

On June 29, 1927, after the painful split that occurred in New York, the majority group of the Habima left for Berlin. They arrived in low spirits, feeling acutely the loss of their leader and one third of their players. The theater realized that it had no home and, consequently, decided to set up temporary headquarters in Berlin and to set out on a tour of Germany, Holland, Italy, and Yugoslavia.

While still in the United States the group decided to settle in Palestine, but there were not funds enough to realize that decision. During the New York visit, a circle of the Habima's friends was established, headed by Otto Kahn, the banker and art patron. This circle raised funds for the troupe's settlement in Palestine. These funds enabled the theater to travel to Europe, since the American tour had left the troupe penniless. But by the time they got to Berlin they were, in effect, stranded.

A group of influential Jews in Germany and Holland came to the rescue and secured the Habima's survival. In December 1927, this group of benefactors founded in Berlin the Mazkirut Habima (the Habima Secretariat), which functioned as the organizational center of the theater. Of all those who were involved in the Habima Secretariat, especially noteworthy was Margot Klausner, the daughter of a wealthy German Jew with a passion for both Zionism and the Hebrew theater. She did most of the organizational and fund-raising work in Europe.

The Habima Secretariat immediately set up several goals: to raise funds for the theater's trip to Palestine; to recruit well-known stage directors; and to help maintain the high artistic standards of the company.[1] The Secretariat established Circles of the Habima Friends in a number of West European countries. The function of these circles was to raise funds and maintain contact between the theater and the public. They also strengthened the national character of the theater as a troupe that wandered from one Jewish community to another.

Lack of funds was not the only obstacle to the Habima's decision to settle in Palestine. Some of the theater's members strongly opposed it. On the whole, there were two major opinions in regard to Palestine. The majority—including the troupe's leading actors, such as Rovina, Meskin, and Chemerinsky—strongly advocated settlement in Palestine. For them, Palestine was the hope of the Habima. The other opinion was held by a small group of players who still believed in the ideals of the Soviet Revolution. When the Habima left Russia, they felt that the theater was leaving an ideal setting to tour "decadent and degenerate Europe." These members were never really committed to Hebrew and Zionism and thought that Zionist ideology was provincial and restrictive.[2] Their attachments to the Soviet regime, and especially to the possibilities which it provided for the flourishing of the arts, were still deep-seated.

While still in Berlin, prolonged and passionate debates concerning the future, purpose, and home of the Habima were held within the collective. Even those players who were in favor of settling in Palestine did not have a clear idea of whether Palestine would be the theater's permanent home. Some actors thought that because the Habima would not be able to operate in Palestine for the entire year, it would probably stay there for six months and spend the rest of each year touring the Jewish communities in the Diaspora. Other members thought that the Habima should visit Palestine for a shorter period—about eight weeks—and then go on a tour of Europe; they conceived of the theater entirely as a wandering troupe.[3]

The last stop of the 1927 European tour was Zagreb, Yugoslavia. The plan was to travel on to Palestine by train through Egypt; but the Habima players held Soviet passports, and the Egyptian government at that time would not grant visas to Soviet citizens. Thus, the theater had to travel to Marseille, and then to Palestine by boat, an itinerary which made the trip all the more expensive.

The Habima in Palestine

The Habima arrived in Palestine on March 27, 1928. On the day of its arrival and in the following weeks, the press published welcome articles. The *Haaretz* wrote that the people in Palestine had long awaited the Habima's arrival there, and concluded that "here, and only here, is the natural location of the Habima and from here the theater will speak to the whole world."[4] *Davar*, the official organ of the Histadrut (General Federation of Jewish Workers), wrote that the arrival of the Habima in Palestine was the beginning of the Fifth *Aliya* (wave of immigration).[5] And *Ktuvim*, the organ of Agudat Hasofrim (the Writers' Association) defined the Habima players as a "group of priests who sacrificed their life for the establishment of Hebrew art."[6]

Of greater importance was the warm reception and support by the audience. Tickets were sold out for every Habima performance. An audience which spoke Hebrew was a totally new and most welcome phenomenon for the Habima. The small Moscow audience had not spoken Hebrew and had admired the Habima primarily because it performed in an exotic and ancient language. Even during its tours, although the Habima had gained many admirers and friends, few who had come to see them knew Hebrew. In Palestine, an even more enthusiastic audience not only spoke Hebrew but also was interested in the rebirth of the Hebrew culture. The existence of a Hebrew audience in Palestine gave the Habima a legitimacy and answered that question which the theater had faced ever since its inception: who are we and for whom do we perform? Hence, in 1928 the theater experienced for the first time an admiring audience which listened, understood, and applauded in Hebrew.

Theaters that performed in Hebrew had existed in Palestine before the Habima arrived.[7] Thus, the commitment of the Habima to perform exclusively in Hebrew was not regarded as an innovation, as it had been in Europe and United States, but rather as one link in the chain of the efforts to create a Hebrew art theater. In Palestine the Habima met for the first time "the real audience, an audience for which a performance in Hebrew was neither a surprise nor a demonstration." Indeed, in Palestine performing in Hebrew was a must and taken for granted by both press and public.[8]

Although the Habima had already achieved world fame in Europe and America, the theater's reputation still had to be established in Palestine. Lufban, an influential critic, wrote that "the new prophet should first be a prophet in his own town" and that the language used by the Habima on the stage could be properly judged only where this language was understood.[9] Similarly, another critic wrote that the Habima had passed the artistic test in Europe but it was in Palestine that the theater had to pass "the judgment of the Hebrew worker who builds the Hebrew national home."[10]

The Habima arrived in Palestine bearing the official name of "The Moscow Theater Habima." This name appeared in all the announcements of the theater and encountered a good deal of criticism. Chaim Harari, then an influential drama critic, wrote that he had been waiting a long time for the Habima, not for "The Moscow Theater Habima." He thought that this adjective was unnecessary and that "a wind of foreignness blows from it." The title "Moscow Theater Habima" was symbolic, in his opinion, and added an international dimension to the Habima, as if the "Moscow Theater" and not the "Habima" were the chief thing. Harari went on to warn the theater not to confine itself to merely artistic values and not to adopt the slogan of "theater for theater's sake."[11]

In Moscow there had been three major innovations: the language in which the theater performed, the content of the plays, and artistic style. However, in Palestine the most important factor was the kind of plays the Habima presented and the ideas they expressed. This was apparent in many articles published during the Habima's visit there. The general tone of the articles was that the Habima would meet its ultimate test in Palestine, and that this test would include a judgment of the theater's artistic achievements as well as how well the Habima fulfilled its mission as a national institution.

This same view was expressed in the reviews of the troupe's productions. Of *The Golem,* the first production presented (March 31, 1928), the *Haaretz* critic wrote: "*The Golem* is not a play of high quality. It has rather cheap moments which probably cause a great deal of enthusiasm among Jews in the Diaspora and among the Gentiles, but Palestine does not like it. . . . Neither will Palestine accept all that ghost business; we here have conquered many ghosts, or we at least make efforts to conquer them."[12] The critics did not like the script of *The Eternal Jew,* though they praised the production. *Jacob's Dream* received a mixed reaction; the *Haaretz* critic, for instance, wrote that the play was more relevant in the Diaspora than in Palestine.[13] *The Dybbuk* was the only production that received unqualified praise, though again one critic added that some of the writers in Palestine opposed the play because they wanted to forget life in the Jewish ghetto and to start anew. Therefore, in his opinion, the importance of *The Dybbuk* was primarily in its modern and innovative artistic form.[14]

These reviews are not surprising if one bears in mind that in Palestine a new society was being created. Most of the Jewish population had migrated to Palestine in the previous three decades, especially after 1918. In 1881, there were only 25,000 Jews in Eretz Israel, most of whom lived in the four holy cities of Hebron, Safed, Tiberias, and Jerusalem. They were fanatically orthodox. The increase of the Jewish population after 1882, and especially between 1919 and 1928, was dramatic. In 1919, there were approximately 55,000 Jews; in 1922, the total was 83,790; and by 1928 there were 156,800.[15] The majority of the Jews who came to Palestine from 1882 on were Zionist pioneers devoted to the cause of establishing a national home for the Jews. For them, the most important task was to create a new society that would be totally different from the Jewish ghetto in the Diaspora. The new society would have different values and a different economic and social structure from those of the shtetl in the Pale of Settlement. Therefore, they saw the Habima as a national institution and not merely an art theater; as such, the theater was expected to present plays compatible with the values and spirit of the new society.

The Habima left Russia with a limited repertoire of five plays. With this repertoire the troupe toured Europe, the United States, and Palestine. Since *Jacob's Dream* and *The Flood* were not artistic achievements and did not fare well, it tended to present only three plays, *The Eternal Jew, The Dybbuk,* and *The Golem.* For three years (1925–1928), the Habima produced no new plays. In Palestine, the troupe reached an impasse: the audience there, though receptive, was small, and with only three productions the company soon exhausted this audience. There was, therefore, an urgent need to prepare a new production—and this meant a new play, money, and a director of a high artistic caliber. Furthermore, since a native Hebrew drama did not exist, the Habima faced the serious question of which plays to present in Palestine.

The first new play was *The Treasure* (or *The Gold Diggers*), written by Sholem Aleichem in 1907. It was directed by the Russian director A. D. Diki, and the first performance took place in November 1928. Chemerinsky first suggested presenting this play, but he met with disagreement from some members who thought that the Habima should steer clear of Sholem Aleichem and the Jewish ghetto and should present plays based on the heroic Jewish past and present.[16] The play was eventually produced, though, because the Habima had little choice—there were few plays of the heroic-historic genre, and plays on the new life in Palestine did not exist at all.

The Treasure was a tragic farce, the story of an entire Jewish community that is misled by rumors that a huge treasure of gold was buried in the town's cemetery by Napoleon's retreating armies. There is no proof that the story is true, but everybody goes mad with gold fever. Then the truth is revealed and there is a cruel letdown. In *The Treasure,* Sholem Aleichem's humor is mixed with a good deal of bitterness and criticism. But in Diki's staging and interpretation the characters were presented in too negative a light. Diki went far beyond the playwright's intention, presenting the life of the shtetl as ugly and deformed. He interpreted the play so that the viewers were led to conclude that an end must be put to the past life in the ghetto, that life in Palestine was the desirable solution.[17]

The Treasure was an artistic as well as a financial success. But the critics were far from unanimous. Some found Diki's interpretation anti-Semitic. And others, though they praised the production and the acting, disagreed with the choice of the play.[18] The *Haaretz* critic, for instance, wrote that if the Habima wanted to become a Hebrew theater in Palestine it should serve the people and its country by making "a convenant with the impoverished Hebrew literature and by reviving it."[19] But the major criticism that the Habima encountered was from the labor movement press. The critic of *Hapoel Hatzair* (The Young Worker) wrote that the tragedy of the theater was that it was not aware of its important mission. In his opinion, the Habima did not stress its Jewish and national character enough. He contended that the troupe's attitudes toward Palestine and Hebrew literature were the attitudes of a stranger, and he concluded by asking, "How can artists, who in their manners and tradition are Russian and not Hebrew, present Jewish and Hebrew art?"[20]

Immediately after *The Treasure,* the Habima prepared its next production, Calderón de la Barca's *The Hair of Absalom,* retitled in Hebrew *Keter David* (*David's Crown*). Calderon's story is drawn from the Second Book of Samuel and the First Book of Kings. The dramatic substance of the play centers on Absalom's murder of his brother, Amnon, and his rebellion against his father, David. Yitzhak Lamdan, the Hebrew poet, translated and adapted the play. In his new adaptation, it became a drama about the fierce fight for succession to the throne and the incestuous relations between Amnon, David's first-born son, and his sister Tamar, which were only hinted at in the original play.[21]

The production was directed by Diki and, as in *The Treasure,* his direction was expressionistic and highly stylized. Once more, despite the brilliant direction and acting, the critics had serious reservations. *Hapoel Hatzair* wrote that the major deficiency of the production was the attempt to give the play a political and universal interpretation and to make it devoid of time and place.[22] But the critics did not speak with one voice. *Davar* accused her critic-colleagues of imposing upon the Habima a narrow conception of a Jewish and national institution, thereby confining its artistic growth. She went on to defend the Habima on the grounds that a Jewish spirit—the spirit that the other critics wanted the Habima to reflect—did not yet exist, but was in the process of creation, exactly like the theater itself.[23]

Many evenings of discussion over the production of *David's Crown* were held in Tel-Aviv. During one such discussion the author Kabak contended that "the Gentile spirit exists in every aspect of the Habima," and, therefore, even its Jewish plays were Gentile. Dr. Harari disagreed with Kabak and reminded him that the Habima had produced a biblical story in a foreign, Gentile way because no Jewish or Palestinian playwright took the pains to write a suitable play.[24]

Shimon Finkel as Amnon and Hanna Rovina as Tamar in *David's Crown* (1929), staged by Alexander Diki.

The interpretation of the play, and especially the portrait of David, stunned the public. David, the great king, poet, and progenitor of the Messiah was, in the minds of the people, a symbol of the unity and glory of the nation, and usually idealized in legend and song. The public held a romantic view of King David that was not only absent from but was contradicted by the play. As a result, some of the press and the audience accused the Habima of abusing national feelings and morals.[25]

The productions of *The Treasure* and *David's Crown* were also presented in Europe during the Habima's second tour there. The Jewish audiences in Europe reacted to these productions differently from the audiences in Palestine. The Habima's interpretation of *The Treasure* was severely criticized. In Warsaw, for instance, the Yiddish daily *Heint* (Today) wrote that Palestine (and the Habima) has condemned the shtetl way of life to extinction in order to build the new life and society, but the Jews in Europe "go along with Sholem Aleichem, loving the Jews the way they are . . . we can laugh at them, but we love them." And he concluded: "What do you want of the Jews in the shtetl? Let them dream! . . . Why does the Habima show so much anger? Why do they cut the living flesh of those people with so much sadism?"[26] On the other hand, the Jewish audiences in the Diaspora were less sensitive to the interpretation of *David's Crown*. Thus, the two distinct audiences—in Palestine and in the Diaspora—applied different yardsticks when they judged the Habima productions, yardsticks that were conditioned by their different social surroundings and, of course, their way of life and vision of the future.

The arguments and controversies in Palestine over the Habima concerned much broader questions than the productions themselves. They touched upon three issues: first, the mission of the Habima in Palestine; second, the nature of the plays the threater should present; third, the task of the drama critics and the yardsticks they should employ in judging the Habima's productions. Needless to say, the controversies over the three issues were extremely significant, because both the society and the theater were in the midst of creation.

A major dispute between the Habima and the critics concerned the relationship between the ideological mission of the theater and its artistic standards. The Habima, because of its Russian origins and theatrical tradition, ascribed an importance to both the content of the play and the manner in which it was presented. The theater wanted to maintain at all costs the artistic stature it had achieved in Russia. It was therefore willing to work only with directors of a high caliber. Diki was chosen because he was a pupil of Vakhtangov and a famous director himself. An enormous amount of money was needed to bring Diki to Palestine and to cover his expenses during the prolonged period that he worked with the troupe. This was a luxury both in light of the theater's financial situation and the poor economic state of Palestine in 1928–1929. Indeed, the critics severely criticized the long rehearsal periods and the amount of money paid to "the Gentile director," especially since they disagreed with Diki's interpretation of the plays.[27] There were others who thought that the Habima was "too Russian" in its artistic work and believed that this might result in artistic fixation and routinized stage manners.[28] And there were still others who did not like the elitist orientation of the Habima, a result of their glamorous past and world fame. These critics thought that the Habima was too separate and removed from the people and the everyday life of the Yishuv (the Jewish community of Palestine until 1948).[29]

In the meantime there was a debate within the collective over how long the theater should stay in Palestine and what its future plans might be. The leading political and cultural figures of the Yishuv were aware of this internal struggle, and a number of them used their influence to make the company settle permanently in the country. This group of representatives of the cultural and political elite of the Yishuv included David Ben-Gurion; Berl Katzenelson, the ideologist of the labor movement; Zalman Rubashov (Shazar); Bialik; and others. All wanted the Habima to settle permanently in Palestine despite extremely difficult conditions: the small size of the Jewish population, and the lack of appropriate conditions for maintaining a company of the stature of the Habima.[30]

Bialik, who had been attached to the Habima from its inception, was the chief proponent of the Habima's settling in Palestine. In an article published in *Haaretz,* Bialik contended that the Habima was an integral part of the new national home in Palestine and that if "we will permit the theater to go abroad it will be a national disaster . . . because the Gentiles will say 'Moscow had sponsored a Hebrew theater but Palestine did not.' " He also wrote that the Habima had the important task of disseminating the Jewish national idea and the Hebrew language. Comparing the Habima's task to that of the Hebrew University, which had been founded in Jerusalem in 1925, Bialik criticized the "broken and shattered" Hebrew of some of the professors which was, in his opinion, "a shame and sign of the poverty" of the entire country.[31]

The warm reception of the Habima by all segments of the Yishuv was more important than the pressures of the political elite. Especially noteworthy was the relationship between the Habima and the kibbutzim, which were then looked upon as the backbone of the new society. The kibbutzim made—and still make—the most appreciative and enthusiastic theater audience. The first Habima performance at a kibbutz took place on May 9, 1928, in Degania—the first kibbutz in Palestine, established in 1909—in the Jezreel Valley. More than three thousand kibbutzniks attended the performance of *The Golem.*[32] The performances at the kibbutzim were given in communal dining halls and frequently in the open, in makeshift amphitheaters. These performances were emotionally charged and were followed by festivities, singing, and dancing the hora. The visits to the kibbutzim made the troupe feel "integrated in the general frame of creating new life in the renovated country."[33]

Despite a very warm reception, the problem of a permanent home was ever present. It aroused endless discussions within the troupe and divided the members into three factions. One, the "Zionist," was headed by Ben-Chaim, Chemerinsky, and Meskin; this faction insisted on settling permanently in Palestine. A second faction, the "Russian," was headed by Prudkin and still felt strongly attached to Russia; to them, Russia was still the home of the Habima. Indeed, in 1928 six actors left for Russia, though three of them returned to Palestine after three months. And in 1932, two additional actors left for Russia, never to return. A third faction, headed by Warshawer, was motivated by pragmatic considerations. Its members believed that the Habima would best serve its purpose as a wandering troupe; thus, they were in favor of setting up headquarters in Berlin. For this faction, maintaining the theater's high artistic standards and assuring its financial support were more important than the functioning of the theater in a Hebrew environment. Palestine was too provincial, they thought, for a theater like the Habima.[34]

This internal conflict took place during a very difficult period of the Yishuv. The fourth wave of immigration (1924–1928) had brought to Palestine more than sixty-eight thousand immigrants, more than one-third of whom were reemigrating. The late twenties were depressing years for the Yishuv; in 1927, for instance, the rate of unemployment was very high.[35] In addition to the small size of the Jewish population (156,800 in 1928), the economic situation and the physical conditions were so harsh that it was extremely difficult to adjust to the new environment. But more important for the Habima was the fact that there was no theatrical tradition. When it came to Palestine, it had to establish its own tradition, but conditions were not favorable for the development and growth of theater. Well-trained people in the theater crafts—directors, painters, designers, composers, and drama critics—were practically nonexistent.

In January 1929, the Habima collective held a series of general meetings to discuss the theater's future plans. Rovina stressed the problem of the small audience and contended that in Europe all of their plays had had prolonged runs, while in Palestine they had been able to give only a limited number of performances. Chemerinsky replied that the theater would rather perform only ten times before an audience which understood Hebrew than give hundreds of performances to an audience that did not speak the language. For him, a responsive audience was the crucial thing. He therefore favored postponing their departure from Palestine, a departure which would break up the already established relationships with their new audience and with the country. Ben-Chaim also objected strongly to another tour of Europe. In his opinion, only in Palestine could the Habima fully express its distinctive ideological mission.[36]

Some members accused Ben-Chaim of putting Palestine first and the Habima second, whereas for them the Habima was first in importance. Other members argued in favor of the proposed tour because they thought the Habima's mission was to wander and perform in the Diaspora. And there were members who favored an extensive tour because they believed that such a tour would provide an opportunity to improve the theater's financial situation.[37] Indeed, most members voted in favor of the tour.

The Second European Tour

In August 1929, eighteen months after it had arrived in Palestine, the Habima left for Europe. Although it seemed clear that the theater would eventually settle there, no one knew how long the tour would last. The extensive tour was originally intended to last several months; instead it lasted eighteen months (till February 1931). The tour included eight countries: Germany, Poland, Belgium, Switzerland, Denmark, Sweden, Italy, and England.

The most urgent problem during the tour was to find and prepare an appropriate repertoire. In November 1929, an evening dedicated to the issue of the Habima's mission and repertoire took place in Berlin at the house of Margot Klausner. Several intellectuals, Jewish and non-Jewish, who then lived in Berlin participated in the conversation. Among them were Bialik; Martin Buber, the Jewish philosopher; Arnold Zweig, the novelist; Alfred Doeblin, the poet; Berthold Diebold, the theater critic; Nachum Goldman, the Zionist leader; and many others. The discussion revolved around one major issue: which way should the Habima go? Should the theater glorify Jewish history and tradition, and hence be the embodiment of Jewish theater for the world, or should the Habima follow the path of all other theaters? Very different answers were given to this question.

Bialik contended that Palestine needed a theater that should be all-Jewish, "the distillation of our national artistic genius." In his opinion, the Habima should not be a theater like all theaters, but a temple of art. Bialik proposed treating the Bible as raw material to serve as a basis for creating plays in the modern spirit. He objected to presenting plays based on the life of the Jews in the ghetto, contending that "life in the Diaspora is for Palestine a closed chapter. It does not offer us even the exotic attraction that it does here in Western Europe." Thus, in Bialik's opinion, the Habima theater had a national task of great responsibility to fulfill: to help in creating the new culture in Palestine and to be the guide leading the people into modern life there.[38]

Martin Buber disagreed with Bialik and suggested:

> Pre-conceived opinions and pre-set aims and theories alone do not create art; subjects from Jewish history etc., and plays written by Jewish playwrights alone do not make Jewish theatre. Cultural achievements are not brought about by a conscious attempt or desire but only a natural process of development can provide them. We have to be open to every influence of great foreign art, poetry and drama; only in this way shall we succeed in the course of time, in finding the synthesis between what has been created by us in the country and the spiritual heritage of the centuries.[39]

Therefore, Buber concluded, "let the Habima translate into Hebrew the best of the world literature, let it be part of the mainstream of the global and universal, let it come out of the confines of a nationalistic theater."[40]

The discussion revolved around these two opposing opinions. Alfred Doeblin, for one, sided with Bialik and considered the Habima to be a purely Jewish creation. He contended: "We cannot create in the universal vein as Buber demands of us. In our situation, we cannot speak of pure art for art's sake. The Jewish people is now engaged in a bitter struggle for its existence. We must be practical and have our art serve the higher national aims."[41]

But the Habima followed Buber's counsel, namely, to deviate from the narrow track of plays on Jewish themes. The theater's next offering was Shakespeare's *Twelfth Night,* which opened in Berlin in September 1930. For years the company has resisted the temptation of performing Shakespeare; it considered it the supreme test of its accomplishment. Consequently, this production showed that the troupe had indeed developed artistically and had outgrown its "exotic" phase.

Twelfth Night was translated by the noted Hebrew poet, Saul Tchernihovsky, and was directed by Mikhail Chekhov, a nephew of the playwright and a former actor and director of the Moscow Art Theater. The production made a great impression on those who saw it. The German critics, who had seen the Habima in previous dramatic productions, were surprised to see the actors' comic talents. *Twelfth Night* was, in fact, the first light comedy in the theater's repertoire. With this production, the company proved that the world's great drama could be successfully presented in Hebrew. *Twelfth Night* was a success everywhere it was presented, including England, although some of the English critics felt that the troupe's approach to the play was anti-Shakespearean.[42]

The next offering, Karl Gutzkow's *Uriel Acosta,* proved again that the Habima was primarily a Jewish theater. This play concerns the tragedy of Uriel Acosta, the Jewish philosopher who wrote a book considered blasphemous by fanatical orthodox rabbis and, therefore, was outlawed as a heretic. The Habima chose this play not only because of its topic, but also because it enjoyed a great vogue in Russia, Germany, and other countries. It was directed by Alexander Granovsky, the former director of the Moscow State Jewish Theater (GOSET) and one of the brilliant men of the Russian theater. Granovsky created a spectacle of color, music, and folk humor with the result that the play became not so much the tragedy of the rebellious nonconformist as a play about Jewish life in seventeenth-century Holland.

Unlike the plays the company had presented in Moscow, none of the plays presented during this period (1926–1931) had a national message. Furthermore, the choice of *Twelfth Night* was a major deviation from the theater's original ideology. This Shakespearean production was the

The Habima's first Shakespearean production, *Twelfth Night* (1930).

beginning of a new trend that would be strengthened in later years when the Habima tried to maintain a balance in its repertoire between Jewish and non-Jewish plays.

It is interesting to mention that some critics were disappointed with the change in the troupe's repertory policy. The critic of *Berlin am Morgen* wrote that with the productions of *Twelfth Night* and *Uriel Acosta* the Habima actors "have severed themselves from that specific uniqueness" that they had had several years before. In his opinion, the Habima "has lost its way in a search for new plays and for a Western manner," as these two plays had shown. He went on to say that the Habima should not strive to create pure art, but rather continue what it had begun with *The Dybbuk:*

> *The Dybbuk* was a highly successful attempt at expressing a culture strange to us Westerners; it formed a foundation of a new theatre which blended idea and form. Perhaps it could not have lasted, but out of it a new theatrical form could have developed. This was the essence of the Habima, and it must not be destroyed while they

make efforts to assume another identity—that of a standard European bourgeois theatre.[43]

In the staging of the productions, the Russian orientation prevailed. All four plays were directed by brilliant Russian directors. Thus, the troupe succeeded in maintaining the high artistic level that it had attained in Russia. The Russian influence was also evident in the sets and costumes used in two of the four productions. Reuven Falk, who had designed the sets for *Jacob's Dream* in Moscow, was invited to do the sets for *Uriel Acosta;* another Russian, Alexander Masjutin, designed the production of *Twelfth Night.* This policy underscored the strong attachment to the Russian theatrical tradition, years after the troupe had left the country. With the two productions that were prepared in Berlin, a twelve-year period during which the Habima had worked exclusively with Russian directors came to an end. In 1931, when the theater settled in Palestine, a new era began—an era marked by work with staff directors—which continued until 1948.

The Habima's second tour of Europe (1929–1931) differed in two major aspects from the earlier one. First and foremost, although none of the actors knew how long the tour would last, it was clear that at its end the Habima would return to Palestine. When the theater left Palestine for this tour, the political and cultural leadership of the Yishuv viewed the troupe as Palestine's cultural ambassador. They were, therefore, disappointed when during the tour the official title of the troupe continued to be "The Moscow Theater Habima," rather than "The Palestinian Theater Habima." Second, this tour differed from the first in the way the Jewish community received the Habima. If the reception on the first 1926 tour was enthusiastic, the reception now was merely appreciative. The novelty of a theater performing in Hebrew and presenting plays with national messages had apparently worn out.

It is noteworthy that the Habima toured Europe a few years prior to Hitler's seizure of power but at a time when the Nazi movement was already spreading. Indeed, when the Habima appeared in Würzburg, Nazi pickets stood in front of the theater distributing leaflets which called the Habima's performances in Germany *Kultur-schande* (a cultural shame).[44] This situation reinforced the theater's belief that there was only one natural and permanent home for them: Palestine.

Despite the differences between the first and the second tours, there were a number of similarities. During both tours the Habima proved that it was one of the most gifted group of actors in the world. The troupe acquired an international reputation and achieved a notable success among Gentile audiences. The leading authorities of the theater world—Max Reinhardt and George Bernard Shaw—applauded the theater. Shaw reportedly climbed on the stage after a Habima performance in London and told the actors to leave England immediately so that they might not be influenced by the English actors. He went further and suggested that English players go to Palestine and learn from the Habima.[45] Many other reviewers also affirmed that the artistic achievements of the Habima could stand up to the most severe professional criticism. Unfortunately, like the first tour, the second was also a financial fiasco. At the end of the tour the theater found itself stranded in Konstanz, Germany, without sufficient funds to get to Palestine.

During both tours, the Habima Secretariat established Circles of the Habima Friends throughout Western Europe to supplement the income received from performances. In the summer of 1929, Margot Klausner established the Agudat Hapatronim (The Patrons' Association) whose members were wealthy German Jews, each of whom were to donate a yearly sum of three thousand marks for three years.[46] The assumption was that within three years the Habima would be officially recognized as a national institution and, like the other national institutions of Palestine, would receive financial support. Indeed, in 1929, the theater was recognized by the Sixteenth World Zionist Congress in Zurich as a national institution and as such was granted a small yearly subsidy of three hundred pounds. However, the financial backing of the Zionist Congress made little dent in the theater's expenses or altered the fact that there was almost no profit from the troupe's performances.

In February 1931, the Habima theater settled permanently in Tel-Aviv. With its settlement, the theater joined the thousands of Jews who had migrated to Palestine from all parts of the Diaspora to build the land and to make a new life for themselves. The Habima saw itself as the pioneer of Hebrew culture just as the kibbutzim were the pioneers of the land and the Hebrew University the pioneer of science and learning. The troupe decided to be an integral part of the overall growth of the new society in Palestine. The transition from international fame to life and work in a small and poor provincial country like Palestine was not easy. The theater faced the serious problem of living up to its international reputation. When the troupe left Moscow the period of glory ended. Indeed, the company was never again to reach the artistic and spiritual heights that it had attained in Russia.

What the Habima brought with it to Palestine was superb training under the greatest men of the Russian theater, a sense of high purpose, and a strong collective spirit. Palestine, on the other hand, offered the Habima what Moscow, Berlin, and New York could not offer—an admiring, cooperative audience, albeit limited in numbers. It is noteworthy that the troupe's financial success in Palestine exceeded that of both its European tours; in its eighteen months in Palestine, the Habima had presented 161 performances with audiences totaling 100,500—proportionately more than one-half of the 1928 Jewish population of 156,800. In Palestine the actors found a sympathetic public that understood Hebrew. Unlike the ephemeral admiration of audiences in Europe and the United States, the public's support in Palestine was regular and permanent. This support was the most significant favorable condition for the operation of the theater in Palestine.

THREE

The Habima in Palestine: 1931–1948

SEVEN

Ideology and Repertoire: 1931–1948

THE Habima established its home in Tel-Aviv, Palestine, in February 1931. The theater's repertoire consisted then of nine plays: five of them had been prepared in Moscow; two in Palestine; and two in Berlin.

Two criteria have been employed in the classification of the repertoire: the subject of the play and the language in which it was written. According to the first criterion the repertoire had two major categories: Jewish and non-Jewish (or universal) plays. The category of specifically Jewish plays was further divided into four subcategories:

1. Biblical plays
2. Folkloristic plays that depicted various aspects of Jewish life in the ghetto or shtetl, for the most part in late nineteenth-century Russia
3. Historical plays that dealt with the problem of maintaining Jewishness
4. Palestinian plays that concerned the new Jewish life in Palestine

Table 7.1 shows the number of plays in each category produced between 1931 and 1948. During this period, the Habima mounted 79 new productions, of which 44 (56 percent) were specifically Jewish and 35 (44 percent) were non-Jewish, universal plays. Thus, in this period the theater maintained a rough repertorial balance between Jewish and non-Jewish plays. Apart from one season (1930–1931), the Habima usually presented at least 2 distinctively Jewish plays every season. The theater averaged 4 productions per season. Table 7.1 also shows that of the 44 Jewish plays, 6 were biblical, 16 were shtetl plays, 18 dealt with the problem of maintaining one's Jewishness, and 4 were Palestinian plays.

Table 7.2 shows the Habima's repertoire between 1931 and 1948 by subject and the languages in which the plays were written.

The vast majority (67 plays, or 85 percent) of the Habima's repertoire consisted of plays that had originally been written in languages other

Table 7.1
The Habima's Repertoire by Type of Play: 1931–1948

Type of Play	*Number*	*Percent*
Jewish	44	55.7
Biblical	6	7.6
Shtetl	16	20.2
Maintaining Jewishness	18	22.8
Palestinian	4	5.1
Non-Jewish (universal)	35	44.3
All Plays	79	100.0

Table 7.2
The Habima's Repertoire by Subject and Language: 1931–1948

Language	*Jewish Plays*	*Non-Jewish Plays*	*Total*	*Percent*
Yiddish	18	—	18	22.8
German	9	5	14	17.7
Hebrew	12	—	12	15.2
English	2	9	11	13.9
Russian	2	6	8	10.2
French	1	5	6	7.6
Czech	—	5	5	6.3
Other	—	5	5	6.3
Total	44	35	79	100.0

than Hebrew. Plays with Yiddish as the original language formed the largest category in this period. After Yiddish plays came plays written in German (18 percent) and Hebrew (15 percent). Of the 11 plays written in English, only 2—Berger's *The Flood* and Irwin Shaw's *Bury the Dead*—were written by American playwrights; all other plays were written by British playwrights. Indeed, in this period, the non-Jewish repertoire was greatly influenced by the European theater, especially by the English and German stages. Lastly, most of the specifically Jewish plays (30 of 44) were written either in Yiddish or Hebrew. Note that all Yiddish and Hebrew plays were distinctively Jewish.

Of an average four new productions every season, at least two were distinctively Jewish plays. The theater's most productive season was 1935–1936 when eight new plays were mounted. Least productive was the season of 1937–1938 when not even one new play was presented because of the theater's extensive tour of Europe. It is noteworthy that except for this eight-month tour of Europe and a tour of the United States in 1948, the Habima operated in Palestine, primarily serving the Jewish community there.

The Habima's Jewish Plays

Biblical Plays

The Habima was originally established as a biblical theater, and the Bible was one of the main symbols of its ideology. But the theater found itself in a dilemma, for no such plays existed, and the few available biblical plays were not of high quality and—more importantly—were written by non-Jews, which meant that they reflected a non-Jewish attitude.

Indeed, from 1931 to 1948, the Habima presented only six biblical plays, of which only two, *Michal Bat Saul* (*Michal, Daughter of Saul*) and *Ahavat Zion* (*The Love of Zion*), were written in Hebrew. These two plays were the only biblical plays that succeeded with the audience.

Michal, Daughter of Saul was written by Aaron Ashman, a Hebrew writer, and opened on January 11, 1941. It depicted the story of Michal, the daughter of King Saul, and told of her love and loyalty to David,

Saul's rival who would later become king. In retelling the story in pseudoclassical style, the playwright made no attempt to draw historical or psychological lessons.

The critics who always paid tribute to the presentation of a Hebrew play praised the virtues of this play and its production. The review of the *Davar* critic was typical: "*Michal, Daughter of Saul* demonstrates that it is possible to write a Hebrew play which, with all its faults, can be presented on the stage, hold the attention of the audience, and serve as a step in the development of our theater."[1] The production was, in fact, highly acclaimed by all critics, who praised Rovina and Meskin, the two greatest actors of the company, who played the principal parts. *Michal, Daughter of Saul* was the first original biblical play to enjoy success with the public; it had a total run of 142 performances.

The Love of Zion, the second Hebrew-language biblical play, was adapted from the novel of the same title by Avraham Mapu, a writer of the Haskala (Enlightenment) movement. The play's action takes place in the period of the Judea Kingdom, when it was surrounded by the Philistines. The play opened in July 1947; the Habima thought that it was the right time to present such a play which, though legendary and biblical, showed the deep-seated attachments of the people to its country. Indeed, *The Love of Zion* succeeded with the public and ran for 90 performances. It failed with the critics, however, who attacked the adaptation of the novel for the stage and the low artistic caliber of the production.[2]

The desire to present biblical plays ran into several difficulties. On the one hand, the theater did not want to present strictly biblical plays without any allusion to contemporary life. On the other hand, it was hard to modernize the plays and at the same time retain their artistic merit. Indeed, the biblical plays failed either due to their small dramatic merit, or due to their attempt to adapt the biblical story so that it would have reference to contemporary life in Palestine.

For example, when the Habima presented the biblical play *Jephtha's Daughter* in 1943, Max Brod, the theater's dramaturge, adapted the play in order to make it more relevant to contemporary life. This attempt was criticized by several critics who thought that the adaptation was banal and that it would have been much better if the play had been produced without any changes.

Shtetl Plays

Sixteen plays of the total repertoire (20 percent) and about one-third of the specifically Jewish plays concerned Jewish life in Eastern Europe, especially in tsarist Russia. Most (fourteen of the sixteen) were written by Yiddish writers in the late nineteenth and early twentieth century. The category of Yiddish plays included seven plays by Sholem Aleichem, two each by Jacob Gordin and Peretz Hirschbein, and one each by Anski, Leivik, and Mendele mocher sforim. The other two shtetl plays were written in Hebrew by Bialik—*Yom Shishi Hakatzar* (*The Short Friday*), and Berkowitz—*Oto Veet Bno* (*Him and His Son*).

The Short Friday, premiered in 1933, was the only one of Bialik's works presented by the Habima in the entire period. Bialik completely renovated modern Hebrew as a literary language and set a new standard for poetic treatment. He was a close friend of the Habima from the very start, but unfortunately, this association did not last very long; Bialik died a few years after the troupe had settled in Palestine. *The Short Friday* was a happy trifle, an amusing anecdote of Jewish life in Russia. Sabbath-breaking is a serious crime among Jews. This play told how Rabbi Lipe came to trangress by travelling on the Sabbath. The Habima's production, staged by Chemerinsky, was well received by both critics and audiences; it ran for 162 performances—much above the average for that time. *The Short Friday* was an excellent example of the great possibilities and importance of adapting Jewish novels and stories to the stage.

Especially noteworthy were the plays written by Sholem Aleichem, the most beloved Yiddish writer, who depicted the internal world of Russian Jewry in the Pale of Settlement. The great success of his novels and plays is due to his mastery of characterization and his sensitivity to genuine folk humor. His literary work concerned the inner dignity and moral grandeur that was submerged beneath the shabby appearances and the apparent permissiveness of the Pale's denizens. In the Jews' passive endurance of humiliations imposed from the outside world, Sholem Aleichem saw a tactic for survival by the Jewish minority in the midst of a hostile majority. He was a pessimist who sought relief from despair in laughter through tears.[3]

The first play by Sholem Aleichem presented at the Habima was *The*

The production of Bialik's *Yom Shishi Hakatzar* (*The Short Friday*) in 1933.

Treasure in 1928. The success of this production encouraged the company to mount *Amcha* (*People*) in 1932. *Amcha* was the story of a poor tailor who comes into sudden riches. The Habima production was a synthesis of fairy tale and realistic folklore, and the notices in the press were extremely favorable. Bialik wrote that the production was "a real joy, a Jewish joy," because everything in it was intimately Jewish.[4] Jacob Fichman, the noted writer, wrote a remarkable review in which he contended that so long as the great Hebrew drama was not yet written, plays like *Amcha* could substitute and fortify the Hebrew repertoire more than any other plays.[5] *Amcha* remained in the Habima's repertoire for twenty years and ran 157 times.

In later years, the Habima mounted six other plays by Sholem Aleichem, of which two were of special importance: *It Is Hard to Be a Jew* and *Tevye the Dairyman*. *It Is Hard to Be a Jew* was the climax of Sholem Aleichem's literary activity. It was first published as a novel in 1912, and then in 1914 as a play. Here Sholem Aleichem deals with the difficulties of Jewish life under tsarist repression before World War I. In a provincial city in Russia, Schneurson, the hero of the play, fears that the doors of the university will be closed to him in spite of the fact that he was awarded a gold medal at graduation from the *gymnasium*. His friend Ivanov, the good-natured Gentile, suggests, while in high spirits, that they exchange names and papers for one year. He wants to show Schneurson that it is not hard to be a Jew, as the latter says. But as the play goes on, the Christian student discovers for himself the hardships and discriminations with which the Jews in Russia have to contend.

It Is Hard to Be a Jew opened at the Habima in 1936 and the reviews were, on the whole, favorable, indicating that the problems presented in the play were still relevant. However, one critic wrote that the play dealt with the problems only superficially;[6] another reviewer contended that the Gentile was portrayed in an extremely and unrealistically human way.[7] The audience in Palestine was attracted to the play, which enjoyed remarkable success with 115 performances.

Sholem Aleichem's most beloved character was Tevye the dairyman, the symbol of the seemingly naive but actually wise and hard-working Jew. An honest man oppressed for no obvious reason by the non-Jewish authorities, he was expelled from the village of his birth. But he never despairs, never falters in his submission to God's will, even though he constantly has to suppress doubts as to the justice God is dispensing to the world and particularly to his chosen people. As the father of seven daughters, he is plagued with a seemingly unending series of misfortunes, but he bears these with an ironic smile, which is the outward expression of an inner feeling of superiority. Tevye is horrified at the thought of his daughter marrying outside of the Jewish fold, yet this blow too he has to endure and he does so with dignity. Another of his daughters falls in love with an antitsarist conspirator and ends with the husband of her choice in Siberia. Tevye believes in the importance of family backgrounds and respectability and yet he has to consent to another of his daughters marrying beneath her social position. The world of Kasrilevka, the typical Jewish shtetl, is changing rapidly and Tevye has to adjust to new social values, but he will under no circumstances alter his moral concepts, which stem from his biblical heritage and his people's historical experiences. His faith in God gives him strength, and he arrives at the optimistic conclusion that, bad as things are, they could after all have turned out worse.

Tevye the Dairyman opened at the Habima on December 25, 1943. The production was highly acclaimed by the two most influential critics of the time, Ezra Zussman of *Davar* and Chaim Gamzu of *Haaretz*. Both critics praised the staging and acting and singled out Bertonov and Finkel who alternated in the title role, of which they each gave a different interpretation. Other distinguished performances were given by Meskin as the priest, and Rovina as Hava. The few reservations that the critics had concerned the adaptation of the novel, and not the Habima's production of the play.[8] *Tevye the Dairyman* awakened the interest of a wider public and soon became one of the Habima's hallmarks and the most popular production in the entire period, with a record of 275 performances.

In addition to Sholem Aleichem, the Habima produced works by other Yiddish writers. In 1935 the theater presented Peretz Hirschbein's *Green Fields*, retitled *Children of the Fields* in Hebrew. This play, written in 1916, revolves around the confrontation of a pious student of the Talmud with simple Jewish country life and his attraction to such life. Levi Yitzhol, the hero of the play, is a symbol of the Jewish tradition of learning. His decision to remain on the farm is not merely the result of his love for a country girl, but also the result of his discovery that Jewish tradition can thrive on a farm even in seeming exile from schools and books. The play depicts the world of the ordinary Jew, the *folksmentsh* in the Jewish farmer, and is a hymn of praise to the simple Jewish life.

Most critics reacted unfavorably. Gurelik of *Haaretz* criticized the literary quality of the play,[9] and Luvrani of *Davar* contended that it was "a primitive propaganda play." He also questioned whether it was worth mounting such an old play that had no relevance to the present.[10] However, the play was staged interestingly by Leopold Lindberg, the German director, and the audience, disagreeing with the critics, kept the production running for 153 performances.

Two plays by Jacob Gordin, one of the most popular Yiddish playwrights, were presented by the Habima: *Mirele Efros* in 1939 and *God, Man and the Devil* in 1940. *Mirele Efros* was written in 1898 and was modeled on Shakespeare's *King Lear;* it concerned the tragedy of a female counterpart of King Lear—a Jewish mother. Mirele Efros is a strong-willed mother who has built up a fine business and runs it in an imperious fashion. When her children grow up, she turns the business over to them. She is then ignored by them and treated disrespectfully, which makes it impossible for her to remain in her own home, of which she has been so proud. At the end, a reconciliation is effected between the proud mother and her ungrateful children, when her grandson begs her to return home to help celebrate his bar mitzvah.

Mirele Efros, a play whose protagonist was the archetype of the self-sacrificing Jewish mother, was a favorite with Jewish audiences for decades. This play stressed the most distinctive characteristic of the Jewish mother—a mixture of practical sense and emotional abundance. The Habima presented the play in 1939 to commemorate the thirtieth anniversary of Gordin's death. The theater had refused for years to present this play because it thought *Mirele Efros* was a *shund* (trash) play that should not be produced by a theater like the Habima. Indeed, some critics expressed their reservations about the choice of the play. They also wrote that the only proper way to present Gordin's play would have been to keep one's artistic distance and mock the way of life presented in the play—not to present a serious and realistic production as the

A scene from Gordin's *Mirele Efros* (1939).

Habima had done.[11] It is noteworthy that the Habima's presentation was ultimately saved from cheap melodramatics by the extraordinary performance of Rovina, who gave the heroine the dignity and depth of her own personality.[12] *Mirele Efros* was enormously successful with the audience and remained in the theater's repertoire for years, with a notable 228 performances.

The success of *Mirele Efros* was not repeated with the production of Gordin's *God, Man and the Devil,* written in 1903 and considered to be his best play. Strongly influenced by the biblical story of Job and by Goethe's *Faust,* Gordin wrestled with the problem of man's dual nature. The production failed with both critics and audiences and closed after 33 performances. The *Haaretz* critic wrote that despite Gordin's important place in the history of the Yiddish theater, it was a "great sin" to present his plays in 1940 and especially by a theater that was seeking to reflect the new era of Jewish life in Palestine.[13] The *Davar* critic criticized the Habima for attempting to repeat the success that the company had had with *Mirele Efros* by appealing to audiences that still remembered Gordin's plays.[14]

Plays on the Problem of Maintaining Jewishness

This category of plays was the most significant in the Habima's repertoire. It consisted of eighteen plays which, for the most part, were written in languages other than Hebrew and Yiddish. Most were written after World War I and predominantly concerned Jewish life in Western Europe. These plays dealt with various aspects of maintaining Jewishness in the Diaspora as well as with problems of assimilation, conversion, and anti-Semitism and were, of course, particularly relevant to the idea of the new life in Palestine.

Especially noteworthy were the topical plays written in German, which were presented by the Habima in the thirties and were related to the rise of the Nazi regime in Germany. They reflected current events which dealt almost photographically with the ruin of German Jewry and coincided with the first influx of refugees from Nazi Germany. Of these plays, two were of special interest: *The Jew Suess* in 1933 and *Professor Mannheim* in 1934. *Professor Mannheim* can serve as an example of all.

Professor Mannheim by H. Wolf was a modern play. Its action takes place in Germany in 1933 and deals with the problems facing the German-Jewish upper class under the Nazi regime. Professor Mannheim, the hero of the play, is an assimilated Jew and a famous surgeon. He is driven out of his position after the new anti-Semitic laws are passed. However, Mannheim returns to his post, after an amendment to the law allows those who fought at the Front to return to their work. When the new Nazi Hospital Commissioner demands that Mannheim sign a document listing those members of the staff to whom the amendment does not apply and who are therefore to be dismissed, he refuses to sign and as a protest adds his name to the list. Mannheim voices sharp criticism of this offense against liberty of conscience; finally, he sees no other solution but to commit suicide. Before his death he explains that he did not see another way out and that he hopes the younger generation will find a better and a more courageous solution.

All plays of the Hitler era dealt with the rise of anti-Semitism and the downfall of the emancipated German Jewry. These dramas stressed disenchantment with the Jewish illusion of assimilation into German society, and emphasized that the desirable and, in fact, only solution to the Jewish problem was for Jews to come to Palestine. The critics did not judge these productions with ordinary artistic yardsticks. *Haaretz,* for instance, wrote that *The Jew Suess* was an important production because it had both dramatic and historical truth.[15] And after the opening of *Professor Mannheim,* the critics emphasized in their reviews the political meaning of the play rather than its artistic merit.[16]

In 1936, the Habima presented two English plays that dealt with anti-Semitism: John Galsworthy's *Loyalties* and Shakespeare's *The Merchant of Venice.* In comparison to *Loyalties,* which was written in 1922 and concerned a case of anti-Semitism in English society, *The Merchant of Venice* was a much more significant production, both artistically and nationally. It aroused a critical controversy among both critics and audiences because it had been associated in the Jewish consciousness with anti-Semitism.

The reviews of *The Merchant of Venice,* which was brilliantly staged by Leopold Jessner (one of the great men of the German theater before the Nazis came to power), were also controversial. The *Davar* critic liked the production and wrote that the sheer fact of presenting Shakespeare on the Hebrew stage was proof of the Habima's wish to be much more than a local Palestinian theater. Unlike her critic-colleagues, the *Davar* writer contended that the interpretation of the play was not anti-Semitic; it presented Shylock as a dignified individual who thrusts back at intolerable wrongs and is a symbol of the oppressed Jewish people.[17] The *Haaretz* critic wrote that the production was the company's greatest effort since it had settled in Palestine. However, he could not understand why the Habima chose this play, since any attempt to purify the play was useless. Furthermore, in his opinion, Shylock did not represent the real Jewish spirit and, in any case, was at odds with the spirit of the new society in Palestine.[18]

There were many public meetings of protest against this production. On June 23, 1936, one month after the opening night, a public trial of Shakespeare, the Habima, and the director was held. The leading figures of the Yishuv participated, including many writers. The trial concluded that neither Shakespeare, nor the Habima, nor Jessner should be accused of anti-Semitism: the playwright did not portray Shylock as having only negative characteristics, and the director had interpreted the play in light of contemporary Jewish reality. The trial also resolved that it was courageous and daring on the part of the company to cope with the problems that Shakespeare raised in his play.[19]

Despite the sensational aspects of the production, the publicity that it received in the press, and the staging by one of the greatest directors of the time, *The Merchant of Venice* ran for only 42 performances, which was then below the average. It is interesting to note that in 1959 the Habima again presented the play, this time under the direction of Tyrone Guthrie. This production also failed, closing after 37 performances, again showing the sensitivity and the extremely emotional reaction of the public to the topic of the play.

Two years later, in December 1938, the Habima mounted another important Jewish play, Max Zweig's *The Marranos*. "Marrano" is the name that has been given ever since the fifteenth century to Christians of Jewish descent. These Jews had a dual life: in public they acted as Catholics, whereas in private they joined in communion with their real faith. Under the mask of their new religion they could procure high positions and become members of noble Spanish families. Their status lasted for about one hundred years, until the fanaticism of the Church reawakened as a result of a long war with the Moors in Spain. A scapegoat was

Leopold Jessner's production of Shakespeare's *The Merchant of Venice* (1936).

needed to bear the burden of guilt, and in 1480, during the reign of Isabella, the Holy Inquisition was established. *The Marranos* was presented in 1938 and the obvious historical parallel between the Spain of Isabella and the Germany of Hitler was unavoidable.

Of the other plays that concerned the problem of maintaining Jewishness in the Diaspora, two were of special interest: *Lo Amut Ki Ehie* (*I Will Live*) in 1944 and *Kiddush Hashem* (*Martyrdom*) in 1947. *I Will Live* was written by David Bergelson, a celebrated Soviet Jewish writer, in 1942, when Germany invaded the Soviet Union and the government relaxed its censorship. The play dealt with the destruction of Russian Jewry during the war; its title was taken from Psalms 118:17.

Avrom-Ber, the protagonist of the play, is an old Jew who is proud of being a Soviet citizen and is also filled with national Jewish pride. He had lost his eldest son in World War I, and then his second son, a commander of the Red Army brigade, in the present war. But the old man does not break down; he believes that the more Jews die, the stronger is their will to live. Avrom-Ber is confronted in the play with Professor Kornblit, a Jewish refugee from Germany, who declares himself a Jew only after the German invasion of Russia. Kornblit, in despair under the Nazi occupation, contemplates suicide. But Avrom-Ber is deeply concerned with the public aspect of such a deed: the Jewish people, despite all persecutions and expulsions, never took their own lives and never ceased declaring to the world: "I shall not die, but live"—a cry Avrom-Ber staunchly reaffirms just before he is put to death by the Nazis.

I Will Live aroused heated controversy. On opening night, Shalom Shofman, the writer, demanded that the play be taken off the stage. He was offended by the miserable way in which the Jewish characters of the play were portrayed. In an article in *Davar* he protested against the theater's anti-Semitic interpretation and presentation. He could not understand how the Habima dared to force Jewish actors to impersonate Nazi officers and in such a beautiful and proud manner. In his opinion, the only way to present a Nazi on the Hebrew stage was as a caricature and a grotesque.[20] Other critics were also unkind to the play, its production and, especially, to the Habima's having chosen it in the first place. The *Davar* critic wrote that *I Will Live* was an example of how not to present "chapters from the Nazi hell."[21] The *Haaretz* critic wrote that the characters of the play were not human beings but "dolls," and went on to define the play as a "melodramatic operetta."[22] The production also raised the question of whether it was possible and desirable to depict the holocaust on the stage—a question that became all the more significant after the establishment of the Israeli State in 1948.

Martyrdom was written by Sholem Asch in 1920. It was a historical drama that dealt with Jewish heroism and martyrdom during the Chmelnicki uprising in the Ukraine in 1648. The Cossacks had given the Jews a chance to survive if they would bow down before the cross, but they replied with the singing of psalms. For the sake of their God, fourteen hundred men, women, and children were slaughtered by the Cossacks. Not a single one of them purchased his life by abandoning his faith. In glorifying the martyrs of the seventeenth century, Asch wanted to bring comfort to contemporary survivors of similar outrages. Asch's play maintained that despite the temporary triumph of non-Jewish physical might, the more enduring victory is that of the Jewish moral elevation and that "Death for the Sanctification of the Name" (Kiddush Hashem) supplied the best testimony that the Jews were unconquerable.

Martyrdom opened in December 1947. It received unfavorable reviews and consequently closed after 29 performances. The critics' main objection concerned the choice of the play and, especially, the timing of its presentation. Gamzu of *Haaretz* wrote that the public in Palestine related to the Habima as "our national theater," and the theater should therefore live up to the public's expectations. In his opinion, it was the wrong time to present *Martyrdom* because the message of the play—that the Jews were ready to accept their fate without struggling—no longer applied to the reality of Palestine, where the Jewish community struggled and fought to establish an autonomous Jewish state.[23] It should be noted that *Martyrdom* opened several months prior to the proclamation of the State of Israel and the War of Independence.

Palestinian Plays

Only four plays in the Habima's repertoire were written in Hebrew and dealt with the new life in Palestine. Although none of the four plays possessed literary or artistic quality, their importance lay in the fact that they were the first attempts made by Hebrew playwrights to confront the new reality.

Modern Palestine was presented for the first time in a full-length drama in the Habima's production of *Shomrim* (*Watchmen*) in 1937. This play drew on the real story of NILI, a pro-Allied organization in Palestine which gathered intelligence and transmitted it to the British in Egypt (in defiance of the Turks, who ruled the country at that time). The Habima changed the names of the real characters and the historical truth.

The reviews of the play reflected the problems which the theater faced in presenting a genuinely Hebrew-Palestinian play. There were critics who maintained that the play did not have artistic merit because it was too close to immediate reality.[24] Others, approaching the production from another angle, contended that the Habima had not yet learned how to portray on stage the new people of Palestine.[25] But despite controversial opinions of the play and its subsequent failure, all critics held that *Watchmen* was an important start of a native original drama and that the failure of a Hebrew play could teach both the theater and the public more than could the success of a foreign, universal play.

The next Palestinian play was Aaron Ashman's *Haadama Hazot* (*This Earth*) which dealt with the days of romantic pioneering by the *chalut-*

zim (the Jewish pioneers) at the end of the nineteenth century. *This Earth* was an epitome and glorification of Zionism. Presented in 1942, it celebrated the fiftieth anniversary of Hadera (called in the play "Yarkia" [Green Fields]), a settlement that was built by early immigrants from Russia.

The play centers in Yarkia, a new settlement in the heart of the swamps. Since the victims of malaria increase daily, the question is whether to abandon or to hold on to the settlement. The physician is convinced that all the settlers will die if they stay, and therefore orders them to leave the place. The settlers who stood up against the Turkish authorities and survived the riots of the neighboring Arabs cannot overcome malaria. As they start leaving, Yoel Yoshpe, the pioneer and hero of the play, rallies them with an effective dramatic Zionist speech which is punctuated by the cry: "Here, on this Earth." He fights the opinion of the doctor and with great difficulty wins the argument; the deserters turn back. In the epilogue of the play one learns that the swamps were drained and malaria eliminated, and that Yarkia is now a thriving settle-

The Habima's production of Ashman's Hebrew drama *Haadama Hazot* (*This Earth*) in 1942, with Aaron Meskin (seated, center) in the leading role.

ment thanks to those pioneers whose bodies lie in the village cemetery.

This Earth presented a sincere and naive treatment of patriotism and the need to hold on to the Jewish settlements. The language of the play evoked a nostalgic and romantic atmosphere and was clearly propagandistic. Most critics were enthusiastic about the production, as the following review indicates:

> Our theatre and literature have neglected not only the romanticism of Jewish settlements but the romanticism of Zionism altogether. The entire Jewish repertoire of the Hebrew theatre, beginning with *The Dybbuk,* is one great paean to the Diaspora, as is our fiction. I am not complaining about it, perhaps this was necessary with the Diaspora in a process of decline. But the theatre and fiction must not deal exclusively with this subject. There is room for the description of a *sinking* world, and also room for the description of a *rising* world. And how much could Zionist propaganda gain had it been able to use artistic instruments. One play is worth more than a thousand proclamations. Bring us the romanticism of Palestine, and the Zionist movement will rise.[26]

Other critics were happy that such a topic was brought to the stage and were fascinated by the playwright's treatment of the subject. One critic wrote that "the play is so honest, so naive and so charged with emotion, the general atmosphere is so attractive, that one is reluctant to approach it with the unpleasant yardsticks of criticism and analyze its details."[27]

This Earth contributed to the popularity of the Habima and attracted large audiences. The public's reaction was enthusiastic; the dramatic speech of Yoel Yoshpe, the leader (brilliantly portrayed by Meskin), invariably brought cheers from the audience. *This Earth* was one of the Habima's hallmarks during the period; the play achieved a notable success with 213 performances.

In 1944, two years after *This Earth,* the Habima presented its next Palestinian play, Aher Beilin's *Banim Ligvulam* (*The Return of the Sons*). This play centers on an American Jewish family who come to Palestine as tourists and, eventually, under pressures from the daughter, decides to stay on and join one of the kibbutzim. As in *This Earth,* the new kibbutz faces difficulties; there is malaria and a lack of water and some of the members intend to abandon the place. But in the end, all difficulties are surmounted and the kibbutz celebrates the opening of the new communal dining hall.

The Return of the Sons was a reportage propaganda play with stock characters, lacking the sincerity and naiveté of *This Earth*. All critics spoke unfavorably of the play, especially of its obvious propaganda. It seemed to many of them that the Zionist organizations themselves were delivering speeches to the audience.[28] The public, however, proved again that it liked to see realistic, reportage plays; consequently, the production achieved a moderate success with 69 performances.

The last original Palestinian play in this period, Aaron Ashman's *Habsora* (*The Annunication*), failed with both critics and audiences and closed after only 25 performances. It was a melodrama, dealing in a superficial and sentimental way with the significance of giving birth to Jewish children in Palestine in light of the destruction of the Jewish people in the holocaust.

Clearly, between 1931 and 1948 the Habima was predominantly a Jewish theater; more than half of its repertoire consisted of distinctively Jewish plays. The category of Jewish plays was varied from the point of view of locale and plot, ranging from the biblical era to modern Jewish history and to contemporary life in Palestine. The Habima wanted to emphasize genuinely Palestinian plays that would reflect the new Jewish spirit of Palestine, but no one wrote such plays. Because the modern Jewish settlement in Palestine was of comparatively recent origin, a native Hebrew drama had not yet had a chance to develop. As Bialik said in 1929: "It is hard to present plays based on the new Hebrew life in Palestine because our new life is not yet crystallized."[29]

In many ways, the repertory problems that the Habima faced in Palestine resembled those that the Russian theater had faced during and after the 1917 revolution. Like the Russian theater, the Habima was expected to express social changes and to project the new ideas of the times. And like Russia, the Habima found few new plays of any dramatic merit; events happened so fast that it was impossible to depict them through good serious drama.

In the period 1931–1948, Yiddish plays constituted the largest category in the repertoire. Many of the Habima's Yiddish plays were shtetl plays, warmly human comedies (or melodramas) depicting Jewish life in Eastern Europe. The successes of *Mirele Efros* and *Tevye the Dairyman* were indeed symptomatic of the period. Sentimental plays on Jewish life were popular with the audience (which in the twenties and thirties consisted predominantly of immigrants from Eastern Europe). But the nostalgic Yiddish plays, though popular, were severely criticized by the critics and intellectuals, who had a totally different concept of the Habima's ideological and artistic mission in Palestine. They not only opposed the choice of these plays but strongly objected to their artistic style and interpretation. Time and again, the critics expressed their opposition to the naturalistic and apparently serious way in which these plays were presented. The critics believed that the presentation of Yiddish plays should create or fortify among the audience the belief that life in the ghetto was abnormal and deformed, and that the only healthy life a Jew could live was in Palestine. Furthermore, in presenting old Yiddish plays in a realistic way, the critics held the Habima was fulfilling a reactionary role by encouraging nostalgia. Instead, the Habima should be educating and preparing its audience for the new life.

The modern Jewish plays (especially the German plays) were better received by the critics. Many of these were morality plays and had a message: the physical survival of the Jewish people is under a constant threat as long as they remain a national minority living among other nations. Only in their national and historical homeland is it possible for them to escape anti-Semitism and their anomalous position. Almost all plays insisted that nowhere—apart from Palestine—could the Jews find comfort and security, and that the tragedy of the Jews' life in the Diaspora lies in their effort to take root among strangers.

As for the Habima's Palestinian plays, they all presented a romanticized reality. They were strictly reportage plays with hardly any significance beyond their immediate subjects. As such, they resembled the Soviet propaganda plays: simplistic, naive, realistic, and employing stock characters. The Palestinian plays, and their successors, the Israeli plays, reflected too intimately a specific reality. As we shall later see, the major problem with the Habima's Israeli plays was the very fact that they were close to reality, and that once this reality changed—and the reality of Israeli society changed (and changes) rapidly—these plays quickly became dated.

EIGHT

The Habima and the Jewish Community of Palestine

CONTROVERSIES and disputes arose between the Habima and the critics on the one hand, and the critics and the audience on the other. These disputes concerned more than the question of what kinds of Jewish plays the Habima should present. The discussions also revolved around the important questions of whether the Habima should also present non-Jewish plays and how many and what kinds of these should be in the repertoire. These questions were not new for the theater; still, it was not easy to come to terms with them.

After the Habima settled in Palestine it began to present plays from the general world repertoire, both classic and modern. The troupe thought that on its European tour, when the theater performed before many Jewish communities, it was especially important to present distinctively Jewish plays to remind them of their national position and problems. But Palestine's Jews—unlike those in the Diaspora—lived a completely Jewish life and therefore did not need only Jewish drama. Once in Palestine, the company thought that its mission should include trying to fill the theatrical vacuum, so to speak, that prevailed there, to serve all the cultural and theatrical needs of the public. It is important to note that in the thirties, apart from the Habima, there were only two theaters in Palestine.[1] The audience, however, wanted to see all kinds of plays, so the Habima took on the task of providing theater of a high caliber, both Jewish and non-Jewish.

Between 1931 and 1948 the Habima presented thirty-five non-Jewish plays—almost one-half of its entire repertoire. The non-Jewish plays were classical, modern, and contemporary.[2] The classical plays included works by Sophocles, Shakespeare, and Racine. The modern classics included productions of Chekhov, Ibsen, and Shaw. The kinds of universal plays varied, though most were drawn from European drama. A high proportion (over one-third) of East European drama on the one hand and a lack of American plays (only two) on the other characterized the universal plays selected (see Appendix 2).

The Habima's move away from its original goal was especially apparent during its first two years in Palestine (1931–1932). In these years, most of the plays produced were universal, such as Shaw's *The Devil's Disciple*, Maugham's *The Sacred Flame*, and Molière's *Tartuffe*. This new trend began to arouse great controversy among critics and intellectuals. In 1934, *Haaretz* wrote that the Habima was standing at a crossroads: It could attempt to create a specifically Jewish-Hebrew theatrical style, or it could continue to borrow from the European theater in both drama and style and thereby become a provincial theater of Palestine.[3] A few years later, the same critic wrote that the Habima was not so much a Hebrew theater as a theater in Hebrew.[4]

Several of the Habima's meetings, in which writers and cultural leaders of the Yishuv participated, were devoted to discussing the Habima's task and repertoire. Such a meeting took place in May 1936. Avraham Shlonsky, the Hebrew poet and then the voice of the young leftist-oriented Palestine, contended that the Habima was much more than a professional theater, because by tradition it had always wanted its plays to express a national message. Therefore, its task was to create an original Hebrew theater, drawing on the works of Mendele mocher sforim, Mapu, Agnon, and other Hebrew writers; "secular" plays (the ordinary universal plays) did not belong in the repertoire. Rovina, on the other hand, represented the actors' position. She argued that as professional actors, the members did not want to confine themselves to one

Somerset Maugham's *The Sacred Flame* (1931).

specific kind of play, especially in a country such as Palestine, where the potential audience was small. The actors, she said, wanted to develop artistically.[5]

It should be pointed out that Leopold Jessner, the noted Jewish-German director who worked with the Habima at that time, took the position of Shlonsky. In Jessner's opinion, Palestine "does not need a theater that presents international plays in Hebrew, but a theater which is Hebrew in its spirit, one that is created out of the life of the country, its history and its problems." He favored the Habima as a political theater, a theater that had a specific (Palestinian) face and reflected its time and surroundings.[6]

In March 1940, yet another meeting—which included major figures of Palestine's intellectual elite—took place. The Hebrew writer Kabak wanted the Habima to be a real public theater, a theater of the people; he opposed "art for art's sake." Kabak was joined by Krupnik, a drama critic who strongly favored the idea that the Habima reflect the particular "face of our generation" and should therefore present mainly Jewish-Palestinian plays. David Zakai, a cultural leader of the Histadrut, emphasized the Habima's role as an emissary of the Hebrew language and stressed the importance of the Habima's players speaking Hebrew in a correct style and with good pronunciation.[7]

There were other opinions, as well. Asher Barash, another leader of the Histadrut, contended that the Habima should also serve the "everyday demands" of the public in Palestine. He therefore opposed those who wanted the Habima to be a "theater of Sabbath," an heroic Jewish theater. And Jacob Fichman, another major writer, criticized the repeated demand of both critics and audience that the Habima present contemporary and relevant plays. He thought the Habima should present not merely non-Jewish contemporary plays, but also classical plays from the world's best drama.[8]

It should be stressed that, on the whole, the critics approached the Habima's productions with one major question: was the play interesting and relevant to contemporary life in Palestine? First in importance was the subject of the play and the ideas it presented. Of secondary importance were such values as literary quality, the dramatic structure of the play, and its artistic significance. The critics' preference (in fact, demand) that the theater present topical plays on relevant contemporary issues was apparent in almost every review that was written. For instance, when the Habima presented Molière's *The Imaginary Invalid,* the *Davar* critic wrote that the play was too remote from contemporary Palestine and that its satiric humor was too French.[9]

Heated discussions concerning the relevance of the Habima's repertoire were held during the short-lived run of Chekhov's *The Cherry Orchard* in 1939, the first Chekhov play to be presented in Palestine. Friedland, who directed the play, gave it a positive interpretation. Instead of mourning the destruction of the orchard he exulted in the housing project to be built in its place. He originally wanted to turn Lopakhin into a representative of the Jewish pioneers who decided to start a new life in Palestine, but he later dropped this interpretation.[10] *The Cherry Orchard* closed after only 22 performances. Indeed, there were critics who thought that in times of war the Habima should not present plays such as *The Cherry Orchard.*

In 1945, when the Habima mounted Gogol's famous 1833 comedy, *Marriage,* Gamzu, then the most influential critic, attacked the theater's artistic policy on the ground that the play was too Russian. Comparing *Marriage* to Racine's classical play *Phèdre,* which was presented in the same year, Gamzu wrote that although *Phèdre* was a much older play than *Marriage,* it was more relevant. Gamzu thought that Gogol's satire

Shimon Finkel as Raskolnikov and Hanna Rovina as his mother in *Crime and Punishment* (1942).

on the old bachelor lured by a matchmaker was an "archeological item," and contended that the Habima's deviation from its both national and artistic mission might destroy the basis upon which it stands.[11]

The Habima responded to the public's demand to present relevant and topical plays. Seven of the thirty-five universal plays referred to contemporary situations. Most of the contemporary plays dealt, in one way or another, with the negative aspects of war. These productions were especially significant because they were mounted either before or during World War II.

Bury the Dead, written by Irwin Shaw in 1936, was presented a year later. Its central theme is the inanity of war and it presents a desperate plea for peace. The play portrays six soldiers who are laid in their graves but refuse to be buried and forgotten. The play was successfully produced in England and the United States by pacifist groups. However, in Palestine in 1937 the play achieved only a moderate success (56 performances). This is partly explained by the public's expectation that the Habima would present contemporary plays bearing on the immediate reality of Palestine. Indeed, several critics disagreed with the message of the play; they felt that is mocked such terms as "nation" and "sacrifice," terms that were precious to the Jewish people of Palestine.[12]

During the 1938 crisis in Europe the Habima presented *The White Plague,* a drama about war and dictatorship written by the Czech playwright Čapek. The play dramatizes the effect of fear in a nation ruled by a dictator. The power of the Habima production rested on its immediacy: it mirrored contemporary political events in Czechoslovakia after the Munich agreement and the invasion of Hitler.

Hanna Rovina in the title role and her five sons in Čapek's *The Mother* (1939).

In the following season, the Habima mounted another Čapek work, *The Mother.* This drama depicts the horrible consequences of war by telling the tragic story of a mother whose husband had died as a war hero and who loses three of her four sons in other catastrophes. The mother who has always advocated a simple and peaceful family life sends in the end her youngest son as she hears that her country has been invaded by the enemy and is in serious danger. *The Mother* reached a wide public with 107 performances. Its success derived in no small part from the immediacy of the play's message, and from the extraordinary performance of Rovina in the title role.[13]

During World War II the Habima presented two war plays: *Morning Star* in 1942 and *Men of Russia* in 1943. *Morning Star* was written by the British actor and playwright Emlyn Williams and depicted wartime London. *Men of Russia* (or *The Russian People*) was written by the Soviet writer Konstantin Simonov and concerned a Soviet village besieged by the German army. The reviews of both productions pointed out that their power rested on their immediacy and not on their literary merit, and that if the Habima presented the plays five years later, many of their deficiencies would have been apparent and the audience's reaction totally different.[14]

Artistic and Box Office Success

It is interesting to compare the artistic success of the Habima's productions with their box office success, i.e., their success with the audience. After all, it is a large audience which makes a production influential. Thus, it is important to examine which productions had wide appeal and what accounted for that appeal.

Table 8.1 shows that of the 79 new plays that the Habima presented in the period 1931–1948, 29 plays (37 percent) failed, 27 (34 percent) had a short run, 11 (14 percent) achieved a moderate run, and 12 (15 percent) were successful or very successful. Furthermore, of the plays that failed, or had short or moderate runs, there was, in each case, practically the same proportion of Jewish and non-Jewish plays. However, of the 12 plays that were presented over one hundred times, 10 were of Jewish interest. Thus, choosing a play of Jewish interest was not a necessary condition for box office success, but the chances of success were much higher if the play was specifically Jewish.

Table 8.1
Jewish and Non-Jewish Plays: 1931–1948

Number of Performances	*Jewish Plays*		*Non-Jewish Plays*		*All Plays*	
	Number	*Percent*	*Number*	*Percent*	*Number*	*Percent*
1–29 (failure)	15	34.9	14	38.9	29	36.7
30–59 (short run)	13	30.2	14	38.9	27	34.2
60–99 (moderate run)	6	14.0	5	13.9	11	13.9
over 100 (success)[a]	10	20.9	2	8.3	12	15.2
Total	44	100.0	35	100.0	79	100.0

[a] A play that reaches 100 performances is judged a box office success in Israel.

An examination of the Habima's productions shows that all the biblical plays, apart from *Michal, Daughter of Saul* and *The Love of Zion*, either failed or had modest runs. Of the Hebrew-Palestinian plays, only one—*This Earth*—was a great success (154 performances). Most of the classical and modern classical plays had short runs. This category included Molière's *Tartuffe* (37 performances) in 1932 and *The Imaginary Invalid* (31 performances) in 1934; Shakespeare's *The Merchant of Venice* (42 performances) in 1936 and *Hamlet* (55 performances) in 1946; and plays by Sophocles, Racine, Gogol, Chekhov, and Ibsen (see Appendix 2).

It is noteworthy that ten of the twelve most popular productions were distinctively Jewish plays, for the most part shtetl plays (see Table 8.2).

Table 8.2
The Habima's Most Popular Productions: 1931–1948

Playwright	*Play*	*Year of Presentation*	*Number of Performances*
Sholem Aleichem	*Tevye the Dairyman*	1943	204
Jacob Gordin	*Mirele Efros*	1939	171
C. N. Bialik	*The Short Friday*	1933	158
Aaron Ashman	*This Earth*	1942	154
Sholem Aleichem	*Amcha (People)*	1932	135
Peretz Hirschbein	*Green Fields*	1935	128
Aaron Ashman	*Michal, Daughter of Saul*	1941	116
H. Leivik	*Chains*	1931	116
Sholem Aleichem	*It Is Hard to Be a Jew*	1936	113
Somerset Maugham	*The Sacred Flame*	1931	111
L. Fodor	*Graduation*	1941	106
Sholem Aleichem	*Upon a Fiddle*	1935	103

A scene from Leivik's revolutionary drama, *Chains* (1931).

Seven of these plays were written in Yiddish, four by Sholem Aleichem. The two greatest successes were *Tevye the Dairyman* and *Mirele Efros*. The subjects of these plays and the superb performances of the actors in the title roles (Bertonov and Finkel in *Tevye the Dairyman*, and Rovina in *Mirele Efros*) accounted for their success. It should be recalled that *Mirele Efros* was a cheap melodrama and that it received unfavorable reviews. However, the audience proved that it preferred a well-acted Jewish melodrama to a poor or mediocre production of a classical or serious play.

The public's preference for melodrama was also reflected in the great popularity of the two non-Jewish plays: *The Sacred Flame* and *Graduation*. *The Sacred Flame* revolves around a woman (again played brilliantly by Rovina) who, after great conflicts, puts her incurably ill son to death. *Graduation* is a human melodrama that takes place in a girls' high school and concerns the relationships between students and their teachers.

Until the company settled in Palestine, all its productions were staged by Russian directors who, for the most part, were affiliated with the

Moscow Art Theater and were familiar with the Habima's work in Moscow. In 1931, the troupe decided to end its dependence on foreign directors and to start developing directors of its own, in part because of the enormous financial difficulties involved in importing directors and in part because of the company's wish to develop its own directors.

This decision was not easy, nor was it wholeheartedly accepted. The company knew that its high standards and fame had been achieved in large part because of the superb training and experience that the troupe had received from its first-rate directors. Many members wondered if those who were to direct had enough knowledge and training to stage productions that would maintain the troupe's standards. But the theater did not have much choice.

The years 1931–1948 are known in the Habima's history as the period of "internal direction," because the vast majority of the productions (seventy-two, or 91 percent) were directed by six members of the collective. Baruch Chemerinsky and Zvi Friedland, both original Moscow members, played especially important roles in the Habima's artistic work. Friedland staged thirty-nine productions (half of the entire repertoire), and Chemerinsky nineteen productions (25 percent). Friedland staged both Jewish and non-Jewish plays; Chemerinsky was responsible for Jewish repertoire only.

Only seven plays (9 percent) were staged by foreign directors. The Habima first violated its principle of "internal direction" in 1934, when it invited Leopold Lindberg, the German-Jewish director, to stage two plays, Wolf's *Professor Mannheim* and Molière's *The Imaginary Invalid.* The next year Lindberg was invited again to direct Hirschbein's *Green Fields* and Leivik's *The Golem's Dream.* In 1936 the troupe invited Leopold Jessner, one of the great men of the German theater before Hitler, to stage Shakespeare's *The Merchant of Venice* and Schiller's *Wilhelm Tell.* The work with Jessner was extremely important for the theater and *The Merchant of Venice* was one of the company's greatest artistic achievements.

From 1937 to 1947 the principle of "internal direction" remained in force. The work with the resident directors had its advantages and disadvantages. The permanent directors, because they belonged to the collective, knew well each member and his or her capability. They could, therefore, guide the actor in giving the best performance of which he or

The actors of Sophocles' *Oedipus Rex* (1947) with the noted English director Tyrone Guthrie.

she was capable. However, the virtual absence of artistic stimulus resulted in the troupe's artistic stagnation. It was also dysfunctional for the audience. Indeed, in the forties, theater critics pointed out time and again that the Habima's productions had become routine. They urged the theater to bring in foreign directors and send its staff directors to Europe to learn from what was being done in the theater centers of the world. As a result, in 1947 the Habima invited Tyrone Guthrie, the noted English director, to stage the Greek tragedy *Oedipus Rex*. This production was artistically the most notable event of the entire decade and "stood like a lonely peak surrounded by mediocrity."[15]

The Habima and Its Audiences

During the period 1931–1948 the Habima went on two extensive tours: to Europe (1937–1938) and to the United States (1948).[16] The theater also visited Egypt several times and performed for the Jewish communities of Cairo and Alexandria in the late twenties and early thirties.

The Habima's extensive tour of Europe lasted eight months (from October 1937 to June 1938) and included nine countries: Lithuania, Latvia, Poland, Czechoslovakia, Austria, Yugoslavia, France, Belgium, and England. The 1937–1938 tour differed from the former tours in one major respect: it was the first tour in which the troupe appeared abroad as a Palestinian theater.

The troupe's belief that it represented the new Jewish life in Palestine was not reflected in the repertoire chosen for the tour: *The Dybbuk, The Eternal Jew, Uriel Acosta,* and *The Golem's Dream.* The first two had been produced in Moscow, and *Uriel Acosta* had been prepared in 1930. *The Golem's Dream,* produced in 1935, was the only new production, but during the tour this production failed and *David's Crown* (produced in 1929) was added to the repertoire. Thus, all the tour plays were old productions, and none of these was a Hebrew or genuinely Palestinian play. It is small wonder, then, that many newspapers and critics in Europe still referred to the company as the "Moscow Theater Habima."

The tour, however, met with enormous success, both ideological and artistic. The critics praised the artistic merits of the theater in general, but of all plays presented, *The Dybbuk* received the critics' most enthusiastic applause. Gordon Craig, the noted English director, theorist, and designer, wrote this review in the *Times:*

> Habima is a group of actors who have preserved their unity—a group which venerates the memory of its leader, Vakhtangov, and even though he is no longer with it, remembers what he told it to do and does it. . . . It is a group which knows well what ensemble means . . . and ensemble means teamwork. . . . And in the theatre they must all be actors of capacity—no amateurs—no stage-struck enthusiasts, but men of purpose who stand together . . . for many years. Habima is composed of such men and has stood firm for twenty years. Europe honors Habima, not for its organizational ability—it has little—but for its capacity to act plays and play the game.[17]

The tour in Eastern and Central Europe assumed a special importance because of the political events and atmosphere there in 1937–1938, especially the anti-Semitism inspired by Nazi Germany. The general feeling of the Jewish leaders and people was that this might be the Habima's last visit to Eastern Europe; it indeed was.

Although the Habima theater was located in Tel-Aviv, it performed all over the country. The Habima was, wherefore, a nationwide operation and attempted to reach almost all communities of Palestine. Mobility—it was described as "a theater on wheels"—was one of its characteristic features. The Habima became mobile as a result of the small size of the country and, more importantly, because of the country's history and sociocultural characteristics. The kibbutzim, which were spread all over the country, had a highly educated population and they played an extremely important part in the Yishuv's political, economic, and cultural life. The Habima, therefore, felt obliged to appear not only in Tel-Aviv and other big cities, but in the rural areas as well.

The theater traveled from one place to another, and performed in all kinds of halls—from movie houses and communal dining rooms of the kibbutzim to open fields where the public sat on the ground. As a result, it had to adapt the setting of the productions to the various stages where it performed. During the 1938–1939 season, for instance, the Habima performed 256 times in fifteen different places; of these, 110 performances were given outside Tel-Aviv. During the 1941–1942 season, the Habima gave 358 performances in thirty-two places, of which only 175 were given in Tel-Aviv.[18] Table 8.3 presents the number of performances and attendance between 1931 and 1948.

Between 1931 and 1948 the number of performances presented per season gradually increased. This increase was made possible by a concurrent gradual increase in the Jewish population of Palestine (from 174,606 in 1931 to 630,019 in 1947). During the 1931–1932 season, the Habima gave 162 performances to a total audience of 98,000 people. It was, therefore, a season in which more than half of Palestine's Jewish population attended the theater. In 1941–1942, the Habima performed 358 times and had a total audience of 228,438. Hence, in ten years the theater doubled the number of performances it gave per season. The audience that attended the theater also doubled in this ten-year period. Indeed, in the thirties and forties the theater sold a number of tickets that amounted to half of the Jewish population. It should be pointed out that the Habima's admission prices were always reasonable, and all income groups (including middle and lower) could pay the admission fees.

Despite the public's support, the Habima continued to face constant financial hardship. Clearly, in so small a community, a theater of such

Table 8.3
Number of Performances and Attendance per Season: 1931–1948

Season	*Number of Performances*	*Attendance*	*Jewish Population*
February to August 1931	76	57,000[a]	174,606
1931–1932	162	98,000[a]	192,137
1932–1933	190	130,000[a]	234,967
1933–1934	200	125,000[a]	282,975
1934–1935	250[a]	150,000[a]	355,157
1935–1936	[b]	[b]	384,078
1936–1937	[b]	[b]	395,836
1937–1938	[b]	[b]	411,222
1938–1939	256	153,068	445,457
1939–1940	250	[b]	465,535
1940–1941	300	[b]	474,102
1941–1942	358	228,438	484,408
1942–1943	[b]	[b]	502,912
1943–1944	[b]	[b]	528,702
1944–1945	[b]	[b]	554,329
1945–1946	324	220,216	580,000[a]
1946–1947	329	220,000[a]	630,019
1947–1948	[b]	[b]	716,678

SOURCE: D. Gurevich, comp., *Statistical Handbook of Jewish Palestine* (Jerusalem: The Jewish Agency, 1947), p. 46; *Statistical Abstract of Israel* (Jerusalem, 1961), pp. 43, 86.

NOTE: In Israel, the theatrical season begins in September and ends in August.

[a] Approximate.

[b] No data.

high stature had to have more than the sympathy of the audience. The Habima depended entirely upon the income from its performances and therefore faced financial risks with every production. Furthermore, the theater's mobility involved enormous expenses and made the company even less financially profitable. Unlike repertory and art theaters that are fully or partly subsidized by cities or government grants, the Habima was not subsidized by any source, private or public.

In the early thirties, the theater's economic situation was precarious. Time and again, the theater and major figures of the Yishuv appealed to the public to support the Habima. In 1932, Margot Klausner of the

The laying of the cornerstone of the first Habima House in Tel-Aviv in 1935. An honorary committee, under the chairmanship of Sir Arthur Wauchope, then the British High Commissioner of Palestine, was formed, and included Dr. Chaim Weizman, later Israel's first president, Tel-Aviv mayor Meir Dizengoff, Bialik, Lord Melchett, and others. Action committees were organized throughout the country to assist with the drive to establish a permanent home for the Habima. The new house opened in 1945.

Habima Secretariat appealed to the national and municipal institutions to ensure the survival of the Habima. She called for an organized public action and for the establishment of a Public Committee.[19] In the same year, leading figures of the kibbutz movement published a memorandum in *Hapoel Hatzair,* the press of the labor movement, calling upon all the kibbutzim to contribute the profits of one day's produce for the building of a new theater hall for the Habima.[20]

At the end of 1932, Klausner and a small group of the Habima friends established Chug Habima (the Habima Circle) in Palestine. The purpose of this organization was to provide the theater with subsidies and to maintain regular contact between the theater and the public. The funds collected were used exclusively to cover the expenses of producing new plays. Within five years, the Habima Circle had nearly twenty-five branches throughout the country as well as several in Europe.[21] The Habima Circle played an important part in the realization of the theater's chief projects: the building of a properly equipped theater, and the establishment of a drama school. Both opened in 1945.

In January 1933, Chug Habima Lanoar (the Habima Youth Circle) was created. Its purpose was to develop among the young people of Palestine a love for the theater and a taste for culture. Like the Habima Circle, the Habima Youth Circle had branches all over the country.[22] There was also a journal called *Bama* (Stage), first published by the Habima Circle in 1933, that dealt with various questions of theatrical art, especially those related to the Habima. In addition to their financial goals, all three—the Habima Circle, the Habima Youth Circle, and *Bama*—sought not only to maintain contact between the Habima and the public, but also to educate both adults and youth.

The Habima and the Ohel Theater

The Habima was not the only theater in Palestine in this period; there was another repertory theater, the Ohel. A comparison between the Habima and the Ohel will highlight the distinct characteristics of the Habima and will consider whether the problems that the Habima faced were unique.

The Ohel theater was founded in Palestine in 1925 by Moshe Halevi, formerly a leading member of the Habima. During 1917, Halevi became imbued with the cultural ideals of the Revolution; although he was not a Communist, he strongly believed in a proletarian theater that would present plays drawn from working-class life. Halevi was especially influenced by the Proletcult movement that was founded in Moscow in 1918 to foster proletarian art, and he was determined to establish such a theater in Palestine. He therefore approached the leaders of the Cultural Department of the Histadrut with the idea of establishing a dramatic studio for this organization.[23]

Halevi travelled around the country, especially to the kibbutzim, to recruit candidates for his studio. The ideal members were "young men, tall and strong as cedars, with fine appearances . . . men who could express the fire burning in the young community which was building its old-new land." As the Habima had done in its early stages, Halevi refused to take actors with professional experience; he wanted a new sort of actor, "an amateur . . . ready to learn and to act in the theater in his free time while earning his living from labor in the fields or in the factory."[24] Halevi gathered forty members for his studio and at the end of 1925 he began to train them.

The name which he chose for the new theater was Ohel, literally "tent." The theater's name had not only a biblical connotation but also a contemporary one—many of the pioneers in Palestine then lived in tents. As part of the Zionist labor movement, the Ohel theater was meant to fit into the dominant cultural and political ideology by being organized as a cooperative, in the same manner as the kibbutzim. The Ohel's founders believed that "Ohel is a kibbutz like all the other kibbutzim, except that its aim is to found not an agricultural settlement but an 'assembly of art' of workers' communities of the country." The Ohel's task was "not only to provide entertainment to the public, but to participate actively in the building of the country and in the revival of the nation."[25]

Ideologically, the Ohel was meant to be the theater of the pioneers of the new society in Palestine. In addition to being a Jewish proletarian theater, the Ohel, like the Habima, believed that it should present biblical plays. Artistically, the troupe intended to apply the Stanislavsky method, in which Halevi, like all other Habima members, had been trained.

At its first public performance in May 1926, the Ohel presented *Nishfei Peretz* (*Peretz Evenings*), several one-act pieces by I. L. Peretz, the noted Yiddish writer. Peretz's stories not only were specifically Jewish but also had explicit social significance; his heroes were the poor and the oppressed seeking a solution to their misery. In his direction, Halevi stressed the oppressiveness and degeneracy of life in the ghetto, as opposed to the ideals on which the new community in Palestine was founded.[26] *Peretz Evenings* was an unqualified success and the press applauded the new venture.

The Ohel's second offering, in March 1927, was *The Fisherman* (originally titled *The Good Hope*), written by the Dutch playwright Herman Heijermans. A play of social import, it concerned the tragedy which strikes the families of Dutch fishermen who, having been sent out to sea in a leaky schooner by their capitalist ship-owner, are drowned. *The Fisherman* was the first play of explicit social comment to be presented in Palestine. Halevi had hoped that the socialist-revolutionary pathos of the play would reflect the revolutionary spirit of the Zionist pioneers, who, like the characters of the play, fought for freedom.

The Ohel's third offering, opening in January 1928, was a biblical play, *Jacob and Rachel* by the non-Jewish Russian writer, Kraschennikov, adapted and translated by the noted Hebrew poet Avraham Shlonsky. In order to make the play genuinely biblical and Palestinian, Halevi taught the actors to speak Hebrew in the manner of Yemenites, whose accent was considered to be authentically biblical.[27] With this production, the Ohel established itself as a theater. The three first productions reflected Ohel's distinctive ideology: Zionist, biblical, and proletarian.

Repertoire

Table 8.4 compares the repertoire of the Habima with that of the Ohel by subject in the period 1925–1948.

The Habima was a larger enterprise than the Ohel; between 1925 and 1948, the Habima mounted 85 plays compared with 62 at the Ohel. The average number of Habima productions per season was nearly 4; the Ohel presented 3. Table 8.4 also shows that the Habima presented more specifically Jewish plays than did the Ohel. From 1925 to 1948 the Habima mounted 48 (56 percent) distinctively Jewish plays, whereas the Ohel mounted 24 (39 percent).

Table 8.5 compares the repertoire of the two theaters by the language in which their plays were written.

Table 8.4
Repertoire of the Habima and the Ohel by Subject: 1925–1948

	The Habima		*The Ohel*	
Type of Play	*Number*	*Percent*	*Number*	*Percent*
Jewish	48	56.5	24	38.7
Non-Jewish	37	43.5	38	61.3
Total	85	100.0	62	100.0

Table 8.5
Repertoire of the Habima and the Ohel by Language: 1925–1948

	The Habima		*The Ohel*	
Language	*Number*	*Percent*	*Number*	*Percent*
Yiddish	19	22.4	13	21.0
Hebrew	12	14.1	5	8.0
German	16	18.8	14	22.6
English	13	15.3	12	19.4
Russian	8	9.4	8	12.9
French	6	7.1	3	4.8
Other	11	12.9	7	11.3
Total	85	100.0	62	100.0

On the whole, there was a great similarity between the Habima and the Ohel in terms of the languages of the productions. The vast majority of the plays presented by both theaters (86 percent of the Habima's plays and 92 percent of the Ohel's plays) were written in languages other than Hebrew. While there was a notable difference in the number and percentage of Hebrew plays (12 plays by the Habima compared with 5 by the Ohel), there were practically no differences between the percentage of Yiddish, German, English, and Russian plays.

However, there was a great difference between the Habima's and the Ohel's repertoire during the first decade of the Ohel's existence (1925–1935). Intoxicated with the idea of building the land as a home for the free Jewish people, the Ohel staged plays extolling the heroism of labor and other socialist-proletarian themes. The other tendency of the Ohel was to produce biblical plays. These two ideological tendencies were reflected in the Ohel's early repertoire.

Searching for original material of national significance, Halevi staged Stefan Zweig's *Jeremiah,* the biblical tragedy of the prophet, in 1929, and a play in commedia dell'arte style on the origins of the Purim festivals (Purim Shpiel) in 1931. *Jacob and Rachel,* a biblical tragedy, *Jeremiah,* another biblical tragedy, and *Queen Esther* (or *Purim Shpiel*), a biblical comedy, made up the Ohel's biblical trilogy.

In the early thirties, the Ohel presented several social and proletarian plays. Especially noteworthy were Karel Čapek's *R.U.R.* in 1930, which dealt with the problem of modern man in the age of technology; Wolff's

Conquerors of the Swamps in 1931; and Leivik's *Shop* in 1932, a play depicting the plight of turn-of-the-century immigrants in the United States forced to work for low pay under inhuman conditions. In these years, the Ohel also presented three important universal plays of explicit social (and class) comment: Ben Jonson's *Volpone,* Maxim Gorky's *The Lower Depths,* and Bertolt Brecht's *Threepenny Opera.* Indeed, the proportion of universal plays presented by the Ohel was higher than that of the Habima, but many of these plays were proletarian or explicitly social, in accordance with the Ohel's ideology.

From the mid-thirties on, the Ohel struggled with the problem of how to be both a proletarian and a Jewish national theater. In 1935, for instance, the Ohel presented *The Mill* by David Bergelson. *The Mill* tells the story of a Jewish flour mill owner who exploits his Jewish workers. This production aroused the ire of both the rightist press and the labor movement.[28] At times the Ohel's efforts to be a genuine workers' theater were so artificial that David Ben-Gurion, then the Secretary-General of the Histadrut, wrote on the occasion of the Ohel's fifth anniversary: "We shall not make ourselves ridiculous by seeing in Ohel *proletarian* art and in the Habima *bourgeois* art."[29]

In later years, the Ohel abandoned its original intention to develop a proletarian art. The atmosphere that prevailed in Palestine in the thirties, with its strong emphasis upon nationalism, was not a proper background for a theater emphasizing socialist ideology and class struggle. The Jewish community in Palestine was then fighting on two fronts, against the Arabs and against the restrictions of the British Mandatory regime, and this called for national unity. In addition, the absence of large industries and therefore of large-scale worker exploitation deprived socialist class-struggle slogans of their validity. Indeed, when the Ohel went on an extensive tour of Europe in 1934, it decided to present its biblical and national rather than its proletarian plays.[30]

The differences between the Habima's repertoire and the Ohel's gradually diminished so that by the late thirties and forties, the two repertoires converged. Like the Habima, which had abandoned its original plan to produce only Jewish plays, and especially biblical and national ones, the Ohel abandoned its original aim of devoting itself to the production of biblical and proletarian plays. In the forties, both were presenting a Jewish repertoire—for the most part Yiddish plays—consisting of historical and romantic plays, together with a non-Jewish universal repertoire consisting of both classical and modern plays.

Artistic Work

The Ohel theater, like the Habima, was primarily influenced by the Russian school of acting and production. However, the major difference between the two troupes was in the training that the Habima actors had received in Moscow and in the number of gifted actors that the older troupe possessed. The Ohel was never a competitor of the Habima as far as acting skill and talent were concerned. Furthermore, it never developed its own unified acting style and never succeeded in building up a good company.

When the Habima first arrived in Palestine, the cultural and political leaders of the Yishuv suggested that the two troupes merge. They argued that the small community of Palestine would not be able to sustain two troupes and that the two would complement each other. However, because of the artistic differences between the two theaters and the Habima's elitist orientation, the Habima never seriously considered this proposal.[31] Furthermore, even the press and the public—in spite of the similarity and competition between the two troupes—never identified the two as being on the same artistic level. As early as 1931, the general opinion was that Palestine had only one important theater with experienced and qualified actors—the Habima.[32] From 1931 to 1948, the Habima was the leading theater, with the Ohel running a poor second. And in the late forties and fifties, when fierce competition existed between the Habima and the Cameri (the Chamber theater, established in 1944), the Ohel ran a poor third.

Despite these artistic differences, the style of both troupes in their first years was that of Russian expressionism. In later years, both the Habima and the Ohel presented plays that were staged in various styles, but, on the whole, their dominant mode of presentation was a mixture of expressionism and realism. Furthermore, the Ohel, like the Habima, worked primarily with staff directors. Fifty-seven (92 percent) of the Ohel's productions were staged by two resident directors, Moshe Halevi and Friedrich Lobe, compared with seventy-two (85 percent) of the Habima productions that were directed by six members of the Habima collective, especially by Chermerinsky and Friedland. However, in this period the Habima also worked with directors of world fame, such as Diki, Granovsky, Chekhov, Lindberg, Jessner, and Guthrie.

Organizational Structure and Support

Halevi, like the Habima members in Miscow, was reluctant to refer to his venture as a professional theater, so in the first years he called it a dramatic studio. The Ohel's members earned their living outside the theater and devoted much of their free time to working in the studio without material compensation; regular salaries were not paid until the mid-thirties. The Ohel, like the Habima, was established as a cooperative, an actors' collective. The theater granted all members equal rights and salaries, and questions of artistic policy were determined by a majority vote of the collective.

The most significant difference between the Habima and the Ohel was in the area of financial and organizational support. The Ohel was founded as the dramatic studio of the Histadrut. More important than the limited financial backing of the Histadrut was its social support; the Ohel was attended en masse by the members of all the labor unions of the Histadrut. Moreover, in 1934, when the Ohel was at the height of its artistic achievements, the *Histadrut* decided that the official name of the Ohel would be "Teatron Poalei Eretz Israel" (Israel's Workers' Theater).

The Ohel remained the Histadrut's official theater until 1958 when the labor organization, after more than thirty years of sponsorship, decided not to continue underwriting the Ohel's heavy yearly deficits. It had come to the conclusion that the Ohel was no longer a workers' theater, but had become another repertory theater (like the Habima and the Cameri). Yet while the official reason for the Histadrut's severing its connection with the Ohel was the change in the troupe's repertoire, the actual reason was the theater's declining artistic quality and diminishing popularity, which had been apparent since the late forties. In the fifties and sixties, the Ohel continued to deteriorate both artistically and financially. Consequently, in 1969, the Ohel was liquidated after forty-four years of existence.

NINE

Organizational Structure: The Actors' Collective

THE Habima was founded as a group theater. Since it was organized as an actors' collective, all actors received equal salaries and took an active part in the general meetings of the collective, where all issues were discussed. But despite its purported egalitarian collectivism, in Moscow it was Zemach, as the General Director, who made the important decisions, a practice that was the major cause of the 1927 split. After the split, most members developed a distrust of authority and were reluctant to delegate decision-making power to one man. It was therefore decided that the sovereign body of the Habima would be the general assembly of the collective. In order to prevent any individual from acquiring personal power, it was resolved that all offices should be held for a limited time and should rotate among the members. Thus, the power struggle with Zemach and the consequent split had a lasting effect on the theater, producing a suspicion of any kind of management, artistic or administrative.

The Habima first arrived in Palestine in 1928. At that time, the dominant political ideology of the Yishuv was collectivist, and the social and organizational embodiment of this ideology was the kibbutz. In addition, most of the people in Palestine were of East European origins and had been brought up in collectivist culture of the Russian political movements of the time.[1] Like the Yishuv, the Habima's collectivist ideology was influenced by Russian culture. When the Habima came to Palestine its collectivist structure adapted easily to its new surroundings.

The institutional setting of Palestine in the twenties determined, to a large extent, the structure of many organizations there. Indeed, political (parties), social (kibbutzim), economic (transportation companies), and artistic (theaters) organizations all had a cooperative structure and adhered to a collectivist ideology. The Jewish community of Palestine was very small (156,800, for instance, in 1928) and the area was governed under the British Mandate. The absence of political sovereignty and an autonomous government that could regulate social, economic, and artistic activities meant that every organization had to take care of itself and be responsible for its own survival. Thus, the Russian-based collectivist ideas and structure of the Habimas were wedded to practical necessity when the troupe settled in Palestine. It was apparent that if the theater was to survive economically, it had to be organized as a collective.

The Habima's collectivism was very similar to early kibbutz collectivism. In the kibbutz, all property is collectively owned and work is collectively organized. Furthermore, "all the essential interests of life are satisfied in a cooperative way."[2] The kibbutz ideology comprised three distinct but related values: group ownership of all economic goods, the primacy of group over individual interests, and group experience as intrinsically valuable. The kibbutz culture stressed the moral value of the group. First, the individual's interests must be subordinated to the interests of the group. Second, the individual's motivations should always be directed to the promotion of the group's interests. Third, group living and group experiences are valued more highly than their individual counterparts.[3] These moral postulates also constituted the social ethic and the basis for the Habima's social structure.

The Constitution of the theater was written in 1928. It remained in force, with minor changes, until 1962. Paragraph 1 specified the goals of the association:

> A. The Association is organized in order to continue in Palestine the existence of the Moscow Theater Habima, established in Moscow in 1917.

B. To establish, direct, and maintain a Hebrew art theater in Palestine and elsewhere.[4]

Again, in 1928, it was not clear whether the Habima should settle in Palestine permanently.

Other important paragraphs pointed out that "the association does not have capital that is distributed into shares,"[5] and that "the association does not pay dividends to its members."[6] As in the kibbutz, the property of the Habima was owned collectively by the members, who were the owners as well as the managers of the theater.

The ideology which underlay the Habima's collectivism was based on an extreme model of participatory democracy, egalitarianism, and voluntarism. The communal ownership of the theater's property derived from the emphasis placed on the moral value of equality. This equality was guaranteed by preventing the rise of invidious distinctions based on salary, power, and artistic skill; there was no system of rank based on differential reward. It would not be an exaggeration to contend that there was a cult of egalitarianism. The Constitution stated: "All members receive an equal salary. . . . Each member participates in the general assembly and has the right to be elected to the Administrative Board or the Revision Committee. In general, all members have equal rights."[7] And the Habima's by-laws, known as the Regulations of Internal Order and Discipline, stated: "All members equally devote their artistic, cultural, and moral powers to the growth and development of the theater and to the achievement of its goals."[8] Hence, all members of the collective received the same salary and enjoyed the same working conditions, regardless of their acting skill, artistic importance, popularity, or prestige.

According to collective ideology, all members had equal voice and share in decision making. All decisions, major as well as minor, artistic as well as nonartistic, were to be reached by a majority vote of the collective. Decisions that concerned the dissolution of the Board of Directors or the inclusion and exclusion of members, had to be reached by a majority vote of two-thirds of the membership.[9] Members were obliged to attend meetings regularly and those who were absent were reproached. Special importance was attached to the rule of ideological collectivism, i.e., members were pledged to accept any majority decision of the general assembly.[10] Before a decision was made, any member of the group had the right to fight for his opinion, but once a vote had been taken, every member was obliged to accept the decision. In addition, special emphasis was placed on conformity to the Constitution and to the unwritten, unofficial norms of the collective.

The ideological and social characteristics of the collective were best reflected in the manner of distributing parts. Many debates and general meetings were devoted to this issue, most of which concerned not merely casting for a particular play but also broader questions related to the organization and ideology of the collective.

Distribution of Parts

As long as Vakhtangov was alive, the Habima actors did not participate in casting decisions. "Vakhtangov was the authority . . . he used to say: 'I want this actor for this part,' and no one dared to question his judgment."[11] In Moscow parts rotated among the actors in successive performances. It was believed that rotation developed the individual actor and also kept the production fresh and alive. There were other practices that assured the principle of equality among the members: "Those who had taken parts in the last production had to yield to those who had not yet had the chance to perform. Those who had taken parts in mass scenes had the choice of offering themselves for better parts, whereas those who had already played major roles were supposed to be cast in mass scenes."[12] Meskin, for instance, who played the leading role in *The Golem,* played a role of minor importance—one of the beggars—in *The Dybbuk.* Members had the right to apply for any role they wanted to play, and at times there could be as many as three candidates for a single part. The final decision was up to the director of the play, though he was obliged to give preference to an applicant who had not yet had an opportunity to perform.[13]

These norms and practices were not formalized or written, but were rather group decisions that were worked out among the members themselves. The members believed that these regulations "guaranteed an opportunity for talent and ability to win recognition." The Habima was determined to avoid the practice of the "professional theatre, where it was determined in advance that given actors would play given types—this actor for comedy, that one for tragedy, and so on." The task of the group was to assign roles in a way that would "develop the skills of our members in every aspect of the actor's art."[14]

There were no star actors in the group. One of the chief beliefs was that the collective, as a group, should always stand higher than the individual player. This was so passionately maintained that members were taught: "If an individual should rise to greater heights than his colleagues, if he was more talented—that was to the credit of the collective, the entire collective, not to the individual himself."[15]

These norms, which were to assure the equality of the member in all respects, artistic as well as nonartistic, are not surprising if one bears in mind the characteristics of the Habima in Moscow. In the first place, the members were young amateurs. Second, because they were all inexperienced, the artistic starting point was basically the same for all members, so they all received essentially the same theatrical education and training. Third, their belief in the members' equality was fortified by the kind of training they received from their teachers, Stanislavsky and Vakhtangov. One of the slogans of Stanislavsky and the Moscow Art Theater was "the social power is in the ensemble." And during their work on *The Dybbuk,* Vakhtangov worked thoroughly with each actor. "It was the heart of Vakhtangov's attitude toward acting that even the most minor character was to project a unique and individual life."[16] This kind of work gave all the actors the feeling that they were creating important roles, though most played very minor ones. Their metaphor for the production of *The Dybbuk* was that of a complex machine each little screw of which was of equal importance to the functioning of the whole. Finally, during its stay in Moscow, the Habima had produced only five plays and therefore most actors had not had an opportunity to prove how talented they were. All these factors contributed to the strong belief in the members' equality in artistic as well as nonartistic matters.

The artistic regulations and practices concerning the distribution of parts, which had taken shape in Moscow, continued to prevail after the company left Russia. Furthermore, after the split over Zemach, the determination to maintain equality among the members was even stronger than it had been in Moscow.

One way of preventing any individual from acquiring personal power was by distributing parts according to official rules. Indeed, the Constitution specified that "each member must abide by the regulations of the collective in regard to acceptance of parts in plays produced by the association, and is obliged to play whatever is given to him."[17] It was also resolved that an actor might study a part that he would like to perform and was to have an opportunity at a rehearsal to demonstrate what he could do with the part. Nonetheless, in Moscow the final decision had been made by the director, but in Palestine it was made by the collective, and once the final decision was made the individual actor had to adhere to it.

In the years 1928–1948, parts were distributed at the general assembly of the collective. Two criteria were significant in assigning roles: seniority and rotation. These standards were considered fair and just by the group and as such guaranteed equality among the members. Considerations of acting skill, physical appearance, and personal charm were regarded as breeding a star system, against which the group fought. Thus, parts were assigned, on the whole, on the basis of formal and bureaucratic rather than purely artistic considerations. The collective tended to ignore the possibility that while considerations of seniority and rotation might be relevant to the regulation of the relationships among the actors within the theater, they were totally irrelevant to the artistic success of the production and to the attraction of audiences to the theater.

In 1928, the collective met to distribute the parts of the theater's next two productions: *The Treasure* and *David's Crown,* both to be directed by the Russian director, Alexander Diki. Bertonov did not get a part in *The Treasure,* because it was not his turn; he had played a major part in the last production of the theater, *The Flood,* in 1925. The part that Bertonov wanted was given instead to Brook, a much less able actor. When Bertonov fought for his right to play the part, the collective resolved that both he and Brook would alternate in the part. However, Diki did not abide by the resolution and insisted that only Bertonov would play the part.[18]

After the premiere of *The Treasure* in November 1928, the artistic work of the troupe stopped for seven weeks, during which there was a dispute over the distribution of parts in the next play, *David's Crown.*[19] Such arguments were not uncommon. Indeed, three general meetings were devoted to the casting of *Twelfth Night,* the next production. In this case, the Repertory Committee suggested several candidates for each part. After a preliminary elimination of candidates, the collective voted for the actors who would play the parts. Sometimes two and three ballots were necessary until one actor got a majority. When Chekhov, the director of *Twelfth Night*, wished to give a part to a particular actor, his decision had to be approved by a majority of the collective.[20]

Actors who were not collective members, though they might appear in the productions, were not entitled to attend the meetings and therefore could not argue and fight for parts as the members of the collective did. Indeed, this was the major reason why actors wanted to become collective members as soon as possible. And for the same reason, the collective was reluctant to accept anyone easily or quickly.

Although until 1931 the Habima's productions were directed by foreign directors, the collective was determined to maintain its authority over casting. In 1930, for example, the title part of *Uriel Acosta* went to an ungifted actor because it was his turn to get a major role, despite the opposition of the director, Granovsky.[21] At times the collective was ready to risk both artistic and financial failure to remain faithful to its regulations. At a 1930 general meeting, the members decided that the collective should have the final word in casting, and that the director be requested to accept the collective's resolutions without any change.[22]

From 1931 to 1948, when most of the Habima's productions were staged by members of the collective, the manner of casting changed slightly. Usually, the director announced the cast he wanted at a general meeting. If there was a disagreement between the director and the collective over a certain performer, the group voted and the actor who received the majority of votes was given the part. Needless to say, at times an actor was given a part because of his power within the collective rather than his acting ability.

Every member also had the right to apply for a part that he wanted to play, and the collective decided how many actors would alternate in that role—another democratic and egalitarian practice. In 1943, when the Habima mounted *Tevye the Dairyman*, Finkel and Bertonov alternated in the title role. A third actor, Vardi, had also applied for the part, but the collective was not satisfied with his work and interpretation.[23] The collective held no less than five meetings between July and October 1943 at which the casting of this play was discussed.

Although the alternation of parts was at times an organizational compromise (i.e., done to satisfy the wish of several actors to perform the same part), it was also functional for the audiences, since it gave them an opportunity to see the same production with different actors and therefore different interpretations. Once again, there were official rules that regulated to the last detail the alternation of parts. For instance, the Board of Directors had to give a player who wanted to alternate in a part the opportunity to perform the part before the collective no later than a week after his application, and at least one rehearsal had to be arranged for him. There was also a distinction between parts alternating equally between two or more actors, and parts played by one chief actor and occasionally by another actor. Regulations specified the rights and obligations of chief players and doubles. The chief player was the actor who worked on the part with the director during the rehearsals, and two doubles who alternated in a part had equal rights if each played no less than fifteen performances. The Board was entitled on special occasions to ask the chief player to perform despite the fact that, according to the original schedule, the double was to perform that evening. However, the double had the right to a compensating performance in the same production on another occasion.[24]

The rotation and alternation of parts, the practice of determining casts by a majority vote, and other regulations aimed at a just distribution of parts prevailed at the Habima for two decades. The collective always maintained that it should have the final word in casting. The members ignored the fact that the theater was not a bureaucratic organization and that its survival and success depended upon the artistic merit of its productions, that factors like acting skill, appearance, charm, and popularity counted for more than principles of justice and equality if their enterprise was to succeed.

The belief in equality was, of course, most passionately held by the less able actors; these principles permitted them to fight for—and often get—parts that different casting principles would have made impossible. The collective's members did not really believe that they were equally gifted, but they strongly believed that because of their common past and theatrical experience and because of the collectivist ideology of the Habima they should all have equal rights and opportunities to take part in the artistic work of their theater.

While still in Moscow, several actors had distinguished themselves as excellent performers. In *The Dybbuk* and *The Golem* critical acclaim went to Rovina as Leah and Meskin as the Golem. During the European and American tours, Rovina and Meskin established themselves as the two great actors of the troupe. Meskin did not have to fight in the general meeting in order to get a part; the collective never disputed or refused to approve parts that were given to him. Rovina was always given the major female roles. Meskin and Rovina were the only two actors whose stardom and acting skill the collective fully acknowledged. All other actors had to fight in order to get major or good parts, especially a small group of gifted actors like Bertonov, Finkel, and Klutchkin, who were not stars of the stature of Meskin and Rovina but nonetheless were able and intelligent performers. The outcome of casting disputes depended on the obstinacy of the player who wanted to perform the part and the support that he was able to get from the rest of the group.

One major casting problem was that most members confused the meaning of two concepts: collective and ensemble. They believed that a collectivist theater was the only real guarantee of ensemble acting. The members did not realize (or, perhaps, ignored) the fact that collective theater and ensemble acting were two different things, at times even contradictory. Indeed, ensemble acting in no way means that all actors have an equal right to play major parts. It means, rather, that each actor performs parts that are commensurate with his talent and ability. Ensemble acting also means that a group of actors complement each other, that every single part, major or minor, is performed with the same devotion and accuracy.

The distribution of parts was related to another important decision made by the collective: the choice of repertoire. Before 1948, plays were chosen by a majority vote at the general assembly. The Board of Directors, and especially the members who were in charge of the artistic policy, usually decided on a list of plays. This list was then discussed by the entire membership, and plays to be presented were chosen by a majority vote. Since both casting and repertoire were decided by the collective, the members tended to choose those plays that would provide them good parts.

Furthermore, the chronological order according to which plays were presented was at times determined by casting considerations. Accordingly, if it was the turn of a certain actor to perform a major role, the next play to be presented was that play in which this actor had the major role.[25] Thus, instead of first deciding upon the list of plays that the troupe wanted to produce during the season and then selecting the artistic team for each of the plays, the Habima reversed this repertoire-planning process and chose its plays on the basis of casting rgulations.

Financial Equality

The actors' belief in equal artistic rights and their attempts to maintain artistic equality were related to, and to a large extent fortified by, the financial equality that prevailed among the members. Furthermore, unlike the principle of artistic equality, which gradually became theoretical, financial equality prevailed in practice as well, until the collective was dissolved in 1968.

Until 1928 all members received an equal salary. The Habima Council was reluctant to acknowledge the demand of the married actors in 1926 to receive a higher salary so that they could support their families.[26] But in 1928, the Constitution provided that "all members receive an equal salary with an additional sum for their children, according to the resolution of the general meeting of the collective."[27] The collective's egalitarianism was also one of the reasons for opposing members' private appearances outside the Habima. The members believed that "if we are a collective, then every single member should live in the same way as his colleague."[28]

But there were members who opposed the principle of financial equality. Rovina, for instance, believed that the salary should be paid according to the theater's need for the player; there were players who could be easily replaced, but there were also players without whose participation the whole production would be ruined. Rovina was supported by another excellent actor, Bertonov, who rejected the "artificial equality of the collective" and contended that the theater should reward its players according to their acting skill and the amount of work they did.[29]

Rovina and Bertonov represented a minority opinion; the majority of players were still strong adherents of collectivism and equality, especially the less able actors, who contended that rewards should be paid according to seniority. Members of the Moscow group also maintained that "if we create differential ranks, we will turn into a professional theater, but the greatness and unique nature of the Habima is not in single stars, like Rovina and Meskin, but in its organization, in the collectivism."[30]

On the whole, therefore, there were two different opinions. One, held by a small group of gifted actors, favored differential payment according to the actor's skill, amount of work, and number of performances. The other view, held by the majority (including the less talented actors), strongly advocated egalitarianism in every sphere of the theater's activity, including remuneration. This group was willing to deviate from the principle of egalitarianism—but only on the basis of seniority and marital status.

In the beginning, acting was the major responsibility of all the collective members. But in the early thirties, several members either supplemented their work as performers with other tasks within the theater, or ceased performing their duties as players and devoted themselves to other responsibilities. Those actors who supplemented their acting duties with other responsibilities demanded additional payment for their services. Furthermore, there were collective members who refused to pay an equal salary to those actors who gave up acting and were engaged only in directing or administration. Nonetheless, the principle of financial equality continued to prevail.

The question of financial equality was further complicated when the Habima began to employ new actors. One major problem was what criterion to use when paying actors who were not members of the collective. In keeping with the Habima's practice, the criteria according to which they were paid were not artistic (i.e., acting skill and contribution to the theater), but marital status and seniority. It was decided that the salary of the permanent nonmember actors would, after fifteen years with the theater, equal that of collective members.[31]

It should be pointed out that since the members were the owners and managers of the theater, it was their responsibility to determine the scale and range of salaries. But the collective never abused this authority. Furthermore, the wage of a collective member was always smaller than the wage that was paid by the Histadrut, which also paid its employees a fixed basic living wage, varied only according to seniority and marital status. In 1928, for instance, the wage of a collective member (seven pounds) was nearly one-fourth of the wage paid to the members of the Histadrut.[32] Moreover, it was not uncommon for the members to receive no wage at all—at times for months—due to the economic problems of the theater.[33]

In summary, all actors received the same wage, regardless of their skill, standing, and amount of work, contingent only on whether or not they were members of the collective. The collective did not regard remuneration as an important motivational reward and ignored the psychological implications of equal pay for all actors. Equal salaries fortified the members' belief in their equal artistic rights and fostered the illusion that they all contributed equally to the functioning of the theater. Furthermore, the theater as an artistic organization did not have a system of sanctions and rewards to motivate the players—especially the young and new players—to aspire to greater artistic achievements; once they became collective members they received the highest salary they could get.

Publicity

The Habima's collectivism and egalitarianism had still another dimension. The group was strongly opposed to personal publicity and to any manifestation of stardom, maintaining that it was the theater as a group, not the individual player, that should get publicity. The members believed that the theater should publicize productions, not those individual actors who played the major roles. When the Habima left Moscow, only Zemach, as the General Director, and Chemerinsky, his secretary, were entitled to speak with the press. Individual players were not allowed to give interviews.[34] But as soon as the theater began its tour, the collectivist ideology was confronted with a different reality. In Riga, the first city on the tour, the members could not understand why reporters insisted on speaking with the "director" of the troupe or wished to interview only the "leading actor." The reporters, for their part, were amazed to hear that all the troupe's actors played major as well as minor parts and received the same salary. It was the first time that the company was exposed to individual criticism and felt its damaging effects: "We had a feeling that these reviews were demoralizing to the collective, that there was little we could do about it. This was the way of the theatre abroad. . . . It seemed as if the collective had become only secondary in importance to a few of its celebrated members."[35] Until then, the group had failed to realize that the reviews could not dwell on the performances of each individual actor, but would criticize at length the performances of the leading actors. Indeed, this happened all during the tour.

When the troupe arrived in the United States, individual criticism and its effects reached a climax. In New York harbor, the players were greeted by photographers who first wanted to know who the stars were; once again, the reporters were surprised when they were told the troupe had no stars. When the Habima left New York, an editorial in the Yiddish daily *Tog* (Day) tried to account for the failure of the visit and for the group's split:

> Who is guilty? Perhaps it is America. . . . The main thing here is fame, names, stars. America does not know what an ensemble is. The American critic writes mainly on the 'leading man' and the 'leading lady' and does not mention the others. This was done with the Habima, and we know how it affected the company. The Habima impressed us all with its unity, with the spirit of an ensemble. The best parts of their show were the mass scenes; they reached the greatest heights when the entire ensemble was on the stage. America came and destroyed it all.[36]

It seems that the Habima had learned a lesson from its tours of Europe and the United States. When the troupe set up its by-laws, a whole chapter dealt with the duties and obligations of the Board of Directors in regard to publicity. Paragraph 19, for instance, specified that "none of the players, except for members of the Board, is allowed to give the press news related to the theater; no one has permission to give any material for the purpose of personal publicity (like photographs, interviews, etc.)." And paragraph 23 stated that "the Board of Directors is obliged to publicize all the plays equally."[37]

Thus, when Finkel gave an interview to the press in Warsaw in 1929, it was considered a violation of the group's norms, and he was openly criticized for his behavior.[38] In Palestine, when the daily *Doar Hayom* published an entire article devoted to Hanna Rovina, it received a letter signed by her in which she protested against the personal appraisal that she had received. She also told them it was the theater's collective that should have received the acclaim. The reporter later wrote that he believed it was the collective that had sent the letter of protest (and not Rovina), and added that since "Moscow is far away from us today, the exaggerated collectivism is undoubtedly also very far."[39]

The Habima continued to object to personal publicity and to any manifestation of stardom. Names of the actors did not appear in advertisements, and theater programs listed all participants in the same size type. The collective was reluctant to acknowledge that the Habima, like every other theater, did indeed revolve around several leading actors, and that it was these leading actors that drew audiences to the theater; until the early fifties, personal publicity, public relations, and advertisements were alien to the collective.

The feeling against publicizing individuals was so ingrained that veteran members of the collective were often antagonistic to the young actors of the troupe who received publicity in the press. When Ada Tal, then one of the apprentices of Friedland's dramatic studio, received favorable notices for one of her first performances, no one spoke to her. Friedland, the director of the play, told her that the hostile reaction of the veteran actors had an educational function: to teach her not to behave like a great actress because of a favorable review.[40] Batya Lancet, another young actress, was exposed to the same reaction when a favorable review of her performance in *Graduation* in 1941 appeared in the press. Indeed, "personal publicity was then a taboo."[41]

The collective did not merely set norms that concerned publicity, but also rules that governed diverse aspects of the members' lives in and outside the theater. The collective claimed the whole of its members' attention and regulated their lives in essential ways. It was intolerant of minority views and actions, and group pressure as applied to "deviant" and "unreconstructed" individuals. A case in point is the strict control on theatrical activity outside the Habima. The Constitution stated that "a member is forbidden to take part in shows, concerts, and public performances that are not organized by the association, without the written permission of the Board."[42]

Many general meetings of the collective and of the Board were devoted to this issue. In 1932, Meskin suggested that the collective itself organize private work outside the Habima, and that 30 percent of any payment for these performances be given to the theater. Other members, on the other hand, opposed outside work on the ground that it would decrease the members' interest in and devotion to the theater. They also contended that these private performances would compete with the Habima's productions, and that the use of the Habima's name by the players for their "private needs" would damage the honor of the collective. Consequently, the Board adopted a resolution which totally forbade members from appearing outside the Habima.[43]

In the thirties and forties, the collective exerted strict discipline over the behavior of its members. There was no clear distinction between one's professional and nonprofessional lives. The collective, like any other intimate and cohesive group, showed the visibility of its norms by penalizing those who deviated from them. During these years (and until 1948) the collective demanded of its members total loyalty and commitment to the theater.

TEN

Organizational Structure: Artistic and Administrative Direction: 1931–1948

FROM 1927 to 1948, the general assembly was the ultimate authority on all matters artistic, administrative, and financial. The general assembly chose the plays, distributed the parts, invited directors, and accepted actors into the theater and the collective. It also approved the annual budget and decided the range of compensation that should be paid to the actors. The frequency of the collective's general meetings was a result of the members' desire to retain a pure participatory democracy.

In order to prevent any individual, or a small group of actors, from acquiring personal power, the general assembly decided that the various offices of the theater should be held on a temporary and rotating basis. The one-year tenure limitation, they believed, would guarantee rotation in the various positions of authority. Moreover, those who occupied powerful positions enjoyed no special privileges; there was no extra financial remuneration and the rewards of authority were not commensurate with the responsibilities entailed. Nor were persons who held these offices relieved of their regular responsibilities as actors. Furthermore, the power of the management was limited by two factors: major decisions were made not by them but by the general assembly, and the management was under the constant and strict surveillance of the general assembly and subject to its power of recall.

Although tenure in office was limited to one or two years, only a small group of actors possessed the necessary skills and knowledge to deal with the diverse problems of the theater. Indeed, from the split in 1927 until 1931, the general assembly elected three boards of directors with practically the same membership: Rovina, Meskin, Chemerinsky, Ben-Chaim, Warshawer, and Gnessin. Clearly, the general assembly was determined to exercise its authority to elect a board every year; equally clearly, the important offices rotated within a small group of actors. Hence, power was not equally distributed, despite the group's ideology.

The foundation of the Habima Secretariat in 1927 brought about changes in the theater's administration. This body had a tremendous effect upon the artistic and administrative management. For the first time, an organization outside the theater assumed responsibility for assuring the financial needs of the troupe. In the beginning, the Secretariat was set up merely as an administrative body. But soon it became evident that it was difficult to distinguish between artistic and administrative affairs. In 1932, Margot Klausner and Yehoshua Brandstater, the heads of the Secretariat, were asked by the collective to participate officially in the management.[1] This was a turning point, the first time that persons who were neither artists nor collective members participated formally in the theater's direction.

This step was not wholeheartedly accepted by those members who were not gifted actors and who were more interested in administrative affairs than in their acting careers. These individuals could not understand the Habima's wish to transfer most of the administrative work to "outsiders."[2] However, the work of Klausner and Brandstater pleased most of the members, who could now devote their time to acting and to artistic affairs. Furthermore, some gifted actors (Meskin, for instance) doubted whether the collective was able to direct itself in an efficient manner, and contended that the authority of the general assembly should be confined and power should be delegated to two or three people who would direct the theater.[3]

It is noteworthy that despite Klausner and Brandstater's work and contribution to the theater, the collective refused to grant them full membership. This reluctance was a proof of the defense mechanisms of the collective against new members and the wish to maintain and preserve power in the hands of a small group of actors. Consequently, in 1936, Klausner and Brandstater resigned from the Board of Directors.

Indeed, the theater ascribed great importance and honor to being a collective member. This is reflected in the by-laws of the collective. Chapter A provided that "in their meeting with the outside world . . . all members of the collective should always remember their responsibilities and duties as members of the Habima." To be a member of the Habima collective was considered to be much more than being a member of an ordinary professional association. The collective was seen as an organic community, as a cohesive group. Accordingly, "the relationships between one member and another should be based on an absolute faith and reciprocal honor." Every member was expected to be "an educator and an example to the newly admitted members," and all members were thought of as being "morally responsible for each other."[4]

Membership in the collective had symbolic as well as pragmatic significance. It was symbolic because membership conferred upon the player rewards of prestige and honor, highly valued by both the theater and the larger society. And membership had a pragmatic significance in that it permitted the actor to participate in general meetings and take part in discussions on every important issue: electing and being elected to the board and various committees, choosing plays, casting, and admitting actors into the theater. The symbolic and pragmatic significance of being a member explains, to a large degree, the elitist orientation of the Habima and its defense mechanism against the immediate inclusion of new members.

In Moscow all actors who were admitted into the theater were automatically collective members. The distinction between actors and collective members was not introduced until 1928. Actors who played in the theater were referred to as "candidates," and they did not have the same rights as full members. But candidates might become collective members after at least one year with the troupe.[5]

It should be pointed out that between 1924 and 1927, no new actors were recruited. Furthermore, as a result of the split, the group lost one-third of its members and arrived in Palestine with only twenty actors. Of these, three left for Russia never to return; hence, the collective had in 1928 only eighteen members (including Gnessin who was readmitted). The theater soon realized that new actors had to be admitted into the company.

In the late twenties, the Habima admitted three new actors: Menachem Binyamini, Shimon Finkel, and Raphael Klutchkin. All three were born in Eastern Europe and had performed in various theaters in Palestine before joining the Habima (see Appendix 1). Of these three actors, Finkel was to become the most influential in regard to the artistic policy of the theater.

Finkel was born in Grodno in 1905.[6] He was educated in a secular high school where he learned Russian and German. His attraction to the theater began rather early; at fifteen he was already a member of a semi-professional group. His main wish was to study at Reinhardt's school in Berlin and to become an actor on the German stage which, in the twenties, was a world center for the dramatic arts. However, in Berlin he joined a group of Hebrew actors and helped them to found the TAI (the Palestinian Theater). At that time, his knowledge of Hebrew was very poor and he was far removed from Zionism. Finkel learned Hebrew in the TAI and in 1924 settled with this theater in Palestine. In 1927, he returned to Berlin, this time determined to enter the German theater. But there he met the Habima, then touring Europe, and under Rovina's influence agreed to join the company. Hence, unlike the original Moscow group, Finkel's attraction to the theater was strictly professional and not ideological. Finkel also differed from the Moscow group members in two major ways: he was younger than most members by at least a decade and, more importantly, he had not been trained in Moscow. As a result, most of the members refused to admit him, and only after a fierce struggle did the Board convince the general assembly to grant him a one-year trial membership; still, he was told that "he still has to prove that he is really worthy to be a collective member."[7] Most members felt that "he was not yet socially assimilated in the melting pot and was not yet worthy to be one of the elite group of Stanislavsky's and Vakhtangov's students," as he himself later wrote.[8]

In the early thirties, six new actors began to play in the theater.[9] Most of these actors were born in the first decade of the century in Eastern Europe and most had played in various theaters in Palestine before joining the Habima. These actors were familiar with the Habima's theatrical tradition because they had been trained and had played in theaters established by former members of the Habima (the Ohel theater, founded by Moshe Halevi, and the TAI, founded by Gnessin—both alumni of the Moscow group). However, they were not trained as thoroughly as the Habima actors. None of these actors was admitted into the collective in the thirties (see Appendix 1).

The criteria according to which actors were admitted into the theater were obscure and ill-defined. From the many discussions and disputes over the issue of including new members in the theater and the collective one learns that at least three criteria were important: age, professional training, and personality.

The actors recruited in the late twenties and early thirties were not much younger than the members of the Moscow group; a few were even the same age. Thus, in 1934, the collective decided that from then on the Habima should admit only young actors, so that the troupe would not consist only of members of the same age.[10]

The professional training of the new actors was also important. The collective believed that the Habima should not admit ready-made actors, i.e., actors who had received their theatrical training in other theaters. The Moscow group maintained that placing the new actors directly on the Habima's stage might damage the theater's prestige and lower its artistic level.[11] Indeed, they were reluctant to accept young actors until the Habima was capable of training them properly and thoroughly.[12] For instance, the discussion over Kutai's admission to the theater lasted several months because many members thought that "only those who were trained in Moscow are worthy actors," as Finkel not so wrongly accused the Moscow members at one meeting devoted to this issue.[13]

The third factor significant in the admission of new actors was the personality of the candidate. When the collective was considering the admission of Amitai, for example, Meskin noted that "Amitai is talented but does not fit into the theater because he will surely be reluctant to perform small parts and will strive to be a star."[14]

The inclusion of new actors also raised important questions concerning the optimal size and the nature of the collective, that is, should it be an open or closed association. According to the Constitution, "the number of collective members is unlimited."[15] However, it seems that most members preferred to think of the collective as a small, intimate, homogeneous, and selective organization. It is a fact that between 1933 and 1944 no new members were accepted. In this eleven-year period, the collective had nineteen members and was the smallest it had been since its founding, or would ever be again.

There were several reasons for the strong opposition to admitting new actors into the collective. The first was the elitist orientation of the Moscow group. Indeed, one important structural requirement for elites is to remain small. Restriction of membership in an organization is one mechanism to preserve the prestige of those who are already members.[16] The elitism of the Habima was based on its pride in the training it received from Stanislavsky and Vakhtangov, and on the fame it had earned during its tours. The elitist orientation also derived from its sense of having a pioneering mission as the first Hebrew art theater. This orientation was shared by all original Moscow members; as one of them contended in 1934, "the new actors are not equal to us and do not have the right to demand a share in the collective."[17] Like other elitist groups, the Moscow group believed that easy extension of membership depreciated the symbolic worth of group affiliation. It not only opposed such extension of membership, but also set extremely high standards of admission.[18] The group maintained that the new members should pass a trial period as novitiates of a sort; in the beginning they should appear only in mass scenes and in small parts and only gradually, after a long process, should they play major roles.[19]

The reluctance to admit new members also stemmed from the wish of the Moscow group to preserve not only prestige but power. In the years 1927–1948, all major issues were discussed and decided at the general assembly. As collective membership expanded, more members participated in the choice of repertoire, casting, boards, committees, etc. True, some members were willing to admit new actors into the collective, but on one condition: "that they not be eligible for election to any of the councils and committees of the theater in the next five years."[20]

There was another reason for the reluctance to admit new members. In the thirties, the collective was highly homogeneous in terms of age, origins, training, and experience. The founding group's formative years had been spent in Russia and these years had a tremendous and lasting effect on its social spirit and organization. The Moscow group had set a pattern of habits, sentiments, and style to which all latecomers were expected to adjust. The collective, in fact, demanded that all new members adapt to the social, psychological, and artistic traditions that it had set. Furthermore, over the years, the collective had developed defense mechanisms against strangers. The group was afraid that the inclusion of new members would lead to changes in the Habima's tradition and spirit, changes that might not be beneficial to the Moscow members.

The collective's expectation that new members would adapt themselves to its traditions and its tendency to resist change were reflected in almost every discussion on the question of new members. Two questions were usually asked about the candidate: was he gifted or able? would he fit into the collective? Dynamic, individualistic, and critical personalities were not welcomed by the collective. Talent and acting skill were, of course, indispensable. However, "moral personality" (to use the Habima's terminology) and an ability to adjust were also important—at times, as important as acting skill.

In 1934, the troupe decided to close the collective for several years but to continue to employ new actors without accepting them into the collective. The theater needed new and young actors, but it was reluctant "to give them rights equal to those of the collective members." It was also decided that new actors would not get salaries equal to those of the collective members.[21] Indeed, for a whole decade the collective did not accept any new members despite continuous applications from the permanent nonmember actors.

In the same year, the collective decided to accept only young actors. The preference for young actors was due in part to the fact that most of the Moscow members were then about forty. The collective also wished to have control over the training of new actors. The theater's aim in training a reservoir of talent was twofold. First, new actors would be thoroughly trained in accordance with the Habima's theatrical tradition. Second, the most able of the trainees would be selected and gradually absorbed into the theater's work.

The resolution to train new actors at the Habima was adopted in 1934, but a long time passed before it was actually put in force. If in later years the Habima had young players to replace the veteran actors, it was solely due to the efforts of one member, Zvi Friedland. Friedland derived great satisfaction from bringing young people into the theater and imbuing them with the sanctity of the profession, as Stanislavsky had taught him. In the thirties, Friedland gave up acting and devoted himself to direction and to teaching. He realized that without a second, young generation, the theater had no future. Unlike the Moscow Art Theater (the Habima's model) which did not want to endanger its chance for immortality and established its own studios for the recruitment and training of new blood, most of the Habima's actors either ignored the need for young actors or feared that the inclusion of young actors would endanger their own positions.[22] Only a few—the great actors—were concerned with assuring a second generation of actors for the Habima.

The Habima's first attempt at establishing a training studio of its own came in 1935, but it was short-lived. Nonetheless, Friedland carried on his work; in the late thirties, he organized his own studio with about ten young students. Friedland was the group's only teacher, and with his devotion to the cause, he succeeded in implanting in his students a passionate love of and a serious approach to the theater. It is noteworthy, that these students later became the Habima's and the Cameri's leading actors.[23]

The Crisis of 1948

In 1936, following the resignation of Klausner and Brandstater from the Board of Directors, the collective resumed its ultimate authority. From 1936 to 1948, the artistic and administrative management was once again under the sole responsibility of the collective. The Board elected in 1938 was perhaps the best Board of this entire period; it remained in power for almost a decade. It consisted of five members: Gnessin, Meskin, Chemerinsky, Friedland, and Finkel. For Friedland and Finkel it was their first term as members of the Board, although both had participated prior to 1938 in the Artistic Committee, and Friedland had been one of the two resident directors.

Finkel's contribution to the theater's repertoire policy was remarkable. He contended that the Habima should not merely present specifically Jewish plays but also classical and universal plays from the world's dramatic repertoire. Indeed, under his influence the troupe produced Shakespeare's *Hamlet* in 1946; Ibsen's *Pillars of Society* and *Ghosts* in 1940 and 1947, respectively; and Sophocles' *Oedipus Rex* in 1947. In this way, as long as Chemerinsky was alive, the Habima maintained a repertorial balance between specifically Jewish and classical and universal plays. In addition, the cooperation of Max Brod, the Czech author, as the theater's dramaturge and literary adviser beginning in 1938, furthered considerably the Habima's artistic development and repertoire.

The Board of 1938 was reelected in 1940, and once again in 1941. In this way, the collective showed its primacy and constant surveillance of the Board. The collective's Constitution assured that the Board would always be responsible and accountable to the general assembly. Apart from a brief interruption (1943–1944), the original Board of 1938 remained in office until 1948.

In 1944, a program aimed at changing the Habima's organizational structure was discussed and eventually rejected by the collective. The initiative had come from Israel Taiber, a businessman with a love of and strong interest in the theater. Taiber suggested establishing an artistic-commercial firm that would take care of administration and finance and whose profits would be devoted to the Habima. His aim was to release the actors from having to deal with administration and finance, allowing them to concentrate on artistic affairs.[24]

The major supporters of Taiber's program were Meskin and Finkel, who were dissatisfied with the rule of the collective. Nonetheless, most members and especially the Moscow group opposed Taiber's program. Their contention was that by submitting the Habima's administration to outsiders, the theater would lose its artistic autonomy. As one original Moscow member put it, "the basis of our existence is our autonomy and independence which we have never sold to anyone." Other members rejected the program on the ground that the outside firm would demand control over the theater's artistic policy.[25]

Chemerinsky's untimely death in 1946 created artistic problems for the theater. He had been a permanent member of the Board since 1927, and had informally assumed the position of artistic director. His contribution to building the repertoire had been invaluable; he chose the Jewish plays and insisted that they constitute a significant part of the repertoire. As one of the two staff directors, he had staged twenty plays, of which seventeen were of Jewish interest. Chemerinsky's authority had been accepted by all members. Had he been interested in the policies and administration of the troupe, he might have become the General Director; he was the only member who had the qualifications and knowledge for this position and whose authority was accepted by all actors.

Indeed, the Habima badly needed authority in general, and artistic authority in particular. The collective's 1928 Constitution was, without any changes, still in force in the late forties. Furthermore, the self-imposed discipline that had characterized the Habima in the twenties and thirties vanished with time, with the result that some kind of authority was all the more necessary. But the reluctance of the members to delegate the authority and power of the collective continued to be a problem for the theater.

Leading actors, like Meskin and Rovina, began to express doubts not merely about the collectivism of the theater, but also about its policies. Meskin thought that the members "did not take into account the new reality that was being created in Palestine"; even more important was the fact that "to date we do not know which type of theater is needed in Palestine."[26] Rovina believed that the problem lay in the fact that "we are not really a collective anymore . . . we lack the artistic authority to decide who can play a part and who cannot."[27] No one had an answer to these serious questions. And as was the collective's custom in such cases, a new Board was elected—consisting of the same members as the former Board. There were no serious attempts to cope with the urgent problems that the theater faced.

In the forties, the veteran members continued to perform all parts, including those of young students and lovers, despite the fact that most actors were nearly fifty years old. They refused to acknowledge the fact that they had aged and could no longer play all parts convincingly. In 1941, for example, the Habima presented *Graduation*, a play set in a high school. The troupe's members were reluctant to give the parts of the students to the young actors; only after a serious dispute (including two ballots) was it decided that two actresses would alternate in the leading part of a high school student, one a veteran and the other a young actress.[28]

Most of Friedland's young disciples began to appear on the Habima's stage in 1940, though in very minor parts. Since until 1948 Friedland was the theater's chief director, he often employed the young actors in his productions. However, they were treated as "stepsons, as children whose father does not want to give them his name."[29] Their status in the theater was an inferior one; in the programs their names appeared with an asterisk and a notation that they were student-apprentices and not actors of the troupe.

The Habima remained impervious to the changes that had taken place in Palestine. A whole generation (that of the Habima's young actors) had matured. This generation had been born or raised in Palestine and spoke a Hebrew language that was different from that used by its parents. This youth found the Habima alien. Furthermore, in 1944, a new theater—the Cameri (Chamber)—was established.[30] The Cameri's founders included several graduates of Friedland's studio who had also performed for a short while at the Habima. These actors left the Habima because they had been allowed to perform only minor and insignificant parts and because they saw no chance of improving their positions or of being accepted into the collective in the near future.

For almost three decades, the veteran actors of the Moscow group played all the major parts, and both audiences and critics grew tired of seeing the same faces on the stage. Indeed, in the forties the press criticized the Habima's conservatism, the closing of the collective, and the reluctance to accept new actors. The *Haaretz* critic appealed to the Habima "to be younger" and "to infuse new blood into its veins." He also wrote that the admission of "young and new forces" who would take the place of the veteran members was a most urgent need of the theater.[31] In 1945, *Davar* ironically compared the Habima collective to other nonartistic cooperatives: "*Hamaavir* or *Egged* [transportation companies] know that if a young man knows how to drive and can pay 2,000 Israeli pounds for his share in the collective, he is a desirable member. But in the theater, there is no share that can equal the seniority rights of the actors who dedicated their blood and sweat establishing the theater. Consequently, it is impossible to accept new members."[32]

As a result of this criticism, six new members were admitted into the collective between 1944 and 1947.[33] But these new members were not really new; they were not much younger than the Moscow members and were familiar faces to the audience. At least one decade had elapsed between the time they began to perform in the theater and the time they were admitted into the collective. Furthermore, none of the new members was an actor of the first rank. With their admission, the collective resolved not to accept any more members for the next five years.[34]

In 1945 the Habima finally opened its first dramatic school, the first attempt in the country at providing aspiring actors with systematic training. The course of study lasted three years; the curriculum included both the theory and practice of acting. The school hoped that through studies and practical work, the young actors would be trained in accordance with the Habima's tradition, imparted to the company by its great teachers in Moscow. The Habima's school lasted only a little more than two years because of the 1948 War of Independence. As a result, only one class was graduated.

The actors trained at the Habima's school began performing in the 1945–1946 season. This group, together with the actors who had begun to perform in 1940, constituted a new category of actors—the Habima's young actors. Between 1945 and 1947, they performed only minor parts in the theater's productions. In the programs their names were still marked with an asterisk indicating their inferior status. The monthly payment that the apprentices received was extremely low in comparison to the collective members' salary, while the salary of the Habima's players was always very low in comparison to the average wage paid outside the theater. The young actors' position improved in 1947–1948, when they were given better parts. Tyrone Guthrie directed *Oedipus Rex* at the Habima in 1947, and he used the young students in important roles; Guthrie was astonished to find the old actors playing parts of young characters.[35]

In 1947, a tour of the United States was proposed. Some members had reservations about the purpose and the timing of the tour, now with the possibility of an independent Jewish state looming on the horizon. Others opposed the tour on the grounds that the Habima was not in its best artistic shape. However, all objections were ignored. Most members believed that an American tour would refresh the company, which had not been out of Palestine since the 1937–1938 tour, feeling that to perform only there would eventually result in the provincialism of the company. They also believed that the large Jewish community in the United States would ensure the tour's financial success.[36]

The Habima went on a tour of the United States in April 1948. It was the troupe's second American tour since the ill-fated visit in 1927. The Habima decided to present four plays: *The Dybbuk*, *The Golem*, *David's Crown*, and *Oedipus Rex*. Apart from *Oedipus Rex*, the plays were old productions that had been prepared two or three decades ago. Once again, the troupe's intent to present the new Israeli theater was not reflected in the repertoire it chose. Not only were no Hebrew plays included, but the Habima's artistic work of the last two decades was also omitted. Furthermore, the company had already presented *The Dybbuk* and *The Golem* in the United States during its first visit.

The Habima opened on Broadway on May 1, 1948, less than two weeks before the proclamation of the independence of the State of Israel. As a result, the theater was unable to celebrate independence at home in the new Israel. The tour was not the expected financial triumph—even after independence—although the performance on the day independence was proclaimed became a festive occasion. Reviewing *The Dybbuk* in the *New York Times*, Brooks Atkinson wrote that "since

The Habima troupe in the United States on the day the Israeli State was proclaimed, May 14, 1948.

they have come from embattled Palestine . . . the Habima represents something more than art at the moment."[37]

Artistically, most performances (especially *The Dybbuk*) were praised. Of *The Dybbuk*'s premiere Atkinson wrote:

> *The Dybbuk* . . . is as timeless as the universe. As a stage composition it is one of the great theatre works of the century. By comparison, the realistic theatre looks poverty-stricken and naturalistic acting seems hackneyed and sterile. . . . It is so vividly stylized and so saturated in music and dancing that the language is not critically important in its appreciation. . . . *The Dybbuk* is to the Habima what *Sea Gull* is to the Moscow Art Theatre—the first success and signature.[38]

The Golem was also acclaimed. The *New York Times* wrote: "What compensates the playgoer who understands no Hebrew is a rich and passionate acting style . . . a style that welds skilled performers into a team and fills the stage with a sense of dramatic rightness."[39] The productions of *David's Crown* and *Oedipus Rex* were not so successful, although they were politely received by the press. However, reviewers also pointed to the theater's shortcomings: the staleness of the productions, the age of the leading actors, and the like.

If the reviews and critics were polite, attracting Jewish and American audiences to the theater was more difficult. The Habima performed in the huge Broadway Theater and found it impossible to fill the house. *David's Crown* and *Oedipus Rex* did not fare well with the audience. And though *The Dybbuk* and *The Golem* were critically acclaimed, audiences wondered whether the theater had not prepared any new productions since its last visit in New York. Because there were people who had seen these two productions during the Habima's first visit, comparisons were unavoidable. The general feeling was that both productions had been far more impressive on the first tour and that the company had deteriorated during the intervening twenty-one years. Worst of all was the reaction of the Jewish audiences and Jewish press. Members of the troupe later admitted that they had made an enormous mistake in ignoring New York's large Jewish community and making no effort to draw them to the performance.[40]

The tour of 1948, like the former tours, was a financial fiasco. The first New York performances were to full houses; then attendance fell off, and the company had to cut short its stay. The original plan—to prepare two new productions under noted American directors—did not materialize. Morale was so low that it was decided to return home immediately. In August 1948, four months after it left Palestine, the Habima returned home. The displeasure of the Israeli public and the Habima itself over th fact that the theater had not been in Israel during the proclamation of the State, combined with the failure of the tour, precipitated a grave crisis, perhaps the worst the troupe ever experienced. The theater was on the verge of liquidation, and performances were suspended for several months.

The crisis of 1948 was the cumulative result of all the theater's problems. The years 1945–1948 were, perhaps, the most difficult that the Habima experienced since it had settled in Palestine. During this period, the troupe presented many Jewish plays and particularly Yiddish plays: Asch's *Warsaw* and *Martyrdom, The Dreyfus Affair,* Sholem Aleichem's *Kitchen Folk,* and Anski's *Day and Night.* None of these plays was an artistic achievement nor did they succeed with the audience. There was also artistic stagnation; the troupe worked for the most part with its two house directors, Friedland and Chemerinsky.

Organizationally, the collective continued to decide all administrative and artistic matters by majority vote, including the choice of plays and casting. The troupe's composition had not changed very much. In 1947, the Habima collective had twenty-five members, sixteen of whom had belonged to the Moscow group and nine of whom had been admitted into Palestine between 1929 and 1947 (see Appendix 3). Therefore, the Moscow group still constituted the majority and held the powerful positions. The fact that the young actors did not get major parts and were not really involved in the theater's life was also one of the major causes of the crisis.

The press was highly critical of the Habima's conservatism and its concern for self-preservation. *Yediot Acharonot* wrote that the theater had been closed both socially and artistically for thirty years and that young and gifted actors had seldom been able "to break through the steel ring of the collective."[41] *Davar* criticized the Habima's tendency to reject talented Israeli-born actors because, presumably, they did not fit in with the Moscow theatrical tradition. He went on to write that "the integration of generations was indispensable and a supreme imperative in all fields, including art."[42] *Haaretz* approached the problem from yet another angle. Its writer contended that a new audience had been born and raised in Palestine, an audience that was seeking a link between the artistic and the historical spirit of the time. By admitting a new generation of actors, the Habima would not merely regain "its internal artistic balance but also the balance between the Hebrew theater and Israel's young generation."[43]

In a series of meetings in September 1948 the members finally admitted that they were incompetent and unable to direct the theater either artistically or administratively. They acknowledged that amateur management by the collective no longer suited the needs, size, and complexity of the Habima.[44] Indeed, the major cause of the crisis stemmed from the theater's collectivist organization, but since the collective had the ultimate power in all matters, the crisis had artistic as well as nonartistic aspects.

The changing psychology and values of the members as well as of the surrounding society all contributed to the problems of the troupe. The group's fanaticism and their ability to endure hardships and sacrifices were compatible with the actors' age and the social climate that prevailed in and outside the theater. But by 1948, the Habima's players were no longer young; their fantacism was gone, the theater had grown in size and complexity, and the values of the larger society were no longer those of Palestine in the twenties. The War of Independence and the establishment of the State of Israel were acting to accelerate changes that had begun long ago.

During the crisis, the members took sides in two opposing groups. One was headed by Finkel who, ever since he had begun to perform in the theater, had fought against its collectivism. The other faction, headed by Rovina and Gnessin, included the majority, especially the Moscow group. The two factions differed in their composition and, more importantly, in their conception of the theater's task and organization.

Finkel's minority group was younger and included members who had not belonged to the Moscow group.[45] They were dissatisfied with collective rule; for them, the theater was primarily an artistic, not an organizational entity. Their major concerns were artistry and standards of production, and they thus favored a professional theater. This group believed that in order to save the Habima while maintaining its standards it was necessary to dissolve the collective. Changing the Constitution, as other members held, was not enough; a more basic reorganization was needed, and this reorganization, they held, could not be brought about by the members themselves.[46]

On the other side was the majority faction. Its members were older and for the most part original Moscow actors. Apart from Rovina and Bertonov, they were the less competent actors. This group saw the theater primarily as a social and organizational unit. Members of this group wished to preserve the collective—though, not for the same reasons. Rovina, the Habima's greatest actress and its symbol, was sincere when she said, "for me the Habima is more than a theater, it is a mother and a nation."[47] She could not understand her comrades who "one bright day decide to destroy an institution that has existed for thirty years."[48] The years of shared experiences had resulted in attachments to the theater that could not easily be abandoned.

In addition, Gnessin was the only member who admitted that the age factor played an important role.[49] In 1948, at the time of the crisis, Gnessin and other members were either close to or over sixty years old, and they realized that the dissolution of the collective would mean their unemployment and artistic death. Furthermore, several members who were not gifted had given up acting and devoted themselves to the theater's administration. For them, the dissolution of the collective would really mean the end of their work. Thus, because of vested personal interests, practical considerations, and sentimental attachments to the theater the majority faction wanted to preserve the collective.

The crisis of 1948 was so severe that the Habima was on the verge of liquidation (the theater remained closed for three months), and official public intercession became necessary in order to stave off dissolution. Indeed, a number of public leaders intervened to save the theater, including Yosef Shprintzak, the Speaker of the Knesset.

The Public Committee was willing to help the Habima on the basis of certain conditions. First, the Habima must concern itself only with artistic affairs; all other considerations must be secondary in importance. Second, the change and reorganization needed could not come from within the collective. Third, the collectivist structure was no longer compatible with the needs of the theater.

The Public Committee had reached the conclusion that the collective had to be dissolved if there were to be meaningful change. The long-term plan was to make the Habima a public or state theater. The Committee had another condition: realizing that some members wanted to abandon the troupe and found a new one, it made it clear that any help for the Habima was made contingent upon its acceptance by all members.[50] It was this condition that ultimately saved the unity of the theater's membership.

FOUR

The Habima in the State of Israel: 1949–1977

ELEVEN

Ideology and Repertoire: 1949–1968

DURING the period 1949–1968, the Habima presented 146 new plays, of which the vast majority (107 plays, or 73 percent) were non-Jewish plays and only one-fourth (39 plays) were distinctively Jewish (see Table 11.1). In this period the theater produced nearly twice as many plays as it had produced in the prestatehood period. This increase in the total number of productions was a result of the growth of Israeli society. The average number of productions per season between 1949 and 1968 was 7—almost twice the average number (4) during the period 1931–1948. The most productive season was 1964–1965, when the theater mounted 11 new plays; the least productive season was 1948–1949, when the company mounted only 4 productions. Apart from the 1960–1961 season, the Habima presented at least one Jewish play every season; in most seasons, more than one such play was presented.

Two important conclusions may be drawn from Table 11.1. First, the proportion of Jewish plays decreased. During the period 1931–1948 Jewish plays constituted slightly more than half (44 plays, or 56 percent) of the total number, whereas in the 1949–1968 period they constituted

Table 11.1
The Habima's Repertoire by Subject: 1931–1968

	1931–1948		*1949–1968*	
Subject	*Number*	*Percent*	*Number*	*Percent*
Jewish	44	55.7	39	26.7
Biblical	6	7.6	6	4.1
Shtetl	16	20.2	4	2.7
Maintaining Jewishness	18	22.8	6	4.1
Palestinian-Israeli	4	5.1	23	15.8
Non-Jewish (universal)	35	44.3	107	73.3
All Plays	79	100.0	146	100.0

only a little more than one-fourth. Thus, the Habima maintained a repertorial balance between Jewish and non-Jewish plays in the prestatehood period, but in the second period lost this balance and became a predominantly universal thater.

Second, and perhaps more important, the content of the Jewish plays presented in the two periods was different. In the first period, only 4 of the Jewish plays were Palestinian; in the second period 23 plays (16 percent) were Israeli plays, i.e., written in Hebrew and depicting contemporary life in Israel. In the second period there was also a significant decline in the number and percentage of shtetl plays. In the 1931–1948 period the Habima presented 16 such plays; in 1949–1968 it presented 4 shtetl plays (3 percent). There was a similar decline in the number and percentage of plays dealing with the problem of maintaining Jewishness in the Diaspora (18 plays in the first period compared to 6 in the second). Finally, there was a significant difference in the type of biblical plays presented. In the first period these plays were strictly biblical; in the scond period, however, they were "modern," that is, they had social or political allusions to contemporary life.

Table 11.2 makes a further interesting comparison of the Habima's plays in the two periods according to the language in which they were written.

In the period 1949–1968 the Habima presented 30 Hebrew plays in comparison to 12 such plays in 1931–1948. Furthermore, in the first

Table 11.2
The Habima's Repertoire by Language: 1931–1968

	1931–1948		*1949–1968*	
Language	*Number*	*Percent*	*Number*	*Percent*
Hebrew	12	15.2	30	20.6
Yiddish	18	22.8	3	2.0
English	11	13.9	46	31.5
French	6	7.6	24	16.4
German	14	17.7	14	9.6
Russian	8	10.2	7	4.8
Czech	5	6.3	1	0.7
Other	5	6.3	21	14.4
Total	79	100.0	146	100.0

period only 4 of the 12 Hebrew plays were Palestinian, but in the second period 27 of the 30 were Israeli plays. At the same time there was a tremendous decrease in both the number and percentage of Yiddish plays: from 18 (23 percent) to only 3 (2 percent) in the second period. Another significant change was the increase in English and French plays: in the period 1949–1968, English plays accounted for almost one-third of the repertoire. On the whole, there was a remarkable increase in the proportion of West European plays and a decrease in the proportion of East European plays.

Between 1949 and 1968 the Habima presented 23 Israeli plays, written for the most part by young Israeli playwrights. Although the category of Israeli plays covers many types of drama, on the whole it concerned three topics: the importance of collective life for Israeli society (kibbutz plays); the holocaust; and the absorption of immigrants. The other Israeli plays included several comedies and satires on contemporary Israeli society, modern biblical plays, and children's plays.

Kibbutz Plays

In many ways, the plays dealing with the importance of collective life for Israeli society were ideologically and socially the most important

Hebrew plays. This category was also the largest, consisting of eight plays.

Yigal Mossinson's *Bearvot Hanegev* (*In the Wastes of the Negev*) is perhaps the most important play the Habima presented in the whole period. It was the first play to be produced after the serious crisis of 1948 and the first Habima play to be presented in the newly born State of Israel. It opened on February 10, 1949, two weeks before the first armistice agreement between Israel and Egypt was signed.

In the Wastes of the Negev focused on the heroic stand of the Jewish settlements in the Negev against the Egyptian army during the War of Independence. Dan, a young member of kibbutz Bikat Yoav (the Valley of Yoav), a besieged kibbutz in the Negev, has returned from evacuating the children of another kibbutz. Avraham, his father, announces that the fields have been set on fire to forestall Arab infiltrators. As the Israeli army retreats, the kibbutz is completely isolated. Baruch, an army officer stationed at the kibbutz, and other members are in favor of further retreat, to which Avraham and Rivka, his wife, strongly object. They are prepared to die if necessary, but they will not give up the land. Since Avraham is in charge, no one is permitted to leave. In the meantime, Dan's wedding is postponed; the wounded must be transported to the north and he is the only available driver. Everyone is reluctant to send Dan on the suicidal mission, but finally his father orders him to go. Dan is killed by the Egyptians, but Bikat Yoav has saved the Negev and protected the country from enemy invasion. As the play closes, the kibbutz prepares to celebrate its regained independence, while Rivka mourns the death of her martyred son.

This play stressed the conflict between Avraham, the civilian and founder of the settlement, and Baruch, the military commander from the city. Baruch sees the situation as hopeless because of the kibbutz's isolation and therefore orders that the kibbutz be abandoned. But Avraham will not leave; to him nothing seems more important than to hold on to the kibbutz, and for this purpose he sacrifices his only son. *In the Wastes of the Negev* portrayed the human sacrifice demanded from the pioneers attempting to realize the Zionist vision.

In the Wastes of the Negev concerned a current event, one that had taken place only nine months before the play opened. Kibbutz Bikat Yoav was actually Kibbutz Negba, which had held up the advance of the

Mossinson's *Bearvot Hanegev* (*In the Wastes of the Negev*) in 1949, the first and most important Hebrew play produced after the establishment of Israel.

Egyptian army long enough to save the Negev from falling to the enemy. The ten-week siege of the Negev was broken by the Israeli army. But the play, instead of giving the army credit, glorified the kibbutz members. Baruch, the army commander, was characterized less favorably than Avraham, the kibbutz leader. At the end of the play, it is Avraham who wins the battle; the members stay on and succeed both in saving the crops and breaking the siege.[1]

A public uproar followed the opening of the production. Many were offended by the negative portrayal of Baruch. The playwright and the Habima were accused of changing the historical truth and slandering the army.[2] Many soldiers and army officers wrote letters of protest to the theater and the press. One soldier who belonged to the unit that had fought in the Negev wrote that the play not only altered historical truth but also offended those who fought and died in the battle.[3]

Despite the controversy, the production was generally warmly received by both critics and audience. At the final curtain on opening night, the audience was so moved and shocked that for a short while there was a total silence. Then cheers erupted and the applause lasted for a long time.[4] Never before—or after—was there such rapport between the audience and the stage.

The reviews, too, were remarkably favorable. The drama critic of *Al Hamishmar* wrote that the play had "great dramatic power, [was] captivating and convincing," and that the whole company revealed "great powers of expression . . . in a central experience of our time."[5] *Haaretz* wrote that the production had both "psychological and factual truth," and that the enthusiasm with which the play was received was a sign of a "strong rapport between the stage and the audience."[6] The *Hamashkif* critic saw in the production a turning point in the Habima's life and in Hebrew drama:

> The first play to depict the great chapter of heroism on the stage . . . the Habima set out on a new path . . . being no longer an intermediary between the world dramatist and the Hebrew onlooker but the home of original Hebrew drama. . . . The Habima has begun the work. . . . The way is now open for every Hebrew stage and for Hebrew authors to . . . draw upon the dramatic content of our lives.[7]

The topic and the timing of the production made it a symbol of the War of Independence. With the critics' enthusiastic send-off, *In the Wastes of the Negev* embarked on a run of 227 performances and turned out to be the theater's most popular production during the entire period (248,007 people—then one-fifth of Israel's population—saw the play).

The next kibbutz play that the Habima presented was Moshe Shamir's *Bet Hillel* (*The House of Hillel*) in 1950. In this play, Hillel, an old-time pioneer and kibbutz member, is contrasted with Naomi, his daughter, and Rafi, her friend. Naomi returns to the kibbutz after her military service and informs her father that she plans to leave the kibbutz and live in the city. Hillel is a fanatical pioneer; for him abandoning the kibbutz is a cardinal sin. He demands that his daughter accept kibbutz life and convinces Rafi that once one is dedicated to the nation's service, one has no right to desert it for private pursuits. The conflict ends with the victory of the ideal: Naomi and Rafi decide to remain in the kibbutz and to prepare new immigrants who wish to join kibbutzim. This production was moderately successful, with 64 performances.

In the fifties, the Habima presented three kibbutz plays by Aaron Megged, one of the most popular Israeli playwrights. *Baderech Leeilat* (*On the Way to Eilat*), which opened in 1951, revolves around a team of water drillers engaged in trying to locate water in the Negev. The younger workers quickly become dissatisfied with the heat, the sand, and the loneliness of the kibbutz which they are expected to found near Eilat—in 1951, Israel's southernmost border community. The uncertainty they feel concerning their mission is mocked by Raskin, a middle-aged pioneer of the prewar period, who despises the softness of the younger kibbutz members. At the end, water is found; only Raskin's heroic efforts were able to restore the group's faith.

Megged's next play at the Habima, *Hedva Veani* (*Hedva and I*), opened in 1954 and focused satirically upon the differences between life in the kibbutz and life in the city. The play centers on the contrast between Shlomik, a peaceful kibbutz farmer, and city folks who desire private and material gain. Shlomik and Hedva, his wife, have left the kibbutz because Hedva prefers to live in Tel-Aviv with her parents. In the city, Shlomik goes through a series of adventures in trying to become a businessman. Although he is an experienced farmer he finds that none of his experience is useful in the city. He is frustrated; the city remains foreign to him. Idleness, bureaucracy, and luxury are incomprehensible to him, and he sees corruption everywhere. At last, he convinces Hedva to return with him to the kibbutz.

Megged's third play at the Habima was *I Like Mike*, in 1956. The play ironically took its title from the American slogan of affection for Eisenhower, "I Like Ike." Tamara, the daughter of the Arieli family is drafted into the army, which her mother thinks is a waste of time. Instead, the mother wants her daughter to marry Mike, a young American Jew whose father is a rich Zionist in Texas, believing that the whole family could live comfortably in Texas. In the end, the ideal wins; the family remains in Israel, Tamara is drafted, and Mike decides to stay in Israel and join a kibbutz. Megged's satire was directed against those Israelis who emigrated from the country in the fifties because of the difficulties that they had encountered there.

Both *Hedva and I* and *I Like Mike* received unfavorable or, at best, lukewarm reviews. The critics' main reservations concerned the dialogue of Megged's plays. Some critics wrote that the dialogue was poor and unimaginative and that the characterizations were less than satisfactory.[8] The *Maariv*'s critic maintained that the entertainment of *I Like Mike* was often grotesque and its humor routine and uninventive.[9] However, the audience was of a different opinion and the two plays had extremely wide appeal; *Hedva and I* ran for 112 performances and *I Like Mike* for 127. This pattern of unfavorable notices together with wide popular appeal and box office success prevailed when other Hebrew-Israeli plays (especially comedies) were presented.

The plays on collective life in Israel were morality plays with a message: abandoning the kibbutz (and the country) was a sin; life in the kibbutz was superior to life in the city; the kibbutz was important because it was the guardian of the country's moral values. All these plays maintained that indulging in personal comfort is contrary to real patriotism. They reaffirmed the belief in the kibbutz as the cornerstone of Israeli reality and implied that without Jewish settlements there could be no future for the new state.[10] All these plays were written by playwrights who were themselves kibbutz members and, therefore, could draw on their own experience and on contemporary events. It is noteworthy that some of these plays stress the generation gap between conservative Zionist fathers and their liberal children, awarding the final victory to the ideals of the old-time Zionists.

The kibbutz plays were reminiscent of the socialist realism of many Soviet propaganda plays: they presented the plot and characters in elementary, black-and-white fashion, with a typical happy ending. They were sincere—perhaps naive—and appealed to the audience because they dealt with current Israeli events.

The fact that all kibbutz plays were presented in the early fifties is not surprising. Until these years, the kibbutzim were at the peak of their power and were viewed with great respect by the rest of the country. To be a kibbutz member was to be a national hero, and the kibbutz was the symbol of the *chalutz* (the pioneer), the prototype of the new Jews.[11] It should be noted that the kibbutz population in Israel never amounted to more than 7.5 percent of the total population.[12] However, because of the kibbutz's political and ideological importance, its members were always prominent within the leadership of the country.

In the fifties and sixties, the power of the kibbutz movement declined. Most of the Asian and African immigrants, who constituted the vast majority of immigrants to Israel after 1948, did not settle in kibbutzim and did not ascribe importance to kibbutz ideals. Hence, the relative strength of the kibbutz movement began to decline, and the late fifties saw the fall of the kibbutz members from their role as cultural heroes. This decline called into question the future of the kibbutz as a wellspring of the country's ideological and political power.[13] The Habima's repertoire reflected these changes in the demography and the ideological climate of Israeli society. No new kibbutz plays were presented by the theater after 1956, and in 1967 when the company revived the 1942 production of *This Earth* it did not have wide appeal (only 46 performances). Furthermore, none of the kibbutz plays (even those which had been popular) was revived by the theater.

Plays on the Holocaust

The Habima presented five dramas dealing with the holocaust, the most crucial experience in modern Jewish life. Of the five plays, only two, *Hanna Szenes* and *Yaldei Hatzel* (*Children of the Shadow*), were written in Hebrew by young Israeli playwrights.

The first play on the holocaust was American, Frances Goodrich and Albert Hackett's *The Diary of Anne Frank.* It was based on the story of Anne Frank, born to well-to-do German Jewish parents who, following the rise of Hitler, found refuge in the Netherlands. In 1942 the Frank family moved into a hiding place provided by non-Jewish Dutch friends at great risk to themselves. The armies of liberation were close to winning the war when the police invaded the place and arrested all of them. The Dutch returned after the war, but of all the Jews who appear in the play only Anne's father returned from Auschwitz. All the others perished, including Anne who died at the age of fifteen at Bergen-Belsen.

Among old heaps of books and newspapers discarded by the Gestapo when they plundered the Franks' hiding place, Anne's diary was found.

The Habima's production of *The Diary of Anne Frank* (1957). The set and costumes were designed by Boris Aronson, the distinguished American scenic designer.

Her father decided to publish it uncensored. Based on the 1952 English bestseller entitled *Anne Frank: The Diary of a Young Girl,* the play first opened on Broadway in October 1956. Three months later, it opened at the Habima.[14] The tremendous success of the play was due to its being an authentic document not intended for any eyes except those of the writer. Anne described in detail the struggle of the people in the shelter to survive, their anguish and hopes.

The critics, on the whole, praised the Habima's choice of the play, its sincerity, and the superb acting of Ada Tal as Anne and Finkel as her father.[15] The *Yediot Acharonot* critic commented that with this production the Habima was "what we always wanted it to be—a dramatic theater loyal to its national mission."[16] The ultimate power of the production rested on the topic and the sincerity with which it was presented. The public was deeply moved by the production and kept it running for 179 performances, making *The Diary of Anne Frank* one of the company's greatest artistic and financial successes in this period.

The next Habima production dealing with the holocaust was *Hanna Szenes* in 1958, a play commissioned by the theater and written by Aaron Megged. *Hanna Szenes* was a story of martyrdom. In 1942 the Allies sent Szenes to her native Nazi-occupied Hungary in order to rescue Jews from annihilation. She disguised herself as a British officer, but was caught by the Germans, tortured, and sentenced to death at the age of twenty. After her execution, Hanna Szenes became a symbol of patriotism. In his play Megged emphasized Hanna's unyielding faith in her spiritual and national mission.

Miriam Zohar as Hanna (right) and Hanna Rovina as her mother in the Israeli drama *Hanna Szenes* (1958).

The most important Hebrew play about Nazi persecution was *Children of the Shadow* in 1962. It was written by Ben-Zion Tomer, a member of the "Teheran Children," the Jewish youngsters who were transferred from war-torn Europe to Persia and from there to Palestine. The play was an autobiographical drama dealing with the effects of the Nazi holocaust on the life of a young survivor who settles in Palestine and tries, in vain, to forget his horrendous past.

The hero of the play is Yoram, a boy born in Poland before World War II and who, with his family, experienced the horrors of war and the Nazi persecutions. Then, separated from his parents, he was brought to Palestine as one of the "Teheran Children." In his new surroundings, Yoram tries to become an integrated kibbutz member and a fighter in the underground. Inwardly, however, he is constantly escaping from his past, that is, from himself. A crisis occurs when he meets his parents whom until then he had presumed dead. At this moment of truth, Yoram realizes that in his efforts to destroy his past he has emotionally mutilated himself.

Tomer's play aroused considerable interest; it was a story about the continuous struggle of many youngsters in Israel to forget their past and to become healthy *sabras* (in current Israeli usage, any native-born Jewish Israeli). But the forgotten past comes back to take revenge on the young people who painfully seek to attain wholeness again. The play maintained that cutting off one's haunting memories of the past does not help to attain full integration within Israel, and that renewed contact with the past may relieve the guilt of forgetfulness and estrangement.

Children of the Shadow was the first Israeli play on the holocaust. This was a literary achievement in itself, as the following review pointed out:

> An outsider will find it strange that Israeli writers ignore a subject which understandably preoccupies their Jewish colleagues the world over—the Nazi holocaust in Europe and its effect on survivors. . . . The play is significant not only for the theme it explores, but because, as a parable, it points . . . at the root of sterility of modern Hebrew writing. . . . The young generation of Israeli writers is culturally rootless. They have cut themselves off from the past of their people . . . disdaining all that comes from the Diaspora, particularly from the shtetl, as degenerate. They see their past in the Bible with all its glamor of Jewish kingdoms and vic-

> torious wars, with heroes and prophets. . . . Between the Bible and the present, there is one blank space.[17]

Other critics wrote that although it was not a great play, it was the most serious attempt made by the Israeli theater to deal with the holocaust, until then a taboo.[18] *Children of the Shadow* stirred its audience, both young and old, and evoked enthusiastic reviews. The production had an impressive run of 206 performances, with a total audience of 82,069 people.

In 1964, the Habima presented Rolf Hochhuth's controversial play, *The Deputy*. This powerful play expressed the playwright's indignation at the silence and indifference of the Catholic Church over Hitler's slaughter of six million Jews. *The Deputy* implied that Pope Pius XII was a criminal for not intervening to denounce and prevent the Nazi atrocities. Hochhuth's documentary drama had its world premiere in

Aaron Meskin as Dr. Rabinowitz (left) and Amnon Meskin (seated) in the leading role, Yoram, in Tomer's Israeli play on the holocaust, *Yaldei Hatzel* (*Children of the Shadow*) in 1962.

Berlin and created a furor there and wherever it was presented. In Israel, the critics' complaint was that the agony and spirit of the topic were missing in the play as it was presented.[19] *Haaretz*, for instance, wrote that the Habima's production did not stress enough the Jewish element, and, consequently, the shock created was too moderate.[20] However, all critics agreed on the special significance that the production assumed in Israel, and emphasized that the play's strength derived from its moral and political ideas.

Plays on the Absorption of Immigrants

Children of the Shadow dealt with the problematic formation of a new identity—an Israeli identity—for a young refugee of the concentration camps. In addition to this play, the Habima presented four plays that focused on the topic of absorbing and integrating new immigrants. These were: *Shahor Al Gabei Lavan* (*Black on White*) in 1956, *Shesh Knafaim Laechad* (*Each Had Six Wings*) and *Rehov Hamadregot* (*The Street of Stairs*) in 1958, and *Hashchuna* (*The Neighborhood*) in 1965. Of these four plays, *Each Had Six Wings* was the most important drama.

Each Had Six Wings was a dramatization of Hanoch Bartov's novel of the same name. It takes place in the late forties and deals with the problems of a group of new immigrants of different origins in an abandoned Arab quarter in Jerusalem. The newcomers are a strange group; they escaped the Nazis yet, at times, they long for the good old days in their native countries. They have difficulties learning Hebrew and in adapting to the Israeli way of life. On the one hand, they carry with them the past, the persecutions, and their dreams of escape. On the other hand, they did not participate in the War of Independence and therefore must overcome many hardships in order to be considered real Israelis.

Each Had Six Wings was based on the author's personal experience. Bartov lived in the immigrants' quarter in Jerusalem for two years, during which he observed closely the life of what is referred to as "the other Israel." Bartov wanted to show that " 'the other Israel' . . . is not so distant from the veteran Israel," and that "we are all simply human beings." The title of the play is borrowed from the Book of Isaiah, where

A scene from Bartov's Israeli drama *Shesh Knafaim Laechad* (*Each Had Six Wings*) in 1958.

angels are described as six-winged creatures. Bartov's intention was to show that every person has one pair of wings to cover the face, one pair to cover the legs, and with the two wings left "they raise themselves above the earthly and the selfish."[21] The play maintained that unity and brotherhood were needed in order to surmount hardships and obstacles to assimilation and integration.

Black on White, written by Ephraim Kishon, Israel's foremost humorist, was an allegorical satire on racial discrimination; all the play's participants are mice, and a conflict takes place between the white mice (the Ashkenazic Jews) living on the first floor and the gray mice (the Sephardic and Oriental Jews) living in the basement.

The Street of Stairs dealt with the same topic; it focused on the problematic relationships between Sephardic and Ashkenazic Jews in Israel. It was adapted by Yehudith Hendel from her novel of the same title. The play takes place in a poverty-stricken neighborhood in Haifa, the Street of Stairs, immediately after the War of Independence. Basically, it is a tragic love story between Avram, a Sephardic sailor, and

Erela, a rich Ashkenazic girl, and ends with their separation and frustration. *The Street of Stairs* found the integration of the two different communities almost impossible, and emphasized the seclusion and solitude of the Sephardic community.

The action of *The Neighborhood,* the last Habima play on the problem of integration during this period, takes place in a poor Tel-Aviv neighborhood in the thirties. It was a play about a tradition that has been ruined and concerned the differences between the generation of the parents, who, for the most part, accept life as it is, and their sons, who seek a new life and new ideals.

All four plays on integration were severely criticized by the press. In the critics' opinion, the major deficiencies of these plays lay in the fact that they were all reportage (almost documentary), lacking any dramatic structure or plot.[22] The review of the *Haaretz* critic of *Each Had Six Wings* may serve as an example: "The plot lacked an objective insight, the characters had no shadows, and the heroes were too generous. . . . An opportunity to dramatize an important human and Israeli situation was dwarfed by the mediocre young Hebrew playwriting. Instead of a fearful tragedy, the play became a pale melodrama."[23] Reviewing *The Neighborhood,* the *Davar* critic wrote that it was reminiscent of the sort of Hebrew playwrighting that prevailed in Palestine thirty years ago. In his opinion, *The Neighborhood,* like many other Hebrew plays, did not make distinctions between "the truth of life" and "the truth of art," and between "journalistic reportage" and "artistic values."[24] But once again, despite the critics' negative reviews, two of these plays—*Each Had Six Wings* and *The Neighborhood*—drew large audiences.

Biblical Plays

From 1949 to 1968 the Habima produced six biblical plays, only one of which (*Saul* by Max Zweig) was strictly a biblical play. The other plays of this genre were written by young Israeli playwrights retelling biblical stories with political and social allusions to contemporary Israeli life. This was certainly the case of Nissim Aloni's *Achzar Mikol Melech* (*Most Cruel of All—the King*) in 1953, the most important Israeli-biblical play in the entire period.[25] The drama takes place immediately after the death of King Solomon and depicts the Kingdoms of Judea and Israel when they were no longer as strong as they had been under King David. The drama focuses upon Rehoboam, King Solomon's son, and Jeroboam, son of Nebat, whom the Bible has branded as an arch-villain and sinner. In the play, Jeroboam's character is a positive one. He is a statesman of peace and social progress who leads a revolt against King Rehoboam, the tyrant who had introduced oppressive taxation and forced labor. Jeroboam, who had spent ten years in Egypt, then the cultural center of the world, is a sophisticate; his chief goal is to broaden the horizons of the people. He therefore speaks against narrow nationalism, religious orthodoxy, and bloodshed. In the end, Jeroboam defeats the selfish and spoiled Rehoboam, King of Judea, and becomes the King of Israel.

The parallel of the play is obvious. Both Jewish states, the biblical and the modern, are isolated and surrounded by enemy states. The small Kingdom of Judea is the new state of Israel, imbued with the spirit of nationalism. The play was a blow to provincial Israeli nationalism: the playwright spoke for the young people of Israel who were tired of war. It also presented the king (the rulers and politicians of Israel) in all their cruelty and spiritual emptiness, and spoke out against religious orthodoxy.

Indeed, the critic of one right-wing newspaper wrote that "the Kingdom of Israel without royal splendour is strange to our national spirit."[26] Other critics wrote at length on the literary merits of the play and its innovative form. The *Haaretz* critic, for instance, wrote that *Most Cruel of All–the King* was unique, being at the same time both a contemporary and a historical play.[27] Others praised the language and dialogue which, while they had a biblical ring, were also modern and poetic.[28] Aloni's play was far superior to all other Hebrew plays that had been presented by the Habima.

The next modern biblical play, Aaron Megged's *Bereshit* (*Genesis*), opened in 1962. Based on the story of Adam, Eve, and the serpent, Megged's *Genesis* was a completely satirical modernization of biblical material. The satire had clear allusions to modern Israel, especially to the priority of personal comfort and material interests over national duties.

Genesis was controversial. Orthodox critics complained that the play was silly and banal.[29] Other critics wrote that Megged's comedy was su-

Raphael Klutchkin as The Serpent and Yehoshua Bertonov as The Keeper of the Garden in Megged's modern biblical satire *Bereshit* (*Genesis*) in 1962.

perficial and presumptuous.[30] However, there were other critics who liked the play and found it original. The *Davar* critic, for example, wrote: "Freedom of conception, a light touch, modern speech and make-up—this mixture of ancient and modern and the excellent performance of the Habima cast provided a comedy about the family of man."[31] Indeed, the production had extremely wide appeal and was presented 233 times with a total attendance of 98,014 people.

The Habima's last two biblical plays in this period, *Masa LeNineveh* (*Journey to Nineveh*) in 1964 and *Haona Haboeret* (*The High Season*) in 1967, failed artistically and did not attract an audience. Yehuda Amichai's *Journey to Nineveh* was a symbolic play-poem that centered on the prophet Jonah whom God had commanded to prophesy Nineveh's destruction. It was a philosophical morality play that drew a parallel between Jonah's attempt to escape God and the middle-class Israelis who avoid their national duties and responsibilities. Audiences as well as critics found the play difficult to follow and to understand.

The High Season, by Aaron Megged, was an allegory of modern Israel and its hero a modern version of the Bible's Job. Here Job represents the remnants of the Jewish people after the Nazi holocaust. He has forgotten all the wrongs done to him, trusts his former enemies, and enjoys the prosperity which comes as a result of this forgetfulness—i.e., he receives reparations from Germany for the murders of the Nazi era. The play was a modern morality drama, a reminder of what happened in Nazi Germany and a projection of what might happen if Jews try to settle there again or to forget the holocaust.

Other Jewish Plays

Apart from *The Diary of Anne Frank* and *The Deputy*, both of which concerned the holocaust, the other Jewish plays were either historical or folkloristic. And except for these two productions, all were artistic and box office failures, though some were very important from a literary or historical point of view. Such a play was *Beketz Hayamim* (*At the End of the Days*), a Hebrew play by Chaim Hazaz, presented in 1950.

At the End of the Days is a historical drama dealing with the influences of the Messianic movement on Jews in seventeenth-century Europe. The central theme of the play is that before the Messiah comes and redemption is achieved, Jewish history and the Diaspora must be destroyed. It is also an ideological play, maintaining that while redemption is the Jewish national revolution, the Diaspora is counterrevolution. *At the End of the Days* received extremely favorable reviews by most critics, who regarded the play as the first really important Hebrew drama and one whose literary merit went beyond the production presented on stage.[32] Yet the cruelty of the play and its powerful message touching upon the roots of the existence of the Jewish people aroused controversy. *At the End of the Days* was presented in 1950, when the State of Israel was just celebrating its second anniversary, and when many people were not yet ready to accept—emotionally or practically—the ideological message of the play (the urgent need to destroy the Diaspora). This explains, at least in part, the fact that the production closed after only twelve performances.

The fate of the other Jewish plays was not much different. Four of them were shtetl plays. *The Story of a Prince* in 1953 was the first Goldfaden play to be presented by the Habima. In the prestatehood period, the theater was reluctant to produce Goldfaden's plays because of their inferior literary quality. *The Story of a Prince* was a musical comedy based on Goldfaden's *Kabzensohn and Hungerman* and belongs to his early comedies which castigate the follies of ghetto life. The play revolves around the tale of a wandering Yiddish troupe. It is noteworthy that all the critics were harsh to the play, though they approved of the Habima's wish to present a nostalgic view of the Jewish ghetto.[33]

The Habima, as Israel's national theater, thought that it should present both old and new Jewish works to a public many of whom were unfamiliar with their own national culture. It therefore decided to stage Zlaman Schneur's *Pandre the Hero* in 1955 and Isaac Babel's *The Sunset* in 1965, both folklorist plays that presented Jewish life in the shtetl in a nostalgic manner. *The Sunset* (the new title for Babel's *Odessa Tales*) was a series of picaresque tales concerning the physical metamorphosis and spiritual demise of the once fascinating universe of Odessa's Jewry.

However, the Israeli-born-and-bred generation rejected the traditions of Yiddish literature, poetry, and theater. Indeed, Yiddish (as a symbol of the Jewish past in the Diaspora) was disdained and ignored in Israel for decades. The Zionist pioneers who settled in Palestine, in their efforts to establish Hebrew as the spoken language and the unifying force of the national revival, engaged in a crusade against Yiddish. Militant Hebraists looked upon Yiddish as the expression of the unregenerated Jews of the Russian Pale. Indeed, Yiddish plays dealing with the *galut* (Diaspora) were not popular; the younger generation especially wanted to dissociate itself completely from that period of Jewish history. It was only in the late sixties that the attitude toward Yiddish and the Diaspora changed.

In conclusion, between 1949 and 1968 the vast majority of the Habima's Jewish plays concerned contemporary Israeli society. With the emergence of the State of Israel in 1948, a Hebrew-speaking generation provided the conditions for the development of genuinely Hebrew plays. Hence, the history of the Israeli drama parallels the history of Israeli statehood. The Habima's Hebrew-Israeli plays, whose authors were part of the younger generation, attempted to portray in a straightforward manner the events and the problems of their own period. For the first time, these plays were truly Israeli—in subject matter, form, and language.

The Israeli plays adopted the patterns of living, spoken Hebrew. They copied the language of the street, the kibbutz, and the army. The language of *In the Wastes of the Negev*, for instance, was extremely colloquial; the whole texture of the play was seasoned with jargon, especially that of the Palmach (an acronym for Plugot Mahatz, the spearhead units of the army).

Most of the Hebrew-Israeli plays presented by the Habima were topical, realistic plays. Despite differences in individual approach and literary merit, these plays had one element in common: for their subject matter they drew upon current events and contemporary reality—the role of the kibbutz, the importance of national unity, the absorption of new immigrants, integration into Israeli society—with which audiences were already thoroughly familiar from nontheatrical sources. They dealt with the central problems of Israel, and their characters were representative of the prevailing social structure and ideologies. Indeed, in the forties and fifties, when young Israelis and new immigrants lost faith in ascetic pioneering as a way of life, this theme became a repeated concern in the Habima's plays. And in the fifties and sixties, city life, waste, bureaucracy, and corruption were dramatized or satirized in the plays presented by the theater. The loss of idealism, social-moral criticism, and the priority of national and social duties over personal comforts and material rewards were recurrent topics.

Prior to the establishment of the Israeli State, the Habima had presented many Jewish historical and folkloristic plays that concerned the struggle of the Jewish people to maintain their own identity in the Diaspora. The theater had also presented plays about the dread of persecution and anti-Semitism and the dream of national redemption. But after 1948 the audience instead demanded new plays that concerned contemporary life and reality in Israel. The new Hebrew drama was therefore an attempt to fulfill the artistic and psychosocial needs of the time.

Judged from the present perspective, it is often difficult to see what the audience liked in these plays. It seems that the audience did not judge these plays for their intrinsic esthetic merit or literary quality, but for their value as social and cultural events. However, the same topicality which endowed the Habima's Israeli plays with liveliness and relevance also limited their scope and tied them too closely to transitory values, problems, and experiences. As the critics pointed out correctly, "the events themselves, rather than the human drama within them, became the focal point of each play."[34] Indeed, once the events passed, interest in them quickly waned; "the plays became stale, like yesterday's headlines."

TWELVE

The Habima and Israeli Society

THE vast majority (107, or 73 percent) of the plays presented by the Habima between 1949 and 1968 were universal plays. The range of the universal plays was very wide and included plays written in various languages, though most were written in English and in French. Especially noteworthy was the growth of the number of the American plays. Between 1931 and 1948, the Habima presented only 2 American plays; in comparison, no less than 26 such plays were presented between 1949 and 1968.

Of the 107 universal plays, 14 were classical, and the rest modern and contemporary. The classical plays inluded 9 Shakespearean productions and 2 Greek classical plays. Included in the modern classical category were plays by Chekhov, Ibsen, Strindberg, G. B. Shaw, Pirandello and others. The contemporary plays were for the most part American. Arthur Miller's work may serve as an example. The Habima mounted three plays by Miller in this period: *Death of a Salesman* in 1951, *The Crucible* in 1954, and *A View from the Bridge* in 1956 (see Appendix 2).

Indeed, in comparison with the prestatehood years, the choice of repertoire in this period was motivated primarily by artistic rather than by ideological considerations. As a result, the Habima ceased to be a distinctively Jewish theater, as it has been until 1948, and became a modern and universal theater, striving to present contemporary plays that had been presented successfully in other theatrical centers, especially London and New York.[1] This policy had its advantages and, of course, its price. In many cases, the theater rushed to acquire the rights to Israel plays that had succeeded in other major theatrical centers without considering the question of whether they were relevant, suitable, or

Hanna Rovina as Medea and Israel Becker as Jason in Euripides' *Medea* (1955).

meaningful within the context of contemporary Israeli society. Time and again, the critics blamed those who planned the Habima's artistic policy for a lack of critical approach in the choice of repertoire.[2] They also urged the theater to stop once and for all casting their eyes toward mediocre foreign plays.[3]

The primacy of artistic considerations over ideological ones was also apparent in the Habima's wish to be like any other modern art theater. Indeed, in 1960, commemorating the hundredth birthday of Chekhov, the theater presented his *Uncle Vanya.* And in 1964, the troupe participated in the international Shakespeare year by presenting *The Comedy of Errors.* These productions demonstrated the Habima's wish to be part of the world's theatrical establishment, but they were mounted at great artistic and financial risk.

The Habima's transformation from an ideologically oriented and specifically Jewish theater into a nonideological art theater was especially apparent in the sixties. The imitation of the repertoire presented in London and New York was almost blind, especially in regard to Broadway hits. Hence, Norman Krasna's comedy *Sunday in New York,* Frank Gilroy's *The Subject Was Roses,* Donald Howarth's *A Lily of Little India,* and Jules Feiffer's *Little Murders* were all presented in Tel-Aviv a year or two after their premieres on Broadway.

The years 1949–1968 were also characterized by the Habima's working with many directors. Table 12.1 shows the Habima's productions according to types of directors in the years 1918–1968. From 1931 to 1948, the Habima worked with nine directors who staged 79 productions, whereas from 1949 to 1968, the company worked with 49 directors who staged 146 plays. Table 12.1 shows that between 1949 and 1968, 59 plays (40 percent) were staged by members of the collective; 49 plays (34 percent) by Israeli directors; and 38 plays (26 percent) by foreign directors. There was, therefore, a significant decrease in the number and percentage of productions directed by members of the collective; in the prestatehood period, 91 percent of the theater's productions were staged by members of the collective, compared with only 40 percent in the period 1949–1968.

The statehood period was marked by three tendencies. First, younger members of the company took over the staging that had previously been done by members of the Moscow group. Second, for the first time in its

Miriam Zohar and Misha Asherov in the leading roles in Hy Kalus's production of Albee's *Who's Afraid of Virginia Woolf?* (1965).

history, the Habima began to employ Israeli directors who were not collective members. Third, there was a tendency to invite foreign directors.

The three major staff directors were all younger actors: Israel Becker, Shraga Friedman, and Avraham Ninio. Friedland, the Habima's major director in the prestatehood period, showed signs of ill-adjustment to the changing climate of both the theater and country. Indeed, Friedland staged only 10 plays between 1949 and 1968—this in comparison to 39 plays (half of the repertoire) between 1931 and 1948. Becker and Friedman preferred to stage Jewish and Hebrew plays, whereas Ninio staged, for the most part, universal drama. Becker was responsible for the tremendous success of several Hebrew plays, both comedies and dramas. Included in his box office hits were Kishon's satire on the corrupt Israeli bureaucracy, *Shmo Olech Lefanav* (*His Name Precedes Him*), in 1953; Megged's comedies *Hedva and I* and *I Like Mike* (1954 and 1956); and Tomer's drama *Children of the Shadow* in 1962. Ninio's major successes

Table 12.1
Productions and Directors: 1918–1968

	Productions									
	1918–1925		*1926–1930*		*1931–1948*		*1949–1968*		*1918–1968*	
Type of Director	*Number*	*Percent*	*Number*	*Percent*	*Number*	*Percent*	*Number*	*Percent*	*Number*	*Percent*
Member of the Habima Collective	/	/	/	/	72	91.1	59	40.4	131	55.7
Israeli directors	/	/	/	/	/	/	49	33.6	49	16.2
Foreign directors	6	100.0	4	100.0	7	8.9	38	26.0	55	28.1
Total number of productions	6	100.0	4	100.0	79	100.0	146	100.0	235	100.0

were Rose's *Twelve Angry Men* in 1959, Gibson's *The Miracle Worker* in 1960, *Gigi* in 1961, and *Irma La Douce* in 1962.

Most important of all was the work with foreign guest directors, some of whom were among the best directors in the world. In this period the Habima worked with Tyrone Guthrie, Harold Clurman (of the Group Theatre in the United States), Lee Strasberg (of the American Actors' Studio), Sven Malmquist (the noted Swedish director), Julius Gellner (the Czech director from England who was later to become for a brief period the Habima's artistic director), and many others (see Appendix 2). Indeed, the artistic highlights of this period were, for the most part,

Julius Gellner's production of Arthur Miller's *Death of a Salesman* (1951). Aaron Meskin (right) as Willy Loman and Ari Kutai (left) as Howard.

Shimon Finkel as Peer Gynt and Shoshana Duer as his mother in Malmquist's production of Ibsen's *Peer Gynt* (1952).

plays staged by noted foreign directors. Especially noteworthy were Robles's *Montserrat* (*Hostages*) in 1949 under Clurman's direction; Miller's *Death of a Salesman* in 1951, staged by Gellner; Ibsen's *Peer Gynt* in 1952 under Malmquist's direction; Marceau's *The Egg* in 1957, staged by Barsac; and Tyrone Guthrie's modern-dress production of *The Merchant of Venice* in 1959.

The troupe—which for almost two decades had worked only with two directors (Chemerinsky and Friedland)—profited from working with these foreign directors, and its acting and producing style became more versatile. However, the tendency to invite foreign directors also had its disadvantages. Although many of the guest directors were distinguished and world-renowned, they were somewhat handicapped when working at the Habima. The language barrier and a lack of familiarity with the company's traditions and acting potential, as well as with the country

Harold Clurman's brilliant production of *Montserrat* (*Hostages*) in 1949. Left to right: Shimon Finkel as Izquierdo, Misha Asherov as Zuazola, and Hanna Rovina as The Mother.

Hanna Rovina in the title role in Leopold Lindberg's production of Brecht's *Mother Courage* (1950).

and its audience, militated against establishing a close rapport between the guest directors and the troupe.

Artistic and Box Office Success

Table 12.2 shows the Jewish and non-Jewish plays in the Habima's repertoire in the period 1949–1968 and the number of their performances.

Table 12.2 shows that nearly two-thirds of the plays (91) presented between 1949 and 1968 either failed or had short runs; 23 plays (16 percent) had moderate runs; and 32 plays (22 percent) enjoyed success.

Table 12.2
Jewish and Non-Jewish Plays: 1949–1968

Number of Performances	*Jewish Plays*		*Non-Jewish Plays*		*Total*	
	Number	*Percent*	*Number*	*Percent*	*Number*	*Percent*
1–29 (failure)	7	17.9	34	31.8	41	28.1
30–59 (short run)	15	38.5	35	32.7	50	34.3
60–99 (moderate run)	6	15.4	17	15.9	23	15.7
over 100 (success)	11	28.2	21	19.6	32	21.9
Total	39	100.0	107	100.0	146	100.0

When, apart from the number of performances, the number of visitors that attended each play is taken into account as another index of popularity, the importance of the non-Jewish plays in this period becomes greater. Table 12.3 presents the Habima's fifteen most popular productions in the period 1949–1968.

Comparing this list with the list of the most popular productions in the prestatehood period (Table 8.2), several conclusions may be drawn. First, of the fifteen most popular productions in the second period only three were specifically Jewish: *In the Wastes of the Negev* in 1949, *The Diary of Anne Frank* in 1957, and *Hanna Szenes* in 1958. The rest of the popular productions were all universal plays. By contrast, ten of the twelve most popular productions in the period 1931–1948 were Jewish, six of which were shtetl (Yiddish) plays. Second, most of the popular plays in the second period were contemporary American plays. Third, despite the differences between the popular plays in the two periods,

Table 12.3
The Habima's Most Popular Productions: 1949–1968

Playwright	*Play*	*Date of Presentation*	*Total Audience*
Yigal Mossinson	*In the Wastes of the Negev*	1949	248,007
Maxwell Anderson	*Lost in the Stars*	1953	224,637
Alexandre Breffort and Margueritte Monnot	*Irma La Douce*	1962	224,095
Peter Ustinov	*Photo Finish*	1963	181,291
Frances Goodrich and Albert Hackett	*The Diary of Anne Frank*	1957	167,873
Félicien Marceau	*The Egg*	1957	154,426
William Gibson	*The Miracle Worker*	1960	152,761
Friedrich Duerrenmatt	*The Visit*	1959	129,714
Alejandro Casona	*The Trees Die Standing*	1959	128,166
Reginald Rose	*Twelve Angry Men*	1959	118,468
William Shakespeare	*A Midsummer Night's Dream*	1949	117,116
John Patrick	*The Teahouse of the August Moon*	1955	115,132
Arthur Miller	*Death of a Salesman*	1951	112,067
Aaron Megged	*Hanna Szenes*	1958	105,583
Herman Wouk	*The Caine Mutiny Court Martial*	1954	103,133

they did display one common characteristic: they were, for the most part, either comedies or melodramas.

Two of the three greatest successes of the period were musicals: the American musical drama, *Lost in the Stars,* and the French musical, *Irma La Douce. Lost in the Stars* was adapted for the stage by Maxwell Anderson from Alan Paton's book *Cry, the Beloved Country.* It had a musical score by Kurt Weill. The story takes place in a little village in South Africa and concerns the relationship between whites and blacks. *Irma La Douce,* the French musical comedy concerning a prostitute, was the third great box office success of the period. It opened in 1962, and was the Habima's first attempt at musical comedy.

The fact that the Habima, the National Theater, presented a play like *Irma La Douce,* elicited censure and criticism, though artistically the production was praised.[4] It should be pointed that *Irma La Douce* followed productions such as Colette's melodrama *Gigi* in 1961 and an ad-

A scene from Maxwell Anderson's *Lost in the Stars* (1953).

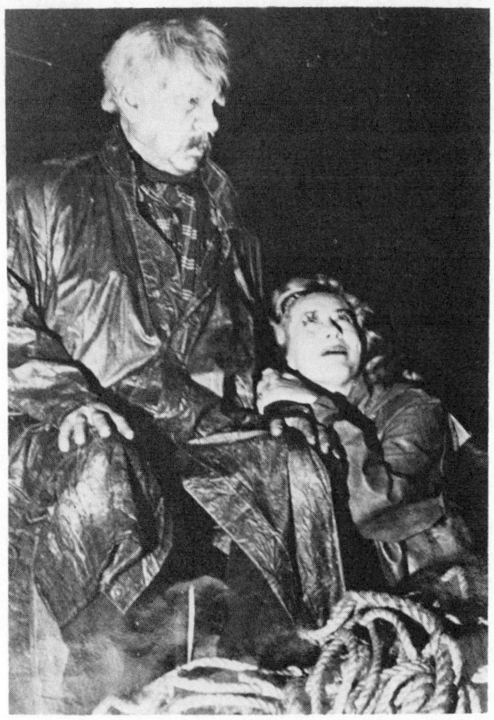

Miriam Zohar as Anna and Aaron Meskin as her father in Hy Kalus's production of *Anna Christie* (1957), the first play by O'Neill at the Habima.

Shlomo Bar-Shavit as Gaston, Dina Doron as Gigi, and Bat-Ami Finkel as Madame Alvarez (from left to right) in Colette's *Gigi* (1961).

aptation of a light English comedy, *A Flat to Let,* in 1962. These latter two productions were denounced by the press, and adverse criticism was leveled at the Habima for lowering its standards and presenting such trivial fare, allegedly unsuitable for Israel's National Theater.[5] The public, however, was of a different mind; all three productions—*Gigi, A Flat to Let,* and especially *Irma La Douce*—played to capacity, and for the first time in years the theater was completely sold out in advance, enjoying a prosperity it had never before known.[6]

Light comedies that were well staged and well acted always proved popular with the audience. This was the case with three comedies: *The Teahouse of the August Moon, The Egg,* and *Photo Finish.* John Patrick's *The Teahouse of the August Moon* (1955) was an excellent American satire directed at the army and at rigid ideas of success, morality, and democracy. The other satire, *The Egg* (*L'Oeuf*) by Félicien Marceau, opened at the Habima in 1957, a few months after it was written.

It was a witty comedy whose point was that if one is to shut out the hardships of life, it is advantageous to penetrate "inside the egg." Emile Magis, the play's hero, confides his secret to the audience by narrating his development from a charming man into a cynical scoundrel. Both productions, *The Teahouse of the August Moon* and *The Egg*, were extremely popular due to the brilliant acting of Raphael Klutchkin, the Habima's greatest comedian.

The third popular comedy, *Photo Finish* (1963), was written by Peter Ustinov. This satire revolves around Sam, a highly successful eighty-year-old author, who encounters in his study three men who are himself, and yet not himself. They are Sam at twenty, an idealistic poet; Sam at forty, a still-struggling author; and Sam at sixty, smugly rich because of his compromise with his early ideals. *Photo Finish* had a wide appeal because it was, in many respects, the life story of almost everyone in the audience. In addition, the Hebrew translation of the play, the staging, and especially Shraga Friedman's outstanding performance as

Shimon Finkel as Mr. Balvaa and Hanna Rovina as The Grandmother in Casona's *The Trees Die Standing* (1959).

Raphael Klutchkin (center, as Sakini) and company in John Patrick's comedy *The Teahouse of the August Moon* (1955).

Old Sam contributed to the success of the production and made it the fourth great box office success of the period.

The other popular productions were, for the most part, contemporary American plays, such as Arthur Miller's *Death of a Salesman,* Reginald Rose's *Twelve Angry Men,* Herman Wouk's *The Caine Mutiny Court Martial,* and William Gibson's *The Miracle Worker.* Despite the fact that these productions were truly American plays (with American locales, themes, and characters), they appealed both to critics and audiences because they were extremely well staged and well acted.

The drama critics often criticized the Habima's choice of repertoire (its tendency to mount comedies and melodramas), and there were frequent disputes between them and the theater over the plays that the Habima, as Israel's National Theater, should present. In order to understand this problem, three major factors should be examined: the particular demographic and sociocultural profile of Israel, the structure of the theatrical establishment, and the theater's finances.

Until 1948, most of Palestine's Jewish population was from Eastern and Western Europe and was highly educated. But the years following 1948 brought vast changes in the country's demographic and social profile. The mass immigration that began immediately after the 1948 War of Independence altered the character of the Jewish population.[7] The bulk of this immigration, and the immigration in later years, consisted of people from Asia and Africa, few of whom spoke Hebrew and all of whom had a cultural heritage different from that prevailing in Palestine. It is of interest to mention that in the late sixties roughly half of the Jewish population of Israel was of oriental (Afro-Asian) origin and almost the same proportion still used one of a dozen different languages as the main instrument of communication. The major problem confronting the Habima—and all the other Israeli theaters—was how to develop a theatergoing habit among the new immigrants from Asia and Africa, most of whom had never before been to the theater.

Miriam Zohar as Anne Sullivan and Daliah Cohen as Helen Keller in Gibson's *The Miracle Worker* (1960).

Furthermore, in contrast to the American and European theater, the Israeli theater (and the Habima, of course) was not limited to the upper socioeconomic strata. Through the publicly sponsored *Omanut Laam* (Art for the People) program, which brought legitimate theater at extremely low prices to immigrant and border settlements, the circle of theater-goers expanded constantly.[8] The social composition of the Israeli audience had an effect on the Habima's repertory policy; it had to take into consideration the artistic taste of an extremely varied audience. Hence, the Habima aimed toward a more conservative, conventional, and varied repertoire, and this tendency clashed with its own ideological and artistic inclinations.

Indeed, despite favorable critical response, the Theater of the Absurd and other more advanced theatrical forms have not been able to overcome the generally conservative nature of Israel's large theater audience. Among the Habima's box office failures were Ionesco's *Exit the King* in 1963, and Pinter's *The Lover* in 1964. These are isolated but undoubtedly representative examples; given the same level of production, avant-garde, absurd, and serious dramas have a much smaller potential audience than the more conventional, "conservative" repertoire, that is, light entertainment, melodramas, and musicals. Thus, the Habima's repertoire came to include all types of plays because it aimed to appeal to and satisfy the varied artistic tastes of its extremely heterogeneous audience.

Another factor influencing the Habima's artistic policy was related to the Israeli theatrical establishment. In the period 1949–1968 there were four major theaters in Israel: the Habima, the Cameri (established in 1944), the Ohel, and the Haifa Municipal Theater (founded in 1961). All four were repertory theaters with permanent troupes, and all were traveling companies. The competition among these theaters and their attempt to appeal to the largest possible audience (urban as well as rural, upper as well as lower class) tremendously affected their repertoire. All four theaters had varied repertoires, consisting of Hebrew and non-Hebrew, classical as well as modern plays. Since none of these theaters wanted to limit its appeal to a special segment of the potential theater-going public, their repertoire was a mixture of plays.

The third factor affecting the Habima's artistic policy had to do with its finances. Only in 1958 was the Habima officially recognized as the

National Theater of Israel and as such granted a yearly subsidy from the government. However, this subsidy never amounted to more than 10 or 15 percent of the annual budget. The Habima's operation was therefore heavily dependent on its success at the box office. Indeed, in 1963, for instance, the Habima had an annual working budget of 1,200,000 Israeli pounds ($400,000), of which 85 percent was covered by ticket sales and 15 percent by subsidies—in part from the American-Israeli Cultural Foundation, the balance from the Israeli government.

Hard box office realities made all the more difficult by the competition with the other theaters combined with its low-priced tickets and increasing production expenses forced the Habima to choose a repertoire with the widest box office appeal. The tendency toward light comedies of the kind usually presented by commercial theaters was especially apparent in the sixties. In 1962, Meskin represented the opinion of many actors when he said: "If we do not place emphasis upon 'commercial' repertoire, we will not succeed; it is neither the mission nor the artistic approach which matters now in Israel."[9] Consequently, all members agreed that from now on the theater's repertoire should cater more to the public's taste.[10] They were right; indeed, it was the box office success of these plays that permitted the production of serious and sophisticated drama.

In the period 1949–1968 the Habima continued to be a traveling nation-wide theater. In the fifties the number of the troupe's performances on the road exceeded that of its performances in its home, Tel-Aviv. During the 1953–1954 season, out of a total of 539 performances, 295 were given outside Tel-Aviv. However, in the sixties, the number of performances given outside Tel-Aviv decreased. During the 1964–1965 season, for instance, the proportion of these performances amounted to only one-fourth (178 out of 682 performances).[11] The late sixties (and early seventies) witnessed a further decrease, which stemmed primarily from the extremely high expense involved in traveling all over the country and the subsequent severe and repeated financial crises that the theater faced.

The number of performances presented per season gradually increased. Table 12.4 presents the number of performances and attendance per season compared to the Israeli population.

Except for the 1948–1949 season (which had an extremely low

Table 12.4
Number of Performances and Attendance per season: 1949–1968

Season	*Number of Performances*	*Attendance*	*Size of Jewish Population*
1948–1949	259	267,502	1,013,900
1949–1950	381	300,166	1,203,000
1950–1951	415	342,943	1,404,400
1951–1952	373	279,030	1,450,200
1952–1953	460	406,617	1,483,600
1953–1954	539	374,717	1,526,000
1954–1955	578	474,582	1,590,500
1955–1956	416	306,718	1,667,500
1956–1957	555	446,616	1,762,800
1957–1958	543	439,293	1,810,200
1958–1959	553	455,274	1,858,800
1959–1960	405	365,610	1,911,300
1960–1961	371	284,964	1,981,700
1961–1962	405	263,945	2,068,000
1962–1963	791	515,330	2,155,600
1963–1964	631	a	2,239,200
1964–1965	682	a	2,299,100
1965–1966	a	a	2,344,900
1966–1967	a	a	2,383,600
1967–1968	a	a	2,434,800

SOURCE: *Statistical Abstract of Israel: 1975* (Jerusalem: Government Printer of Israel, 1975), p. 19.
[a] No data available.

number of performances and attendance figures because of the 1948 crisis), there was a gradual increase in the number of performances and in the size of the audience that attended them. It is noteworthy that during the 1952–1953 season, the Habima gave 460 performances with a total audience of 406,617, whereas during the 1962–1963 season it performed 791 times before an audience of 515,330. The increase in the number of performances from the 1962–1963 season on was a result of the opening of a second theater hall—the Little Hall, seating 300 people—in July 1962.[12]

However, the rise in theater attendance (measured by number of tickets sold) was not commensurate with the increase in Israel's population during these years. At best, the number of tickets sold amounted to one-fourth or one-fifth of the population, as in the 1958–1959 season. A comparison of the Habima's attendance in the prestatehood period with that in the 1949–1968 period shows that there was an increase in the total number of tickets sold, but a decrease in the percentage of the tickets sold relative to the total population. This relative decrease was the combined result of the influx of a vast number of immigrants who never attended the theater, a decline in the Habima's popularity, and, most important of all, the competition of the other theaters, especially the Cameri.

The Habima and the Cameri

Changes in both the institutional and demographic setting of the Jewish community of Palestine, and the ideological and artistic state of Palestine's two major theaters, the Habima and the Ohel, played an important role in the origination of the Cameri theater.

In the early forties, both the Habima's and the Ohel's repertoires consisted of either European or of old Yiddish plays; native Hebrew plays were rare. In both theaters almost all plays were directed by staff directors. As the actors of both troupes aged, they continued to perform all the major roles and did not accept young actors into the theater. Thus, both the Habima and the Ohel became conservative in their repertoire and artistic style.

Furthermore, the two theaters remained impervious to the changes that had been taking place in Palestine. In the forties, a new generation came of age. It was a generation that was either born or raised in Palestine and, therefore, spoke a Hebrew different in sound, syntax, and vocabulary from the Hebrew that their parents spoke. In addition, the mid-thirties had brought to Palestine a large number of immigrants from Germany, Austria, and Czechoslovakia who were fleeing from the Nazis. These immigrants were better educated than the immigrants who had come from Eastern Europe, and they had been exposed to the best European theaters (especially the German), which had traditions very different from those of the Russian theater to which the Habima and the Ohel adhered.

The Cameri theater was founded in 1944 by Yosef Millo and four other actors.[13] Millo was born in Czechoslovakia in 1916 and came to Palestine when he was five years old. Although educated in Palestine, he was a product of Western culture; he spent several years in Europe, where he became acquainted with the work of Brecht and Reinhardt, work that greatly influenced him. In Palestine he worked in the Wooden Troupe Marionette Theater and acted and directed in the *Matateh*, the satirical theater. Millo also applied to the Habima, but was rejected.

The Cameri's founders were young and, in contrast with the Habima actors, they had been influenced by the theater of Western Europe. The group's intention was not to establish a new theater, but rather to present several plays that would differ artistically from those presented by the Habima and the Ohel. In October 1944, after rehearsing for four months, the group presented its first production, four one-act plays by Oscar Wilde, the Quintero brothers, and others—a choice guided by the available acting talent.[14] Critical reaction to the first production was lukewarm; it was presented only 33 times and was seen by 11,800 people. Most newspapers ignored the new venture, and several critics who attended the performance were skeptical about the intentions and artistic future of the group.

The second production of the *Lahakat Hamaarchonim* (the One-Act Play Group), as the group was then called, was an adaptation of Bialik's story "Aluf Batzal, Aluf Shum" ("Master of Onion, Master of Garlic"), which was staged in high-comedy fashion with music by Jacques Offenbach. It opened in 1945 and ran for only 26 performances. Despite the lack of real success, the group found some friends—especially among German-Jewish immigrants—who were ready to help in financing the venture. It was decided to found a theater called the Cameri (the Chamber).

Determined to establish a "vanguard theater" that would be different from both the Habima and the Ohel, Millo decided to stage Goldoni's *The Servant of Two Masters* in 1945 in the commedia dell'arte manner, a style unknown in the country until then. This production marked the beginning of a new theater; its artistic style was something innovative at that time, and critics as well as audiences were charmed by the fact that they saw new and fresh faces on the stage after years of seeing the same actors in the established theaters. *The Servant of Two Masters* was presented 148 times, an above-average run for that time. With this success, both artistic and financial, the Cameri established itself.

Repertoire

Table 12.5 shows the repertoire of the Habima and the Cameri between 1944 and 1968.

Table 12.5
Repertoire of the Habima and the Cameri by Type of Play: 1944–1968

	The Habima		*The Cameri*	
Type of Play	*Number*	*Percent*	*Number*	*Percent*
Hebrew plays	33	20.1	20	13.8
Jewish plays (other than Hebrew)	17	10.4	3	2.1
Universal plays	114	69.5	122	84.1
Total	164	100.0	145	100.0

Table 12.5 shows that there was no significant difference in the number of plays presented by the two theaters (164 at the Habima compared with 145 at the Cameri). The average number of new plays presented per season was 7 at the Habima and 6 at the Cameri. However, there were significant differences between the Habima's and the Cameri's repertoires. In the first place, the Habima presented more Hebrew plays than the Cameri did. Second, Habima presented 17 Jewish plays, whereas the Cameri presented only 3 such plays.[15] Third, the proportion of the universal plays presented at the Cameri was much higher: 84 percent in comparison to 69 percent of the Habima's repertoire. Thus, the Habima was more Hebrew and Jewish and less universal in its ideological and artistic orientation than the Cameri.

Table 12.6 classifies the repertoire of the Habima and the Cameri by language.

Several conclusions may be drawn from Table 12.6. Almost half of the Cameri's repertoire was written in English in comparison to one-third of the Habima's repertoire. Second, only one Yiddish play—Sholem Aleichem's *Wandering Stars*—was presented by the Cameri, compared with

Table 12.6
Repertoire of the Habima and the Cameri by Language: 1944–1968

	The Habima		*The Cameri*	
Language	*Number*	*Percent*	*Number*	*Percent*
English	50	30.5	66	45.5
Hebrew	33	20.1	20	13.8
French	26	15.9	12	8.3
German	16	9.8	12	8.3
Russian	8	4.9	7	4.9
Yiddish	7	4.3	1	0.7
Italian	4	2.4	4	2.7
Spanish	4	2.4	4	2.7
Other	16	9.7	19	13.1
Total	164	100.0	145	100.0

seven Yiddish plays by the Habima. Third, the Habima presented more French plays than did the Cameri. Apart from these differences, both theaters presented approximately the same percentage of German, Russian, Italian, and Spanish plays.

It should be pointed out that a significant difference between the Habima's and the Cameri's repertoires prevailed in the early years of the Cameri, especially between 1945 and 1948. Of the fifteen plays that the Habima presented in these three years, two were Hebrew (Israeli), two biblical, six Jewish (Yiddish), and five universal plays. Thus, two-thirds of the plays were of Jewish interest, and half of them were old Yiddish plays. At the Cameri, of the thirteen plays only one, *Hu Halach Basadot* (*He Walked through the Fields*), was a Hebrew-Israeli play; the others were all universal plays, predominantly American. In the season of 1946–1947, for instance, the Habima presented such plays as *The Dreyfus Affair*, Sholem Aleichem's *Kitchen Folk*, and Mapu's *The Love of Zion;* whereas the Cameri presented Thomas's *Charley's Aunt*, Kaufman and Hart's *You Can't Take It with You*, and Werfel's *Jacobowsky and the Colonel*, all light comedies.

In its early years, the Cameri presented modern and avant-garde plays, such as Lorca's *Blood Wedding* and Anouilh's version of the Greek tragedy, *Antigone.*[16] However, it soon became apparent that serious and avant-garde plays did not have wide audience appeal. Consequently, Millo decided to present plays that would reach the masses, and not just a small intellectual elite. In 1947, the Cameri mounted two American plays: *You Can't Take It with You* and Shelley's *Pick-up Girl.* Millo was right, and both plays were smashing box office hits; the former ran 135 times, and the latter 176, unusually high figures for that time.

The Cameri's chief source of repertoire was the American theater; it devoted itself almost exclusively to producing Broadway hits, both comedies and dramas. During the 1948–1949 season, for instance, the Cameri presented Van Druten's *I Remember Mama,* Miller's *All My Sons,* Krasna's *Dear Ruth,* and Kanin's *Born Yesterday,* all American plays. The Cameri adapted this American orientation with the help of two American-Jewish directors who settled in Israel, Peter Frye and Hy Kalus.[17]

The Cameri not only presented more American plays, but was also more progressive, more modern in its artistic orientation. It was the first theater in the country to produce contemporary and socially significant plays by Steinbeck (*Of Mice and Men*), O'Neill (*Desire under the Elms*), and Tennessee Williams (*The Glass Menagerie*), all of which were presented in the early fifties. And in the sixties, it was the first Israeli theater to present avant-garde plays by Pinter (*The Caretaker*) and Albee (*The Zoo Story*).

Apart from the fact that the Habima mounted more Hebrew plays than the Cameri, there were no qualitative differences between other types of plays. Almost the same playwrights wrote for both theaters.[18] These playwrights were, for the most part, young, and belonged to the new Israeli generation. The topics of their plays reflected to a large extent the ideas and social tendencies of the new reality. The language that they used was a living, not a "literary," one.

Chronologically, the first of the new Israeli plays was Moshe Shamir's *He Walked through the Fields,* which opened at the Cameri in May 1948, during the War of Independence. The play's story, characters, and language were all anchored in the younger Israeli generation (especially the kibbutz-born pioneers) which, for the first time, could see itself on the stage as it really was. Mossinson's *In the Wastes of the Negev,* which opened at the Habima in February 1949, was chronologically the second Israeli play. Both plays signaled a new era in Israeli playwrighting; their topic and timing made them symbols of the War of Independence. Indeed, both plays scored a tremendous artistic and box office success.[19]

In the fifties, both theaters presented realistic, topical Israeli plays. Both the Habima and the Cameri presented plays that concerned the moral issues of the War of Independence, the confrontation of the older-generation idealists with the younger "careerists," the conflicts between new immigrants and older residents, and the problem of integrating Israeli society. The similarity between the Habima's and the Cameri's Hebrew-Israeli plays continued to prevail in the late sixties (and today) for the simple reason that the same playwrights wrote for both theaters.

The difference between the Habima's and the Cameri's repertoires that existed in the late forties disappeared in the fifties and sixties. The Habima and the Ohel had had different ideological missions when they were established, but in later years they departed from their original purposes and became similar. So, too, the Cameri soon departed from its original task of presenting modern chamber plays and original Hebrew plays. Indeed, a great similarity between the repertoire of the Habima and the Cameri prevailed not only in regard to the Hebrew-Israeli plays that they presented, but also in regard to their universal plays.

Artistic Work and Style

One of the Cameri's original aims was to establish a new theater; Millo wanted to show that the Habima and the Ohel were not the only types of theater possible. In 1947, *Pick-up Girl* was a milestone for the Cameri, because the translation of the play was replete with words which had hitherto been kept off the stage. The realistic staging and the naturalistic acting of Hanna Maron, who performed the title role of a girl of the streets, were startlingly new.[20] The realistic style also characterized *He Walked through the Fields* in 1948. Apart from the fact that the play's language was living and natural, Millo's staging was as direct and matter-of-fact as the milieu and characters. The acting (especially of Hanna Maron and Emanuel Ben-Amos) was also devoid of any sentimentality. The leading roles were performed by young native actors whose appearances and voices were natural for the parts.

The Cameri's first actors were in their twenties, and most were born or raised in Palestine. They spoke fluent Hebrew in a natural way and with a clear diction. In their age, education, and outlook they reflected

Israeli's young generation. Indeed, one of the Cameri's greatest contributions was that "it breathed a spirit of youth into the Israeli theatre, and liberated the art of acting from its theatrical stiff-jointedness. . . . It transformed the theatre into a popular institution, in the good sense of the term. . . . And it set the seal of art on the manifestations of Hebrew linguistic freedom, now that the language had become a vernacular."[21] Thus, the Cameri's artistic innovations were threefold: the type of plays it presented, the language (pure Hebrew-Israeli accent and clear diction), and a natural, realistic style of staging and acting.

Audience and Support

It will be recalled that the Habima's establishment in Moscow was an improbable undertaking because there was no Jewish public and no chance that there would be such a public. The Cameri's position in regard to audiences was totally different. By the forties, when the Cameri was founded, a new generation had come of age in Palestine. The ideas of this generation were different from those of its European parents. Its Hebrew language was natural and forthright, unlike the labored and heavily accented language spoken by its parents. This generation regarded with a certain disdain the plays presented by the Habima and the Ohel (Yiddish, romantic, and historical) with their expressionistic style, and the aging actors of these troupes with their accented speech.

Hence, unlike the Habima, when the Cameri was founded there was a public that was seeking to express its own culture and values on stage as well as off. Indeed, the type of repertoire that the Cameri presented in its first years, its innovative artistic approach, and its style of acting had a special appeal to the younger generation in Palestine. In 1948, with the presentation of *He Walked through the Fields,* the Cameri established itself as the theater of youth par excellence.

The Cameri also succeeded where the Habima failed, namely, in creating for itself the image of a dynamic, modern, quality theater, even when the actual repertoire and level of production did not justify this image. With the aid of superb public relations—a factor totally neglected by the Habima—the Cameri succeeded in attracting an audience to all its productions. By the fifties and especially the sixties, the Cameri had established a loyal public for itself. True, when the Habima presented a good play or had an interesting production, it also attracted large audiences. But when the older theater presented an uninteresting play or the production was artistically poor, it was much more severely criticized by the press and audience. This resulted partly from the press's higher expectations for the Habima as the National Theater, but also because of its unpopular image and its lack of public relations. In addition, unlike the Habima (and the Ohel), the Cameri was never burdened with the cooperative-collective system which gave actors the power to decide which plays to be presented and how they should be cast.

Indeed, the Cameri's productions were on the whole, more popular than the Habima's productions. Table 12.7 shows that two-thirds of the plays presented by the Habima between 1944 and 1968 either failed or had only short runs, in comparison with less than one-half at the Cameri. Especially significant is the difference between the two theaters in the number and percentage of plays that either totally failed or totally succeeded. For instance, fifty-one of the Habima's plays failed in comparison to twenty-five of the Cameri's plays.

Table 12.7
Habima and Cameri Productions: 1944–1968

	The Habima		*The Cameri*	
Number of Performances	*Number*	*Percent*	*Number*	*Percent*
1–29 (failure)	51	31.1	25	17.2
30–59 (short run)	56	34.2	43	29.7
60–99 (moderate run)	24	14.6	32	22.1
over 100 (success)	33	20.1	45	31.0
Total	164	100.0	145	100.0

The Cameri theater had a tremendous effect upon the Habima in artistic matters. Its progressive repertoire forced the Habima to present similar plays, and the natural, fresh acting style of the Cameri's young actors affected the Habima's actors. The Cameri also affected the Habima in social matters. The Cameri's success and image as the theater of Israeli youth altered the attitude of the Habima's veteran actors toward its younger actors and, as a result, the latter's position in the theater's artistic work significantly changed in the fifties.

But most important of all was the competition between the Habima and the Cameri. For the first time in its history, the Habima had real competition, and it was fierce. The Ohel theater was a competitor of the Habima only in its first years, but the Ohel was never considered by the press and public as being on the same artistic level as the Habima. The Cameri, on the other hand, became a serious competitor of the Habima from the moment it was founded. By 1958, when the Habima was granted the title of Israel's National Theater, it was not the singular institution it had been in the thirties and forties. Then, the Habima had been not only the leading theater, but also a major cultural endeavor of the Yishuv. The Cameri's advent and popularity had changed all that: in the fifties and sixties the Habima was only one of Israel's theaters, and not always the best one.

THIRTEEN

Organizational Structure: Artistic and Administrative Direction: 1949–1968

THE crisis that the Habima faced in 1948 was the worst that the theater had ever experienced; the troupe was on the verge of liquidation and official intercession by public figures became necessary to stave off the theater's dissolution. In November 1948, a new Board of Directors was elected. It consisted of five members: three—Rovina, Gnessin, and Bertonov—represented the collective; two were representatives of the Public Committee. Thus, for the first time, public figures participated in the management as full-fledged members, possessing equal power.

The 1948 crisis brought about a series of reorganizations. In the first place, the actors' collective no longer had ultimate power. The earlier system, according to which the actors voted on the choice of repertoire and casting, was abolished. Now the management of the theater was in the hands of an elected board. As a result, the general assembly, which had had the final word in every matter, now became a forum where the members received basic information on the theater's affairs. Indeed, between 1949 and 1953 the collective had no voice in artistic or administrative affairs. After three decades of active involvement in the theater's direction, the actors' chief responsibility was to perform.

A second reorganization concerned the division of authority between the artistic and administrative management. For the first time, the theater had an official Administrative Director, Michael Frid, who was not a collective member. All artistic affairs—the choice of plays, casting, inviting stage directors, and the like—were resolved by the Board. The direction of the Habima between 1949 and 1953 was quite effective. Under the new Board, the troupe developed artistically and the repertoire was altered to include more modern and contemporary plays. The troupe now worked with foreign directors of high stature. The theater's administration and finance also improved.

Another significant change was related to the composition and authority of the Repertoire Committee. After the 1948 crisis, the Board appointed a Repertoire Committee composed of noted writers, such as Nathan Alterman and Leah Goldberg. Its task was to read, select, and suggest a list of plays to the Board.

The Public Committee also tried to introduce differential payment based on acting ability. Until 1948, financial equality prevailed at the Habima; the talented and great actors of the troupe received no greater salary than the others. But this proposal got no further. Among other reasons, it was too late to introduce differential artistic (and financial) ranks among a group of actors who had lived and performed together for more than thirty years. So all actors who were collective members continued to receive equal wages until the last day of the collective.

However, beginning in the fifties, there were exceptions to the rule of equal pay to all members. Actors who excelled in their performance, for instance, and were responsible for the wide appeal of a production received a special reward. And there was another "deviation" from the principle of equal salary. In the fifties, actors who were members of the Board of Directors, and members who, apart from their responsibilities as actors, also directed, received special remuneration for this work.

The Habima's Generation Gap

The most significant result of the 1948 crisis concerned the position of the young actors in the theater. In 1948, the actors' collective consisted of twenty-five members, sixteen of whom belonged to the Moscow group; the other nine had been admitted in Palestine between 1928 and 1946 (see Appendix 3). In this year there were also about ten young actors, all of whom had been trained at the theater. Although their position within the theater had improved in 1948, when they had been given better parts to perform, they were still not members of the collective. When the Habima toured the United States, most of the young actors were left at home. During the War of Independence, they were drafted and became the nucleus of the military entertainment units, in which they earned fame and popularity. And when peace came, they represented the new heroes of the country—they had been born or raised in Palestine and they had fought in the War of Independence.

The young actors' popularity improved their position within the Habima. The first postwar production in which they performed the major roles was *In the Wastes of the Negev* in 1949. This production also marked the end of the appearance of the asterisk near the young actors' names, indicating their inferior status in the theater's programs. After *In the Wastes of the Negev,* the Habima's young actors continued to receive better parts in the productions.

The young actors constituted a cohesive subgroup within the theater. This subgroup was of a significant size; in the early fifties it numbered nearly fifteen actors, while the collective itself had only twenty-five members. The relationship between the older and the younger actors displayed characteristics of an intergenerational conflict.

The two groups constituted two generation units and represented two distinct subcultures.[1] First, there was the age difference. The members of the Moscow group had been born in Russia at the turn of the century and had come to maturity during the Russian Revolution. Most of the younger actors were born in the 1920s and matured during the War of Independence. The Moscow group had been raised and educated in Russia; the younger actors in Palestine. Some of the younger actors were members of youth movements and some had even been members of kibbutzim. And, finally, compared with the younger actors, to whom the Hebrew language was natural, the Habima veterans spoke Hebrew with a very heavy Russian accent.

Indeed, several critics pointed out that the diction of the Habima veteran actors was markedly inferior. Gamzu, the *Haaretz* critic, wondered how the theater could fulfill its task of teaching the varied audience of

Palestine to speak Hebrew properly if most of the actors themselves spoke Hebrew with a heavy Russian accent. He went on to contend that that accent had become a major handicap due to the fact that the proportion of Jews coming from Eastern Europe was decreasing while the proportion born or raised in Palestine was rapidly increasing. Gamzu expressed his fear that this demographic change might cause a deep breach between the Habima and the Israeli-born people.[2]

The differences in age, education, and cultural tradition between the Habima's two groups were reflected in their different conceptions of the theater and of their role as actors. The Moscow group was ideologically oriented, doctrinaire, rigid, and emotional. The veteran actors cleaved unquestionably to the old Russian methods, and were still living under the spell of past ideas and theatrical traditions. The younger actors, in contrast, were more pragmatic, less ideologically motivated, and their commitment to the theater was more professional than emotional. Furthermore, the Moscow group had a broad definition of their role as actors; the Habima was for them more than a theater; it was an artistic community, a home. Work in the theater was a sacred duty, a calling. The veteran actors always felt that the younger members were not sufficiently committed to their sacred task.

The Moscow actors' conception of the theater had a tremendous effect upon the younger actors' education and approach. However, the younger group did not—and could not—have the same images and role-definition as the veteran actors; they were educated and lived in a totally different social and historical setting. Furthermore, the Moscow group had graduated from one of the best dramatic schools in the world, the school of Stanislavsky and Vakhtangov, a factor which contributed to their self-esteem and elitist orientation. Consequently, they always stressed that the younger actors had a long way to go before they could become "true" actors.[3]

Indeed, despite the fact that the younger actors were trained at the Habima's dramatic school, they advocated a different kind of acting. The Moscow group, on the whole, still adhered to an expressionistic style and their approach was far more theatrical. The younger actors' approach, on the other hand, was more natural and realistic. Their acting style was greatly influenced by their experience in the army entertainment units, through which they had acquired a new approach to the audience. They therefore asserted themselves with a style of acting which was natural, immediate, and direct.

In 1953, four years after it had taken over, the Public Committee suggested setting up a temporary board of directors that would be comprised of two members from the government, two from Tel-Aviv Municipality, two from the Public Committee itself, and three from the Habima collective. This board was to direct the theater for one year, during which its juridical and organizational structure (a cooperative) was to remain in force. After the one-year trial period, a new organization for the Habima would be discussed, though the final word would belong to the collective.[4]

The collective rejected this proposal and instead suggested a board on which members of the collective would be a majority. Those members who still favored collective rule criticized the work of the Public Committee. They believed that "we should maintain our independence at all costs and pass it on to the younger actors who come after us." Therefore, they were in favor of admitting new actors in order to strengthen the collective. It is noteworthy that the main discussants in this meeting were the less able actors who had traditionally been the strongest supporters of the collective. These actors complained that the Committee "segregated itself" and "ruled over the collective." On the other hand, the great actors advocated the Committee's continued intervention in the theater's direction, but they represented a minority. At the end of this crucial 1953 meeting, the collective decided that all resolutions about the future of the theater had to be approved by the general assembly.[5] With this resolution, the collective again asserted its wish to have control over the theater's affairs.

The collective's distrust of the Public Committee was primarily motivated by fear on the part of the ungifted actors that once the collective was dissolved, their careers as actors would be over. It also grew out of the deep-seated attachment that most of the members had for the collective which they themselves had directed for three decades. As a result, the Habima's veteran actors suggested that some of the younger actors be accepted into the collective. In the early fifties, the Moscow group finally acknowledged that it was getting older and that if the Habima was to continue to function, younger actors had to be admitted. Furthermore, some of the leading actors had passed away, and by 1952 the collective had only 22 members.[6]

New members had to be admitted to keep the Habima alive. And it had to be done soon, especially in light of the fact that some of the Habima's new actors joined the Cameri in the late forties, and the collective feared that other young members might do the same. In addition, in 1952, the number of actors not belonging to the collective almost equalled the number that did. Most of the members truly wished to strengthen the collective and avert its dissolution. Consequently, in February 1953, the Habima's collective accepted eight young actors into its ranks.[7]

The admission of the eight new actors was the most important recruitment by the theater since its foundation. The younger actors totally changed the social composition of the collective. There were now thirty actor-members, thirteen of whom were from the Moscow group, ten Palestinians, and seven young Israelis.

But the admission of the new members was dysfunctional from the organizational point of view; it reinforced the theater's collective, which during the previous four years had, in effect, been powerless. It also made clear that the Public Committee's attempt to dissolve the collective and bring about a basic reorganization would not succeed. Indeed, the Committee realized that the theater wished to maintain its organizational structure, and the Committee members consequently announced their resignations. Hence, in 1953 the Habima collective resumed its former power and authority.

With the direction of the theater back in the hands of the collective, there was once again a lack of artistic and administrative authority. However, in comparison to the period 1927–1948 when the actors' collective was the sovereign body, between 1953 and 1968 (when the collective was dissolved) it was the Board of Directors that had ultimate power. The general assembly's power had already begun to decline in the late forties. Nonetheless, it did not give up its power easily, and the decade of the fifties witnessed a power struggle between the general assembly and the Board of Directors. In 1958, for instance, when the issue of which body—the collective or the Board—should have the authority to accept new actors was discussed, most of the members favored leaving this authority in the hands of the collective where it had always been.[8] Indeed, up until the dissolution of the collective, it remained the responsibility of the general assembly to accept new actors into the collective.

The decade of the fifties also witnessed the last attempt of the Habima's veteran actors to maintain their powerful positions in both artistic and administrative management. The veteran actors (especially the Moscow group) could not accept the idea that casting was no longer determined in the general assembly. Moreover, they could not accept the idea that the younger actors were getting better parts and were taking over; they maintained it was not right to give younger actors parts that veterans were still qualified to perform.[9]

Official Recognition as Israel's National Theater

As soon as the theater's direction was handed over to the collective, the custom of electing a Board of Directors every year or two was resumed. As in the past, the failure of a Board was attributed personally to its members rather than to the principle of electing boards and to the membership's reluctance to accept the Board's authority. Consequently, every time the theater faced a crisis, the membership insisted on electing a new Board, hoping that it would solve the problems of the theater.

In 1954 the new Board consisted of five members: Bertonov, honorary president; Meskin, chairman; Warshawer, for administration; Finkel, for repertoire; and Bat-Ami, for finance. There was also a Repertoire Committee and an Artistic Committee. Almost half of the membership was involved, in one way or another, in the artistic or administrative management of the theater, though none of the younger actors held an official position.[10] This Board remained in force for three years, during which the Habima struggled to become a state theater.

The desire to become a state theater and to be fully subsidized by the government derived, at least in part, from severe recurring financial crises. The press and public opinion generally supported this wish. *Yediot Acharonot*, for instance, wrote that the Habima was an integral part of Jewish national history and should therefore be sponsored by the state.[11] *Lamerhav* contended that the Habima was neither a private-commercial theater nor an experimental studio but a national-cultural property, and the public should therefore help find a solution to the theater's financial deficits.[12] And *Haaretz* wrote that by virtue of the Habima's mission and glorious past, it should be supported in order to maintain its high artistic standards.[13] All newspapers regarded the Habima as much more than an art theater; it was a national institution and an important component of the Jewish cultural heritage.

But several newspapers wrote against transforming the Habima into a fully subsidized state theater. The *Davar* critic, for example, wrote that the nationalization of the Habima would not solve the problems of repertoire and audience. In his opinion, the release of the theater from its dependency on the box office would not release it from dependency on audiences.[14] Others stated that the Habima was not the only theater in Israel, and that its current repertoire and artistic level were interchangeable with and even lagged behind those of the Cameri; there was therefore no justification for transforming the Habima into a fully subsidized national theater. In the opinion of these critics, the only justification for this title would be if the Habima were first a high-level theater, presenting important plays with an outstanding ensemble of actors—and a theater without a deficit.[15] Indeed, because the artistic achievements and popularity of the Habima did not exceed those of the Cameri, the Habima troupe decided to try to convince the government to recognize only their theater as *the* state theater because "it was the only theater that has a glorious past and tradition."[16]

The Habima's members were quite disappointed that they had to apply and fight for official recognition. They had believed that this recognition (and subsidy) would be awarded immediately after the establishment of the State of Israel in 1948. The founding group kept reminding the public and government that the Habima had been supported by the Soviet regime long after all other Jewish organizations had been liquidated. They thought that it was a paradox that the Habima had been an official Soviet state theater in its first years, whereas now, forty years after its founding, it was still not supported by the Israeli government.[17]

All the actors wanted the Habima to become a state theater, although there were different ideas of what this title meant. For most members, it meant no more than assuring the theater's financial existence without any public or government interference in artistic policy and administration. However, for a few actors, such as Finkel and Meskin, becoming a state theater meant dissolving the collective and choosing for the new theater the best actors in the country.[18]

In October 1958, on its fortieth anniversary, the Habima was officially recognized as the National Theater of Israel. The committee appointed by the government recommended that the Habima be transformed into a state theater; this included structural reorganization as well as full subsidy. However, a cabinet committee decided that the Habima should be made the National Theater. Official recognition did not bring about any significant change in the theater's organization or operation. In addition to the honor of being the National Theater, the new status meant that the Habima would receive a yearly subsidy of 100,000 Israeli pounds ($56,000), nearly 8 percent of the annual budget. The government also decided to set up a Public Council, with advisory authority, for the Habima.

The Habima's actors were disappointed, both with recognition as the National Theater rather than the State Theater, and with the amount of yearly subsidy. The struggle to transform the Habima into a publicly owned state theater and, hence, to establish it on a new organizational and artistic basis, had failed. Indeed, the cooperative structure not only prevailed for another decade, but also contributed greatly to the deterioration of the artistic, financial, and administrative state of the theater.

The Last Years of the Collective: 1958–1968

The new members who were accepted in 1953 exerted a tremendous influence upon the theater, both because of their number and the fact that they were accepted not as a scattered aggregate of individuals, but as an organized subgroup with shared values and interests. It was the first time that the collective had admitted a whole set of actors as a group. In the past it had preferred to accept new members individually and gradually. The members had been reluctant to admit organized groups because of the fear that these groups might introduce changes that would not be beneficial to the collective. In addition, it was easier for the collective to exert social control and assimilate new members by admitting them individually rather than in groups. The younger actors not only performed the major parts in the theater's productions and provided three of the four staff directors, but they also participated in the management and influenced artistic policy.[19] The real turning point in the position and impact of the younger actors occurred in June 1958, when they removed the members of the Board and made sure that the new Board represented their own interests.[20] The new Board elected in June 1958 is known in the theater's history as the "young Board."

The "young Board" brought about changes in the artistic policy and administration. First, a young administrator (a former army officer) was brought to the theater to take over administration from the collective. Second, and perhaps more importantly, under this Board the repertoire was more modern and included several contemporary plays. Thus, during the 1958–1959 season the Habima presented O'Neill's *A Touch of the Poet*, Osborne's *Look Back in Anger*, Max Frisch's *Herr Biedermann*, and Duerrenmatt's *The Visit*. Three of the plays presented under this Board turned out to be smash hits: *The Trees Die Standing* (130 performances), *The Visit* (134), and *Twelve Angry Men* (136). Third, the Board dismissed most of the actors who did not belong to the collective. These actors had become a strain on the budget, especially since approximately one-third of the collective's members were elderly actors who could no longer perform but who remained on the payroll because the theater did not have a pension system.

Despite the artistic achievements of this Board, in December 1959, when the collective gathered for its annual meeting, it decided to elect a new Board.[21] The custom of removing an old Board and electing a new Board in the hope that the new one would cope more effectively with all the problems continued to prevail—even when there was no need to do so. It should be pointed out that as far as the composition of the various Boards was concerned, the collective was really democratic, willing to give a chance to any member who wanted to be on the Board. Indeed, only a very few of the members were never elected to the Board.

The Board elected in 1959 included some new members and was given authority for only one year. Under this Board the theater faced problems of artistic and administrative mismanagement. Apart from one play, *The Miracle Worker*, that was a hit, all other plays failed.[22] This Board proved repeatedly that "six members on the Board are like six separate Boards."[23] This was especially so since members were elected as individuals, not as a group sharing the same ideas and artistic approach. Consequently, in April 1961 the Board resigned. There followed a series of general meetings at which the members expressed their discontent with the state of affairs which resulted from the rule of collective Boards. The members now favored delegating the authority of both the collective and the Board to one member who would then function as the theater's director.[24] Some members, such as Meskin, contended that the crisis was spiritual rather than merely financial. Finkel, like Meskin, ascribed the continuous crisis to the collective structure. Finkel also maintained that the Habima's problem was that it had long ago lost its distinctive repertoire and artistic approach and become "a mixture of all the other theaters."[25]

Most members, especially the younger actors, advocated a strong and authoritative Board, headed by one artistic director. Friedman, the leader of the younger group, summed it up: "We are first and foremost actors, and, therefore, any Board composed of actors is bound to fail."[26] Of the five names suggested—Meskin, Rovina, Finkel, Becker, and Friedman—only Finkel was willing to be a candidate. He was elected Artistic Director of the theater by a large majority of the members. As Artistic Director, Finkel demanded—and was given—full powers, including veto authority, over all artistic matters.[27]

Finkel was Artistic Director for one season, during which he ran the theater like a fully subsidized repertory theater (which it was not), adhering to a strict schedule of premieres. In fourteen months, he presented eleven plays, which were extremely varied; in contrast to his former contentions, the choice of plays did not stem from any distinct repertory line or artistic approach. Of the eleven plays that he chose, nine failed both artistically and with the audience; only two—*Gigi*, a French melodrama, and *Genesis*, an original Hebrew play—succeeded with the audience (see Appendix 2, plays 176–186). Finkel was accused of choosing plays for leading actors rather than choosing interesting plays and then selecting actors for them. As a result, in June 1962, fourteen months after his election, he was removed from office by a majority vote of the collective.

Finkel's term of office was productive in at least one respect; it resulted in the collective's resolution that from now on the theater should have an artistic director. Indeed, in 1962, when a new constitution was prepared, the Board was vested with the authority to propose to the general assembly a candidate for the post of Artistic Director, although his authority was to be decided and approved by the general assembly.[28]

The Habima's next Artistic Director was Julius Gellner. A stage director of Czech origin, Gellner had been living and working in London. He did not speak Hebrew but had the advantage of long association with the troupe; between 1949 and 1962 he had staged twelve plays at the Habima, some of which were among the more memorable of the theater's productions. The collective elected Gellner in June 1962 by a very small majority. The older actors opposed his election on the grounds that he did not speak Hebrew; the younger actors opposed him on the grounds that he was neither young nor up-to-date in artistic matters.[29] Unlike Finkel, Gellner was elected for a two-year period, but he was not given full powers and had to get the approval of a council for every major decision.

The choice of Gellner soon proved unfortunate. Apart from the fact that he was not familiar with Israeli culture and was opposed by many of the actors, Gellner faced from the very start a public opinion that resented the fact that the Israeli National Theater had as its Artistic Director a man who did not speak Hebrew. Of all the plays presented during his two seasons as director, only two were great successes: *Irma La Douce* (originally planned by Finkel) and *Photo Finish*, both light comedies. Their presentation, therefore, aroused much resentment on the part of those who could not separate the Habima from its past and tradition and thought that such trivial fare should not be presented by the National Theater. Of more artistic importance were *The Deputy* and *Children of the Shadow*, both Jewish plays, and Duerrenmatt's *The Physicists*, all of which succeeded. Gellner made another mistake when he accepted the offer of The Little Theatre Inc. in the United States to tour there in 1964.[30] This tour, like all former tours, was a financial fiasco.

Gellner's failure as Artistic Director was not only a result of his personality or the repertoire that he chose; it was also an inevitable result of the Habima's organization which made him a victim of various pressure groups within the collective. The fundamental problem was the actors' reluctance to accept the authority of someone whom they themselves had elected.

The Habima's second experience with an Artistic Director having been unsuccessful, the theater returned in 1964 to collective rule. As was customary, a new Board was elected—this time an extended Board of seven members. This extended Board was the last attempt on the part of the actors to direct the theater. The Board of 1964 proved unable to adopt a single resolution because the seven members represented seven different artistic opinions. The extended Board faced a serious dilemma. On the one hand, it realized that the theater needed one artistic director instead of elected boards, but it was unable to solve the problem of finding a suitable person for the post and convincing the membership to accept his authority. On the other hand, the members of the Board were afraid that if the collective appeared unable to direct itself, the government might appoint an "outsider" to direct the theater.[31] Hence, the dilemma was that the actors realized they were incompetent as a group to direct the theater, but at the same time were reluctant to delegate power or accept the authority of an outsider. For an actors' collective that for almost half a century had directed itself, it was not easy to hand over authority to an outsider.

In October 1965, the extended Board resigned, and the direction was handed over to a Board of Executives of three members: Bat-Ami, the Chairman of the Board; Zvi Rozen, who was vested with the powers of an Artistic Director; and Asher Sherf, the Administrative Director.[32] The collective believed that because the three were not actors they would handle affairs objectively—especially the choice of plays and casting—without the vested interests that motivated the actors when they had been members on the Board. This Board was given its powerful position because of the distrust and suspicion of Boards that consisted of actors, and because none of the actors was willing to assume official responsibility any more.

The three-member Board directed the theater for three years, rather than for three months, and was responsible for the deterioration of the Habima to an unprecedented degree. Indeed, in the late sixties the Habima faced a series of social, artistic, administrative, and financial crises. The collective did not intervene in the Board's work, not because

Nachum Buchman as Othello and Tikva Mor as Desdemona in Patrick Dromgol's production of *Othello* (1966).

it was satisfied with it but rather because resentment with the conduct of affairs had led to indifference among the actors.

Socially, the collective was quite a heterogeneous organization, consisting of three major strata based on age and social origins. The first stratum was composed of the Moscow group; its average age was over sixty and it had eleven actors. The second stratum consisted of players who had joined the theater in Palestine between 1928 and 1947; this group also had East European origins but was younger than the Moscow group by about a decade. The third stratum comprised actors in their late thirties who had been born or raised in Palestine and joined the collective between 1953 and 1965; they made up fourteen of the thirty-five actors.[33]

Artistically, there were no guidelines; the repertoire was chosen on a play-to-play basis, and plays were usually chosen to satisfy the leading and powerful actors of the troupe. Several productions did succeed both artistically and with the audience (such as *Othello* in 1966, and *Tango* and *Becket* in 1967), but these successes were as accidental as the failures and did not stem from a general artistic plan. The majority of plays presented in these years failed, both artistically and financially.

The Habima needed a strong and efficient artistic leadership. The theater was cognizant of this urgent need, but finding a suitable candidate to handle its artistic management was not a simple task, especially since the members were not willing to accept authority. In these years, the press repeatedly criticized the Habima's "management by clerks," and strongly urged the theater to appoint an artistic director who would remain in the post for an extended period of time and would be given full authority in artistic affairs.[34] Indeed, the Board did approach two persons for the post of Artistic Director, Alexander Bardini, the Polish

Oded Teomi (left) as King Henry the Second and Misha Asherov in the title role of Jean Anouilh's *Becket* (1967).

director, and Hy Kalus, the American director, but neither of these negotiations was fruitful.[35]

In the late sixties the Habima also faced a serious financial crisis, the cumulative result of its system of finance. As has been mentioned, all the actors received equal salary. But in the sixties, more than one-third of the troupe was sixty years old or over. These actors no longer participated in the artistic work. Thus, the theater's budget was burdened with salaries paid to actors who had not been seen by the public for years, a burden which made the financial situation of the theater all the more unstable. Only in 1966 was a pension fund established; as a result, ten actors retired. In addition, during the Six-Day War in June 1967, the theater's deficits increased because the government insisted that the theater remain open and perform even to empty halls—to keep up public morale. At the end of 1967, the theater closed the Big Hall in order to renovate and equip it with a better system of acoustics. As a result, for more than two years the troupe performed in the Little Hall (which seated only three hundred people) and in other halls in the city which it had to rent for its performances.

The idea of making the Habima a public theater was first broached in the mid-fifties and then again in the sixties. But it took almost a decade for the idea to gain wide support in government circles. When at the end of 1968 the Habima found itself facing a grave crisis and was threatened with liquidation, the Ministry of Education and Culture (under Zalman Aran's leadership) was finally prepared to take over. This was part of a government policy based on three principles. First, repertory theaters perform an important public service, and since they cannot exist on a commercial basis, the public ought to take on the responsibility for their support. Second, subsidies should amount to one-third of the theater's annual budget. And third, since the cooperative form of organization had proven unable to assure efficient artistic management, the subsidies ought to be granted on the condition that the theaters become publicly owned.[36] The government decided that the Habima as a publicly owned theater would be guaranteed full artistic freedom and that public supervision would be limited to administrative and business matters. It also resolved to consolidate the theater's debts and deficits.

The government's resolution to ensure the existence of the Habima contingent upon the dissolution of the collective caused long and stormy discussions within the troupe. Eventually, the majority decided in favor of giving up ownership for the sake of becoming a state theater. The actors understood that if they wanted to ensure the Habima's existence there was no alternative. Furthermore, the example of the Haifa Municipal Theater (the first public theater in Israel, founded in 1961) strengthened the arguments of those who had advocated fully supported public theaters. The fact that the Haifa theater remained free from municipal interference in its choice of repertoire and manner of production placated those who feared that public support might limit the theater's artistic freedom.

In December 1968, the Habima acquired the status of state theater. The theater kept its old name—the National Theater Habima—and the public did not associate the new framework with any changes in continuity, since the actors' ensemble was not affected. All the actors who belonged to the collective were given life contracts. Thus, the Habima, after fifty-one years of existence as an actors' cooperative, became a state theater—a public trusteeship with a Board of Trustees, General Director, and Artistic Director appointed by the government.

FOURTEEN

The Search for an Artistic Identity: 1969–1977

In 1969, following the dissolution of the actors' collective, a new era in the history of the Habima began. It is noteworthy that of the twenty-four actors who were collective members only two, Rovina and Meskin, had belonged to the Moscow founding group. These two excellent players represented the continuity in the theater's operation. The new structure of the theater had an important impact upon the actors; after a period of fifty-one years, during which they had owned and managed the theater, their sole responsibility now was to perform. This transition from active participation in the theater's work to performance only was difficult and was not wholeheartedly accepted by the members.

The change that took place in the Habima's organizational structure was only one step in a series of changes that had been brought about by the government's policy. Indeed, in the period 1969–1970, the entire structure of Israel's theatrical establishment changed. Of the three repertory theaters in Tel-Aviv which had been cooperatives, one—the Ohel theater—was liquidated; the other two—the Habima and the Cameri—became public theaters. The Habima became Israel's State Theater, and the Cameri the Municipal Theater of Tel-Aviv. In addition to the Ohel, five smaller troupes which played a considerable part in Israel's vibrant and multifaceted theater went out of existence. At present, there are no cooperative theaters left and there remain very small permanent companies. Thus, the public theater has become the main, if not the sole, purveyor of theatrical activity in Israel. Until 1969, the country had only one public theater, the Haifa Municipal Theater, while a few years later it had four publicly owned theaters. The Habima receives its entire subsidy from the government, whereas the Cameri, the Haifa, and the Beer-Sheva theaters receive their subsidy in two equal parts from the government and the respective municipalities.

The Habima in Transition

The new era began with a series of reorganizations and appointments. In late 1968, Zalman Aran, then Minister of Education and Culture, appointed Gabriel Zifroni as the Habima's General Director. Zifroni was a member of the Editorial Board of *Maariv*, Israel's most popular newspaper, and had considerable interest in the theater. Zifroni demanded two things before he accepted the position. First, that the government consolidate the Habima's debts (which amounted to six million Israeli pounds) in order to enable the theater to turn over a new financial leaf. Second, he demanded that the government own all the shares of the theater so that the actors could not have any part in its ownership. Both conditions were met and his appointment was supported by the leading actors of the troupe.

In 1969, a Board of Trustees was appointed. It was chaired by Moshe Zanbar, then head of the Bank of Israel, and included thirteen members, most of whom held top positions in business and administration and only a few of whom were from the fields of education and culture. Nonetheless, it was important that the Board include influential civic leaders in order to improve the theater's management and public image.

The Habima also accepted into its ranks the three directors of the Zavit theater, which was dissolved in 1968 after ten years of existence. Shmuel Omer became the Habima's Administrative Director, and in 1976 he succeeded Zifroni as General Director. Shmuel Atzmon and Pnina Geri joined the acting company. Pnina Geri later became the Director of the Habimartef (the Habima Basement), the theater's third stage, which assumed the character of an experimental theater mounting modern and contemporary (Israeli and universal) plays.

The most important appointment was that of David William as Habima's Artistic Director. William was a young English director, the former director of the New Shakespeare Company in Regents Park who had also worked in many theaters in the provinces. William was appointed by the former Board (before the dissolution of the collective). He did not speak Hebrew and had never visited Israel before. William's appointment was a great disappointment and was severely criticized in the press and by public opinion, which assumed that the new era of the Habima as a State Theater would start with a suitable artistic director, namely, with Israeli artistic leadership.

David William demanded, and was given, full artistic powers. Due to time pressures, the repertoire which William chose for his first season (January to August 1969) did not reflect any particular artistic line. The troupe presented Noel Coward's *Blithe Spirit*, Ben Jonson's *Volpone* (under his staging), and Pirandello's *Six Characters in Search of an Author*. The most important thing was to keep the theater going and to provide work for the actors, many of whom worked outside of the Habima. In addition, William had to choose plays that did not require many actors because the Big Hall was closed for renovation and the theater was forced to perform only in its Little Hall, where even successful plays could not make a profit.

Indeed, the major artistic efforts were directed toward the celebration of the Habima's fiftieth anniversary, which was postponed from October 1968 due to the closing of the Big Hall. The serious defects of the Big Hall resulted in the rebuilding of the house. Wooden seats were replaced with comfortable armchairs; the acoustics were improved with the help of local and foreign experts; the hall was enlarged, and revolving stages with electronic control systems were installed. This project cost 10 million Israeli pounds (then almost $2.5 million), instead of the estimated 4.5 million. Despite enormous monetary problems and numerous interruptions, it was completely and successfully renovated. It opened in March 1970, almost two years after it had closed.

The three plays that were chosen by William for the Habima's fiftieth anniversary reflected how unsuitable he was for the post of Artistic Director of Israel's National Theater. William presented Dekker's *The*

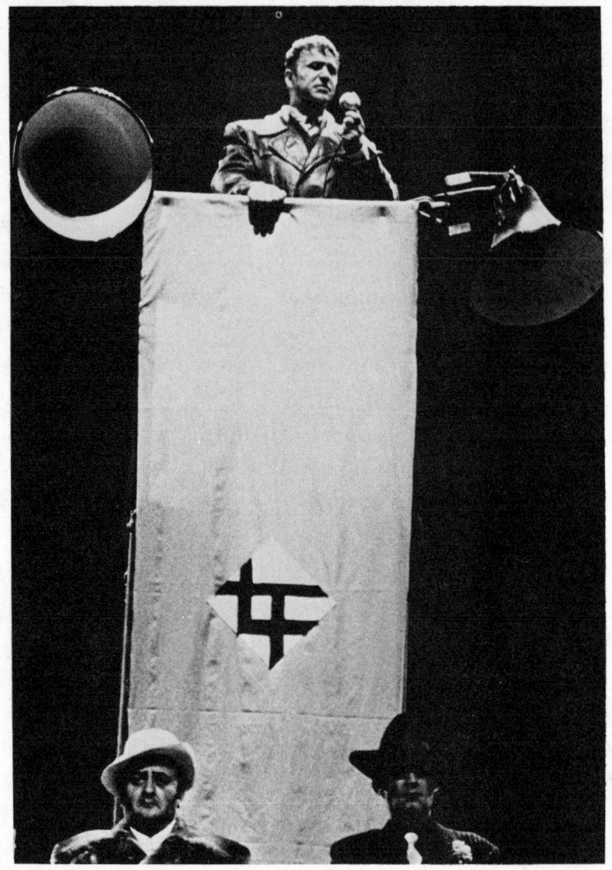

Misha Asherov in the title role of Brecht's *Arturo Ui* (1970), staged by the English director Michael Blackmore.

Shoemaker's Holiday (under his direction), Chekhov's *Seagull*, and Brecht's *Arturo Ui.* This repertoire was severely criticized by the press, especially the choice of Dekker's comedy for the official opening night of the house. The general feeling among both critics and audiences was that to present *The Shoemaker's Holiday* on such a festive and national occasion was the equivalent of presenting Gordin's *Mirele Efros* or Goldfaden's *The Witch* for the opening night of the British National Theater.[1] Furthermore, none of the three productions was an artistic achievement, and all three closed after several performances.

Another mistake made by William was his inattentiveness to the theater's budget and finances. He invited distinguished directors and designers for these productions. Michael Blackmore was brought from London, where he had staged Brecht's play with great success, and John Hirsch, another noted director, was imported from Europe to stage *Seagull.* William proved once again that a foreign director (even an artistic figure of the first rank) cannot function as the Director of Israel's National Theater. Several weeks after the premieres of the three productions he resigned and left the country. He had served as Artistic Director for a little more than a year.

Interestingly enough, the end of the 1969–1970 season was, unexpectedly, better than its start. William had invited from England a young director, Michael Meacham, who staged brilliantly two plays: Edward Albee's *A Delicate Balance* and David Storey's *Celebration. A Delicate Balance* was perhaps the Habima's best production of the entire decade. Its cast included the theater's best actors and the production proved again the artistic potential of the Habima actors when they worked in a good play with a good director.

David William's successor as Artistic Director was the veteran actor, Shimon Finkel. It was the second time that Finkel served as Artistic Director. In 1961, he had been elected—and ousted—by a majority vote of the actors' collective; in 1970, he was appointed to the position by the Board of Trustees for a period of three years with full control. Finkel was an intellectual actor, extremely knowledgeable in theater arts and one of the Habima's leading figures. He was appointed at the suggestion of the actors, who fully supported him because they knew that he was committed to theater based on actors' capabilities.

Finkel's artistic credo consisted of two components: the serious classical tradition and the modern one, the Jewish and the universal. His artistic approach was a synthesis of original (Israeli), Jewish, classical, and modern drama.[2] Finkel's position was not easy, either socially or artistically. The Habima was a shambles; William's resignation left the theater with no plans for the future and the morale of the actors very low. In addition, Finkel had to fight negative public opinion as a result of the arrest of the former Board of Directors who were accused of corruption and unlawful use of property.

Finkel served as the Habima's Artistic Director for five years

(1970–1975).[3] His first season (1970–1971), which was the best of the five that he planned, reflected his artistic endeavors (see Appendix 2). In this season, Finkel produced eleven plays which included classics (Bernard Shaw's *Saint Joan* and Ibsen's *Peer Gynt*), modern drama (Ionesco's *The Chairs*), and light comedy (Alan Ayckbourn's *Relatively Speaking*). The repertoire also included Jewish works, such as Elie Wiesel's *Jews of Silence*. Finkel's first production, *Jews of Silence* in November 1970, aroused considerable interest in Israel and abroad because it coincided with the renewed struggle of Russian Jews to obtain permits for Israel. This production was successfully presented in Brussels, at a conference aimed at promoting the cause of Soviet Jewry, and in other cities in Europe.

In a period of five years, Finkel mounted forty-eight new plays, almost ten productions per season. Of these plays, nine were Jewish, nine were original Israeli dramas, and the rest universal, both classical and modern. Included in the Jewish plays were Hebbel's historical drama *Herod and Miriam*, Sholem Aleichem's *Stempeniu*, and an adaptation of

Shlomo Bar-Shavit and Lia Konig in the brilliant production of Ionesco's *The Chairs* (1970).

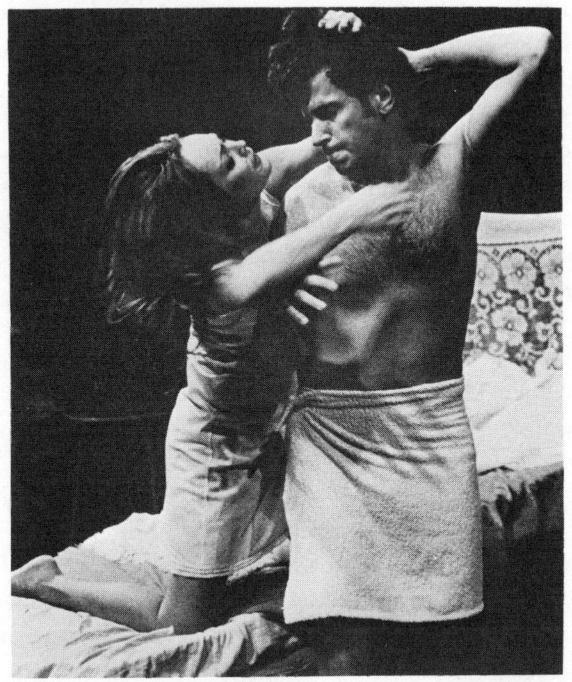

Daliah Friedland as Margaret and Elie Cohen as Brick in Michael Meacham's production of Tennessee Williams's *Cat on a Hot Tin Roof* (1973).

Hachnasat Kala (*A Bridal Canopy*) by S. Y. Agnon, the noted Hebrew writer and Nobel Prize winner.

The category of universal plays was more varied; it consisted of classical, modern, boulevard, and avant-garde plays. It is of interest to mention that none of the classical plays either succeeded artistically or was acceptable to the audience. Among the classical plays that failed were Strindberg's *A Dream Play* (1971), Marlowe's *Doctor Faustus* (1973), Shakespeare's *The Merry Wives of Windsor* (1973), and Büchner's *Danton's Death* (1974). The group of modern plays was rather successful, artistically speaking. It included David Storey's *Home* (1972); two plays by Tennessee Williams, *The Rose Tattoo* (1971) and *Cat on a Hot Tin Roof* (1973); and O'Neill's *Long Day's Journey into Night* (1974).[4]

Finkel was committed to a repertory theater and gave priority to the acting ensemble, at times at the expense of the other components of a successful production, such as the literary merit of the play and the staging. His first principle in building the Habima's repertoire was full employment and satisfaction of the actors.[5] Finkel soon faced a serious dilemma: if he selected repertoire with dramaturgical and literary considerations playing the decisive role, he encountered difficulties in obtaining adequate artistic manpower and risked inferior performance. On the other hand, if he chose plays on the basis of the availability of artistic manpower, he found it difficult to put together an interesting and well-balanced repertoire and risked public criticism. Generally speaking, Finkel gave priority to the "how" over the "what."

The European and the American theaters are relatively free to choose their repertoires according to the merit of the plays, knowing that they will have no major difficulties in finding suitable directors and actors. In most Western countries there is an abundant supply of capable actors and directors. This situation does not exist in Israel; because of the very intensive theatrical activity and the popularity of theater, there has for many years been a serious shortage of actors and directors. The demand for acting and directing talent far exceeds the supply, particularly in the public theaters which have their own permanent ensembles. Only to a small extent is it possible to import guest directors. Because of the scarcity of these artistic "production factors," the Habima was not free to act as theaters abroad usually do, namely, to shape the repertoire principally on the basis of literary considerations.

Finkel chose plays primarily according to the available acting talent. For instance, the Habima refused for decades to present Tennessee Williams's plays because it believed that they were not "literary plays" and there were actors who opposed the ethics and morality that they represented. Until 1971, no play by Tennessee Williams was presented by the troupe. Finkel however, decided to mount *The Rose Tattoo* and *Cat on a Hot Tin Roof* because they provided good parts for the company's leading actors. Finkel was strongly committed to an actors' theater (in part, because he himself was an actor) and therefore built the repertoire around the leading actors of the troupe. Between 1970 and 1975, the theater revolved around a small group of six actors.[6]

Despite his shortcomings as Artistic Director, Finkel presented some excellent productions. Among his artistic highlights were the following Jewish and Israeli plays: *Hazoanim Shel Yafo* (*Gypsies of Jaffa*) by Nissim Aloni, Israel's foremost playwright, in 1971 (107 performances);

Yosef Yzraely's adaptation of Agnon's *A Bridal Canopy,* with Yzraely's brilliant staging, in 1972 (159 performances); *Ho, Ho, Julia* by Ephraim Kishon, Israel's foremost humorist, in 1973 (251 performances), a satire on Shakespeare's *Romeo and Juliet;* and, most successful of all, Aaron Wolfsohn's satire *Al Kalut Daat Utzviut* (*On Frivolity and Hyprocrisy*) in 1974 (319 performances). The last play was written in Old Hebrew in 1776 during the Haskala (Enlightenment) movement in Germany and ridiculed shtetl superstition. It was directed by Omri Nitzan, a young Israeli director who was trained in London, in the commedia dell'arte style with elements of the Purim Shpiel and so had a special appeal among young audiences.

The most popular productions, Israeli and universal, were comedies, the kind of fare ordinarily presented by commercial theaters. Especially noteworthy were the British comedy on marriage and adultery by Alan Ayckbourn *Relatively Speaking* (1971), with 165 performances, and the Brazilian satire on religious hypocrisy *The Dog's Will* (or *The Virgin's Game*), staged brilliantly by Yosef Millo in 1972, with 187 performances.

A scene from Nissim Aloni's Hebrew play *Eddie King* (1975), a modern play based on *Oedipus Rex.*

The Israeli audience, like most audiences in the world, is attracted to comedies and melodramas. The drama critics, however, were harsh to both plays. Their criticism was similar to that leveled at the Habima in the early sixties, when it presented *Gigi* and *Irma La Douce*. The critics' contention was that the National Theater should by no means present this light repertoire. But, as in the past, the audience completely ignored the drama critics and proved again that it preferred well-staged and well-acted comedies and melodramas to poor or mediocre productions of serious and classical plays.

The Habima presented comedies and melodramas not merely because of the absence of complete financial support (the annual subsidy amounts to two-thirds of the theater's budget), but because Finkel believed that the troupe, as Israel's National Theater, should serve all social strata, not only the intelligentsia and the upper classes. The repertoire that he chose was highly varied because it had to serve an audience heterogeneous in terms of ethnic origin, education, and income. Therefore, Finkel supported a "flexible, popular, and opportunistic repertoire."[7] In addition, Finkel maintained that a varied repertoire was the best guarantee of the actors' artistic development.

Finkel went too far in his policy. In his last season, 1974–1975, the Habima underwent a metamorphosis and became a producing organization with one premiere after another, indistinguishable in taste and style from other theaters. Plays were chosen for leading actors regardless of their literary or dramatic quality. Finkel's eclectic policy fortified the critics' view that the Habima lacked a discernible platform and a specific artistic identity. The theater encountered hostile public opinion that resented the fact that the troupe received a very substantial subsidy from the government and yet presented such an uninteresting repertoire. The critics correctly maintained that it was not enough to present plays by Marlowe, Pinter, or Albee; it was more important what particular plays by these writers were presented and in what artistic style they were staged and acted.

It is of interest to mention that in June 1973, at the end of Finkel's first term as Artistic Director, a group of eight young artists submitted a proposal to the Habima's Board of Trustees, suggesting that they take over the theater's artistic direction. This group included three stage directors (David Levin, Edna Shavit, and Yosef Yzraely—all three had staged at the Habima); two drama critics (Boaz Evron of *Yediot Acharonot* and Moshe Nathan of *Maariv*); and three playwrights (Yosef Bar-Yosef, Hanoch Levin, and Yaakov Shabtai). The group suggested a collective direction, with Evron serving as Artistic Director.

The "Group of Eight" wanted to take over the Habima's direction because of its large pool of acting talent and its substantial subsidy. They did not merely want to replace Finkel, but to establish a new kind of artistic policy. Their main contention was that both the theater's successes and failures were accidental because they did not stem from a clearly defined artistic program. The group's main idea was to establish an interdependence between the processes of repertoire planning, producing, and directing. To this end they brought writers of their own who would write, translate, and adapt. Members of this group did not complain of not getting work at the Habima, but rather that their work there was insignificant and inconsequential because it lacked a permanent frame and continuity.[8]

The proposal of the group was rejected outright by the Board of Trustees for several reasons. First, the Board was skeptical of collective managements, especially after it took so long to dissolve the actors' collective. The Board assumed correctly that this collective direction would not last long. Second, and perhaps more importantly, the Board and the actors feared that this group of ambitious artists would first serve their own needs and only then the theater's and the actors' needs.[9] The truth was that the actors were strongly opposed to the group, partly because they did not consider its members great artists. Some of the group members had done some excellent experimental work but they were far from established artists. The Board and actors believed that if these artists wanted to achieve their revolutionary artistic ideas, let them establish a theater of their own. Why risk the Habima, the country's oldest and most established theater?

However, the next Habima's Artistic Director was Yosef Yzraely, one of the leaders of the "Group of Eight." It seems that the Board realized reluctantly that the "Group of Eight" represented the country's future artistic leaders. Here, as in the case of actors, the demand for first-rate directors exceeded the supply and this often resulted in Israeli directors undertaking artistic tasks which were beyond their capabilities. This held true for Yzraely when he assumed his important position in 1975.

Yzraely was born in Jerusalem in 1939 and was a graduate of the Royal Academy of Dramatic Arts in London and the Carnegie-Mellon Institute in the United States. He had directed in most Israeli theaters, including the Habima. Yzraely was an interesting director and rather experimental in his approach, which was affected by the work of Peter Brook and Peter Stein. Among the highlights of his career were Ostrovsky's *Enough Stupidity in Every Wise Man*, Strindberg's *Creditors*, the modern Hassidic production *Only Fools Are Sad*, and Agnon's *A Bridal Canopy*. However, all the classical plays that he directed failed, including Ibsen's *Peer Gynt* and Shakespeare's *The Merchant of Venice*.

Yzraely was appointed Artistic Director for three years. Shlomo Bar-Shavit, the Habima's best actor, was appointed Vice–Artistic Director. His function was to serve as a liaison between Yzraely and the actors, some of whom had strongly opposed Yzraely from the very start. The artistic management consisted of Yzraely, Bar-Shavit, and two staff directors, David Levin (also a member of the "Group of Eight") who excelled in his staging of *The Chairs*, and Omri Nitzan, the young director trained in London who had produced the smash hit *On Frivolity and Hypocrisy*.

The expectations for Yzraely, as a young, Israeli-born, experimental director, were great. Yzraely's artistic line was "to return to the sources, i.e., Jewish tradition and Israeli drama." He believed that the role of the Habima, as Israel's National Theater, was to focus on contemporary Israeli drama supplemented by the Jewish literary tradition. In his opinion, the Habima's mission was "to continuously examine the Israeli identity and the world we live in." This was a particularly important function because of the theater's operation in a society in which there was a "double strangeness": on the one hand, the Israelis are like "tourists" within Western culture; on the other hand, they are still "guests" in their indigeneous culture. Yzraely wanted both continuity and change: "continuity in the Habima's actors, and change in taste, method, and conception."[10]

Unfortunately, Yzraely disappointed the Board, the actors, and the public in the first season that he planned, 1975–1976. The repertoire that he chose and the subsequent artistic work revealed the disparity between his interesting theoretical ideas and practice. In contrast to his manifest artistic line, only three of the eight plays that were presented were Jewish and Israeli. The first was Sholem Aleichem's *The Treasure*, a mediocre production that was only a shadow of the Habima's brilliant 1928 staging of the play. The other two were not interesting or important plays. Yzraely presented Allen Ginsberg's 1960 autobiographical drama, *Kaddish*, and *Hagag* (The Roof), a contemporary melodrama by a young playwright. None of these plays succeeded artistically or with the audience (see Appendix 2).

Furthermore, the two plays that Yzraely himself staged, Ibsen's *The Enemy of the People* and Max Brod's adaptation of Kafka's *The Castle*, totally failed. The only plays that were successes during this season were Brecht's *Mother Courage* (because of Lia Konig's outstanding performance in the title role), and Labiche's farce *The Italian Straw Hat*, under Omri Nitzan's dynamic staging.

The Habima troupe in Labiche's comedy *The Italian Straw Hat* (1976).

The next season that Yzraely planned, 1976–1977, was neither different nor better. Again, the repertoire was eclectic, a mixture of classical and modern plays. The theater mounted Shakespeare's *Richard III* and Brecht's *The Good Person of Szechuan*, both average productions, and a revival of Albee's *Who's Afraid of Virginia Woolf?* In addition to the failure of the repertoire, Yzraely soon reached an impasse in his relations with the actors, who were dissatisfied with his approach and policy. Yzraely's plans and ideas remained unfulfilled and he had to resign, less than two years after he had assumed his position. Yzraely was succeeded by his Vice–Artistic Director, Shalomo Bar-Shavit, for one year, at the end of which the Board appointed David Levin, one of the resident directors, as the Habima's next Artistic Director.

The Habima as a National Theater

The fact that the Habima has had four Artistic Directors in the short period of eight years and that none of them succeeded—despite the fact that they represented different artistic platforms and tastes—is indicative of the serious problems faced by the Habima in terms of artistic leadership. The Habima's major problem today is its lack of a clear conception of the mission of Israel's National Theater in the seventies. This problem is actually not a new one, though it is more severe and urgent at present than it was ten or twenty years ago. Phrased differently, the Habima's problem at present derives from its lack of a specific and definite artistic identity.

Until the late forties and the establishment of Israel, the Habima was a repertory theater based on ensemble acting (in the real sense of the term) and was committed to a national Jewish repertoire. Most of the plays presented were distinctively Jewish and this special type of repertoire was used as a means of creating and strengthening a sense of national solidarity and consciousness. The Habima was an essential instrument in the country's attempt to gain national stature. However, in the early fifties, as a result of the changes that took place in both the demographic and theatrical structure of the country (the emergence of new audiences and new theaters), the Habima lost its distinctive identity, in terms of both content and style, and became just one of Israel's many theaters, indistinguishable from them in terms of repertoire or producing style.

It is noteworthy that when Tyrone Guthrie staged his second production at the Habima, *The Merchant of Venice* in 1959 (the first was *Oedipus Rex* in 1947), he observed that "the Habima, like everything else in the country, was greatly changed. It was far less Russian and far younger." Guthrie went on to say:

> Something in my opinion, has been lost in the gradual dilution of the company's very Russian individuality. The new productions are more up to date and, in most respects, much more efficient. But they are more like the productions of any other theater. . . . The reforms have been inevitable; but at the present time the Habima has lost its old distinctive style and has not yet found a new one.[11]

Guthrie's observation is true today even more than it was in the past. The Habima's lack of specific artistic profile is especially apparent when it is compared to other repertory theaters in Israel. At present, Israel's theatrical map is composed of five subsidized repertory theaters, all touring companies with permanent ensembles of actors. These are the Habima, Israel's National Theater; the Cameri, the Municipal Theater of Tel-Aviv; the Haifa Municipal Theater; the Chan Theater in Jerusalem; and the Beer-Sheva Municipal Theater. In addition to these public repertory theaters, there are a number of private producers, most of whom specialize in musicals, revues, comedies, etc.

The Cameri, the Habima's major competitor, is now Israel's most popular theater. Its repertoire consists for the most part of universal plays, mainly English and American, with few Israeli (not Jewish) plays. Trying to reach the largest potential audiences, the Cameri's repertoire is rather commercial, and its style of production quite popular. This troupe has a good ensemble of actors and its level of professionalism is high. Most of the performances are given in Tel-Aviv, although the theater also tours.

The Haifa Municipal Theater is the most "Israeli" theater in the sense that it devotes itself to the development and presentation of contemporary Israeli drama more than does any other theater. Its Israeli repertoire amounts to over one-third of its entire repertoire (at the Habima, it is less than one-fifth, and much lower at the other theaters). The Haifa theater adopted this policy in 1970, when Oded Kotler, a young actor and director, was appointed Artistic Director. Another feature which distinguishes this troupe from the other theaters is that it works with resident writers and directors. Its major shortcoming is the lack of a sufficient number of gifted and professional actors.

The Municipal Theater of Beer-Sheva lacks a distinctive artistic identity, being Israel's newest theater. Its repertoire, like that of the Cameri, consists of non-Jewish plays. However, the Beer-Sheva theater performs a highly important function; it serves as the cultural center of this city, Israel's fourth major city, and of the Negev, the southern part of the country.

There are two theaters in Jerusalem: the Jerusalem Theater, built by and named after its patron, Sherover, and the Chan Theater. The Jerusalem Theater does not have a permanent troupe of actors and, in fact, serves as a theater house for individual guest performances (not only for other theatrical companies). The Chan, by contrast, has a distinctive artistic approach. Its ensemble consists of a small group of young and extremely talented artists, and it is, in fact, Israel's youngest theatrical troupe. Their work is usually experimental in both content and style. This group worked for several years with Michael Alfreds, an excellent English director, who produced one of Israel's best productions in recent years, *The Servant of Two Masters.* The Chan constitutes almost the entire "off-Broadway" of Israel.

In comparison to these public theaters, each of which has a discernible artistic approach, the Habima, trying to compete with them, presents a repertoire which is a mixture of all of them. There is only one exception (though a minor one): the Habima presents more Jewish plays than the other theaters. But the Habima should be significantly different from all other theaters in both its repertoire and producing style (as it had been until 1948). As Israel's National Theater, it should not merely be distinguishable in taste, method, and acting style but should also strive to serve as their model. Eclectic policy and unevenness in artistic work should not be permitted at the Habima. Furthermore, since the Habima is not guided by any clearly defined artistic policy, it is difficult to assess its success and, more importantly, to determine whether or not it fulfills its goals as a National Theater.

There are many different concepts of the "National Theater"; its meaning varying from one country to another. National Theaters can be distinguished by two criteria: first, their attitude toward native and national drama and literature and, second, their attitude toward the audience. Variations in the origins and purposes of National Theaters account for their different attitudes.

The National Theater of France, the Comédie Française, is the oldest National Theater in the world; it was officially established in 1680 by Louis XIV. Its founding purpose was to preserve the traditional classical plays, particularly the works of Corneille, Racine, and Molière. This theater has survived three hundred years of social, political, and artistic changes. It has always served as a monument to French literary and theatrical achievements. Tradition and stylized acting were emphasized at the expense of progress in playwriting, in acting, and in production. Indeed, as one observer noted, "the weight of tradition is . . . burdensome, as it tends to stress the old merely because it is old and rejects the new for the same reason."[12] However, in France there are several national theaters that are subsidized by the state, not all of them located in Paris. Especially noteworthy is the TNF, the Théâtre National Populaire, established in 1951, which is committed to the aim of public art education and maintains a policy of low ticket prices. Still, the common purpose of the National Theater branches is to make the great French classics available to people from every region and income group.

The British National Theater (formerly the Old Vic), established officially in the late forties, presents another type of National Theater. This theater does not present only English drama. It presents a broad spectrum of the world's best drama and is always on the highest level of professionalism. Seriousness of artistic purpose, high standards, and efficient management are the characteristics of this theater. Therefore, it is considered an honor as well as a national service to play at the National Theater at financial sacrifices. London's West End theaters offer much better salaries. The Royal Shakespeare Company can also be considered a National Theater. This troupe is devoted to preserving in performance the artistic integrity of Shakespeare's lifework. Its headquarters are in Stratford, Shakespeare's birthplace, but the theater maintains branches in London, too. The performances of this theater are distinguished by textual fidelity: Shakespeare's word remains sacrosanct.

It should be noted that in both France and England, the National Theaters were based on impressive literary and dramatic traditions. The Habima, however, is more similar to the Irish and Czech national theaters than to the French and English. Its cause received an impetus from a body of very pronounced political and national attitudes and its origin can be traced to a strong national consciousness. The purpose and development of the Habima, the Abbey Theatre, and the Czech National Theater stem from a combination of cultural and political motives. In all three societies, the nationalist movement involved a revival of native language and literature in which the theater has played an important role.

However, unlike many other National Theaters, when the Habima was established (and, to a certain extent, even at present) it did not have access to literary and dramatic traditions equal to those enjoyed by France, England, and Ireland, nor did the Habima have a native literary tradition (in Hebrew) to preserve and transmit from generation to generation. The Hebrew language was not spoken and Hebrew drama was nonexistent. Furthermore, the problem of the Habima as Israel's National Theater stems from the rather unique social and cultural make-up of the country. In Israel, the need for a popular and varied repertoire is greater than in other countries because the theater-going public is much less elitist in its educational and social composition than are European or American audiences.

In addition, unlike the English-speaking theater, for instance, which is at an advantage in being able to pool its dramatic resources, the Hebrew theater has no such opportunities. The American theater would be much poorer if it had not been able to draw upon Bernard Shaw, Shakespeare, Marlowe, and O'Casey. The Habima—and the Hebrew theater—must be content with translation, which is much more than translating the script; it requires the translation of spirit, conventions, manners, etc.

At present, the Habima does not present enough Hebrew plays. The proportion of Jewish and Israeli drama should amount to more than one-fifth of the entire repertoire. The Habima was always more concerned with its actors than with its writers or directors, and therefore it fell far short of its goal as a National Theater in developing and stimulating "grass-roots" drama. The presentation of Jewish and Israeli drama is especially important in Israel because it is an immigrants' society. The Habima must present the past to a people unaware of its history and national culture. This calls for commissioning plays on Jewish themes and adapting to the stage the great Jewish literary works, many originally written in Yiddish.

This does not mean that the Habima should present only Jewish and Israeli repertoire. It rather means that the Habima should produce good plays ordinarily not accepted by the other theaters. The theater should keep alive the classical heritage, Jewish and universal, and call the audience's attention to new forces in the world theater. Rather than imitating other theaters and being a mixture of all of them, the Habima should strive to establish its own distinctive identity and be different from all the other Israeli theaters in both content and artistic form. The end result should be that the audience will become able to distinguish a Habima production from productions of other theaters in the same way that English audiences can distinguish between a production of the National Theater or the Royal Shakespeare Company from productions of the West End theaters.

The Habima's attitude toward its audience is not less important than its attitude toward indigenous drama and literature. A common characteristic of National Theaters is that they are subsidized by the state in order to provide inexpensive tickets to their populace. In some countries, the National Theater approximates a nation-wide operation through its regional structure (it has branches outside of the capital) and touring companies. In Norway, for instance, there is a distinct state traveling theater. Indeed, the National Theater should not only serve the needs of the country's capital or large cities, but also theatrical needs throughout the country.

Unfortunately, ever since the Habima became a state-subsidized theater, it stopped being a nation-wide operation (as it had been until the sixties) and there has been a continuous decline in its audiences. Despite the fact that it receives a substantial subsidy from the government, the ticket prices are not cheaper than those of other theaters, and it tours the country less extensively than do other companies. In the season of 1973–1974, for instance, the Habima gave 539 performances of which 82 (15 percent) were given outside of Tel-Aviv. In the 1975–1976 season, out of a total of 604 performances, only 54 (9 percent) were given outside of its home.[13] Furthermore, most of these performances were given in other large cities, like Jerusalem and Haifa, which have theaters of their own, and only few were given in the kibbutzim, small towns, and border and development areas. By contrast, in the fifties, almost half of the Habima's performances were given outside of Tel-Aviv, and in the sixties they amounted to one-fourth of its total appearances.

Moreover, there has been a continuous decline in the total number of performances given per season and in audience attendance. The best season in recent years was 1974–1975, during which the theater gave 626 performances. On the average, the Habima gives between 460 and 620 performances per season (in three halls).[14] This number equals the number of performances given by the Habima in the late fifties, when it performed in only one hall and, more importantly, when Israel's population was half of its current size. The Habima's audience at present is half of its size ten or twenty years ago. In recent years attendance has ranged from 200,000 to 250,000, equaling the same audience the Habima had in the forties.[15] Moreover, in the late fifties and sixties, the Habima could reach an audience of 400,000 to half a million people, twice as large as today's audience.

The Habima had a subscription system for a short time. Two years ago, subscription was reestablished, but not enough is done to develop new audiences, particularly among the younger generation. The subscription audience is highly important not merely because of the small but steady income that it guarantees, but because it provides for a regular contact between the theater and its audience.

The first house of the Habima theater, opened in 1945.

The second (renovated) house of the Habima, opened in 1958.

As long as the Habima was a nation-wide operation, a popular and conservative repertoire was understandable. But at present, since it does not tour and its operation is limited to Tel-Aviv, it could at least become somewhat more daring in subject matter, style, and technique. Instead of serving as a cultural stimulus for the city, the Habima is reflecting the most settled and backward of tastes. Thus, the theater falls short of fulfilling two of its important goals as a National Theater: being a nation-wide operation and presenting a high-level repertoire.

The publicly owned theaters have still not acquired the sound financial basis promised to them. Civic leaders serving as the theater's trustees are now demanding that the government and the municipalities ensure the theaters' financial health. In spite of the obvious need for larger support, subsidies do not seem to be a cure-all and there is always the danger that their main effect will be to reinforce the status quo. The problems of the Habima as Israel's National Theater are not financial problems. They are not even, in a sense, problems of the theater; they are problems of society. The major question is what kind of National Theater society needs and wants, and this question of policy should not be left to the actors or to the Artistic Director (whoever he is) to decide. If the Habima is a real public theater, then public officials should participate actively in determining its artistic goals and the means to achieve them.

The third and current house of the Habima, opened in 1970.

The interior of the Big Hall (seating 1,000 people) of the Habima.

Conclusion

THIS study of the Habima as the Hebrew national theater described and analyzed the causes, patterns, and consequences of the Habima's development from its foundation in Moscow in 1917 to the present.

The history and development of the Habima theater paralleled in many respects those of the Zionist movement. The Habima was founded in Russia in 1917, several months prior to the Balfour Declaration affirming the Jewish people's right to establish a Jewish national home in Palestine. The 1920s were the formative years—in many respects the most important period—of both the theater and the Jewish community of Palestine. In the 1930s and 1940s both the Habima and the Jewish community of Palestine grew in size and strength. In 1948, with the establishment of the independent State of Israel, a new era began for the newly born state and for the Habima.

The importance of the Habima theater is to be ascribed not to its distinctive artistic style, but rather to its success in a venture in which many of its predecessors had failed, namely, the institutionalization of a permanent Hebrew art theater. Indeed, one of the Habima's greatest contributions was its success in establishing and institutionalizing both a Hebrew art theater and the role of the Hebrew actor. This new role had ideological and artistic ramifications: the actors conceived of themselves as contemporary prophets, as emissaries of the Zionist philosophy and Hebrew language who employed artistic rather than political means.

More specifically, the Habima's innovations were four: a strong commitment to perform exclusively in Hebrew, an ideologically oriented repertoire focusing on biblical and national plays, extremely serious and high-level artistic work, and a permanent organization in the form of an actors' collective.

In examining the social, historical, and cultural setting of Russia in the twenties within which the theater operated, some unfavorable conditions, such as the lack of a Jewish audience and the illegality of the Hebrew language and Zionism have been noted. But despite these negative factors, the Habima's institutionalization and legitimate existence in Moscow was made possible by the enlightened and tolerant policy of the Russian regime toward the theater, the official recognition of the Habima as a Soviet state theater, and, most important of all, by the social and moral support of the Russian cultural elite and the training of the Habima by the best teachers in Moscow. The Habima was able to institutionalize its innovative venture because of peculiarities of the Russian political and cultural setting on the one hand, and the actors' single-minded devotion to the cause on the other.

The strong emphasis upon thorough and systematic professional training and upon high-level artistic standards set the Habima off from both amateur Hebrew- and Yiddish-speaking troupes. The Habima's members professionalized the role of the Hebrew actor: they were professionally trained; they maintained standards of excellence in performance and production; and they were engaged in full-time theatrical activity. Indeed, the Habima's members were the first to consider themselves professional Hebrew actors, and the first to be so identified by the larger society.

The development of a Hebrew art theater occurred in Russia, and not in Palestine, because Russia provided the sociocultural and professional conditions for that development. A Hebrew art theater did not—and could not—become institutionalized in Palestine in the first two decades of this century because of the lack of theatrical tradition and knowledge and the absence of a group of people who were consciously willing to identify themselves as practitioners of the acting profession. Moreover, in Palestine theatrical and artistic activities were not important values in their own right and did not constitute integral parts of the culture.

The process of institutionalization that the Habima underwent from 1917 on had a specific pattern and consequences; the term secularization best describes this process. Broadly defined, secularization refers to the process by which sectors of society and culture are removed from the domination of religious institutions and values. Secularization "affects the totality of cultural life and of ideation, and may be observed in the decline of religious content in the arts, in philosophy, in literature."[1]

The Habima's secularization took place on three levels: ideational, symbolic, and organizational.[2] The ideational level concerns the Habima's ideology and repertoire. The symbolic level concerns the members' mode of participation in the theater as well as the audience's relation to the theater. The organizational level concerns the Habima's organizational structure.

Secularization on the Ideational Level

The Habima's secularization on the ideational level was reflected in the gradual decline in the salience of specifically Jewish (biblical, Messianic, and national) ideas and a corresponding rise in the importance of artistic considerations as the determinants of the theater's artistic policy and the content of its repertoire. More specifically, there are four indicators of the Habima's secularization on the ideational level. First, there was a gradual decline in the proportion of Jewish plays presented by the theater; second, a secular change in the contents of those Jewish plays presented in the different periods; third, a gradual decline in the percentage of the representation of the two Jewish languages—Hebrew and Yiddish; and fourth, a change in the language employed by the actors on stage.

The decline in the percentage of specifically Jewish plays in the repertoire indicated the increasing importance of artistic considerations (at the expense of ideological considerations) in guiding the theater's artistic policy. In the Moscow period, the Jewish plays constituted 84 percent of the entire repertoire; in the transitional period 75 percent; in the Palestinian period 55 percent; and in the Israeli period only 27 percent. At present, the Jewish plays constitute approximately one-fifth of the entire repertoire.

The Habima had been founded as an ideologically oriented theater, a theater of "prophetic pathos" and "sacred attitude," to use Bialik's words. The theater's repertoire in Moscow had been compatible with its original ideological mission. The Moscow plays had stressed the eternal Jewish quest for the Messiah and the yearning for national redemption. In comparison with the Moscow plays, the Jewish plays presented in Palestine were, for the most part, of two kinds: shtetl plays and plays that concerned the problem of maintaining Jewishness in the Diaspora. Many people in Palestine strongly opposed the choice of Yiddish shtetl plays; they particularly objected to the serious and naturalistic interpretation of these plays and to the depiction of the ghetto in nostalgic and sentimental terms. In Israel, the Habima's Jewish plays were of yet a different kind. Although intimately Israeli and written in Hebrew, these plays were secular, topical, and realistic. They concerned contemporary problems of Israeli society, such as the decline of the kibbutz and patriotism and the issue of absorbing and integrating the various immigrants who were coming to Israel.

The Habima's secularization and transformation from an ideologically oriented and specifically Jewish theater into a universal, modern one was also reflected in the company's most popular productions in each of the different periods. In Moscow, the popular plays were *The Dybbuk* and *The Golem;* in the transitional period, *Uriel Acosta;* in Palestine, *Tevye the Dairyman* and *Mirele Efros*. But in Israel, the most popular productions were, for the most part, universal and modern, such as *Lost in the Stars*, *Irma La Douce*, and *A Dog's Will*.

The decrease in the percentage of plays written in the two Jewish languages also serves as an indication of the Habima's secularization. In Moscow, 4 of the 6 plays (66 percent) were written in Yiddish and Hebrew. In Palestine, 30 of the 79 plays (38 percent) were written in these two languages; in Israel, only 33 out of 146 plays (23 percent).

Finally, the language spoken by the Habima actors on stage also underwent a process of secularization. The creation of the Habima involved, as had been mentioned, a linguistic revolution; as an outgrowth of the Zionist movement, the theater regarded as one of its most important missions the revival and dissemination of the Hebrew language among the Jewish people. But since Hebrew was almost a dead language and there was no available model for spoken Hebrew, the actors had to invent it. Therefore, the language which the Habima players used on stage was not really a spoken language; it was rather a stylized sacred Hebrew but it fitted perfectly the biblical and Messianic plays that they presented.

When the Habima settled in Palestine, the Hebrew language used by the actors became more and more secularized, especially when the theater began to present non-Jewish universal plays in Hebrew translation. Thus, when the troupe presented its first universal classic play, *Twelfth Night* (1930), it proved that the world's great drama could be successfully presented in modern Hebrew. After the establishment of the Israeli state, the language of the theater became extremely secularized. The new on-stage language reflected the emergence of a new, Hebrew-speaking generation and a new genre of Hebrew-Israeli plays. These plays adopted the patterns of a living, spoken Hebrew; they virtually copied the language of the street and used the jargon of the period—especially the language of the army, the youth movements, and the kibbutzim. Thus, unlike former periods, there was now no differentiation between the language spoken on stage and off.

The growing importance of artistic over ideological considerations and the Habima's deviation from its original ideological mission were the unanticipated consequences of changes within the theater and changes in the values of the theater's surroundings. On the whole, the Habima's secularization on the ideational level meant that the theater could no longer justify its existence in political and ideological terms as it had done in Moscow and in the early period in Palestine. Furthermore, this secularization was an indication of the Habima's full institutionalization. A social activity is fully institutionalized when it is "widely accepted as a value in its own right."[3] Indeed, the Habima came to regard itself, and to be regarded, as an important value in its own right. Ideas such as "theater for theater's sake" that had been rejected by the founding group were now regarded by both the theater and the larger society as legitimate values.

Secularization on the Symbolic Level

The secularization on the symbolic level involved changes in the internal as well as in the public image of the Habima. In Moscow, the theater had displayed many characteristics of an ideological group; involvement in the theater was total and all-inclusive. Members were required to divest themselves of all personal and family interests.[4] The Habima actors attributed sacred qualities to their studio; they saw it as a temple, where the actors—like priests—were dedicated to the mastery of their art. For the founding group, work at the theater was more than a job; it was a sacred task, a calling. Consequently, the major rewards for this work were intrinsic: self-realization and the great honor of being the first Hebrew actors. The Moscow group lived for rather than off of the theater,[5] and it strongly opposed material rewards, careerism, and fame—all important in other theaters.

However, the aging of the Moscow members, the changing values of the theater's social surroundings, and the inclusion of new and young actors led to a shift in basic attitudes toward the theater. In later years, the mode of the members' participation was secularized. Involvement in the theater became restricted, and there was a clear line of demarcation between life in and outside the theater. Gradually, being a Habima actor became just one segment in the status set of those working in the theater—and not necessarily the most salient segment.

It seems that the Habima's secularization was interrelated with a broader process of routinization.[6] The Habima began its operation as a charismatic movement; it was innovative, revolutionary, and tremendously exciting. Like other charismatic movements, it operated at an extremely high emotional pitch. The Moscow period, though very short (it lasted only eight years), was the Habima's charismatic and most significant phase. These were the formative years in which the theater's artistic and organizational foundations were established, and they had lasting psychological and social effects on the members and on the troupe.

However, charisma never lasts. Indeed, every charismatic movement has a transitory nature; after its success, it must find stable forms of organization that will secure its orderly continuation.[7] The demise of the Habima's charismatic period began as soon as the theater left Russia, and was especially clear by the time it settled permanently in Palestine in 1931. However, as long as the original founding generation participated actively in the theater's work (until the late forties), the charismatic elements of the theater could sustain themselves, if not on the basis of the members' present experience, then at least on the memories of their great experiences and the excitement of the past.

The charismatic elements, and especially the mode of participation and relation to the theater, changed drastically when the Habima's second generation of actors began to perform. This new and younger generation had not participated in the great events of the formative years. They only knew these events through the stories of their elders. That which to the first generation had been truly extraordinary and exciting became in the second generation part of the ordinary and the routine; this included the existence of the theater. Furthermore, the younger generation could not relate to the theater emotionally, ethically, or religiously in the same way as the founding members had because it had grown up in a completely different social and cultural setting. Consequently, there was a generation gap between the veteran (Moscow) and the younger (Israeli) actors, each group representing a distinct generational unit.

In addition, routinization was made inevitable by the very fact that the Habima ceased to be an exotic phenomenon as soon as it had established itself as an ongoing activity. In Moscow, the theater prepared six plays in a period of eight years. The preparation of each play was therefore prolonged and emotionally exciting. In later years, the preparation of new plays became routine and could no longer involve the emotional and religious attitude of the Moscow years. The theater's routinization was also apparent in the orderly rehearsals for each play (with a pattern of six to eight weeks of preparation) and nightly performances—two routines that had not prevailed in Moscow.

Lastly, changes in the mode of participation were also a result of the process of aging. Excitement, total involvement, and single-minded devotion are all characteristics of unattached youth, as the Habima's founding members had themselves been in the Russian period of the theater's history.

Secularization took place not only in the actors' relation to the theater, but also in the audience's relation to the theater. In Russia, the Jewish audiences had related to the Habima as a wonder, because it was the only place where one could publicly hear or speak Hebrew without risking arrest. When the Habima settled in Palestine, the emotional attitude toward the theater continued to prevail, but the sheer fact that it performed exclusively in Hebrew was not the only criterion for judging its activities, nor was it a sufficient cause for glorifying it. The audience's relation to the theater consisted of a judgment both of its artistic achievements and of how well it performed its national mission. However, since the Habima was the major cultural institution and the best theater in Palestine, audiences used to attend the theater even when its productions were not as good or as interesting as they might desire. It was a norm to attend the Habima, a norm that was all the more significant because the Jewish community of Palestine was not a sovereign entity. Attending the theater in the Yishuv period was, therefore, much more than a form of entertainment.

The most significant change in the audience's attitude toward the Habima occurred with the establishment of Israel in 1948, when the relation to the theater became more rational and pragmatic than emotional. This took place as a result of changes in the country's institutional and demographic setting. In the first place, a new Israeli generation came of age, a generation that had been raised in Palestine and therefore found the Habima's Yiddish and romantic plays and its artistic style alien to Israeli culture. In addition, with the establishment of the new state a large influx of immigrants from Asia and Africa came to Israel, immigrants who had never before attended the theater. For these two audiences—which constituted the majority of the country's population after 1948—the Habima did not have the same symbolic meaning that it had had in the past. The new Israeli generation went to see a Habima production only when it was an artistic achievement. Its judgment of the troupe was rational, and was based primarily on artistic, not on symbolic or ideological, considerations. Furthermore, attending the theater (not merely the Habima) was no longer a sacred norm; the theater had become a totally secular form of entertainment, deprived of the national and ideological meaning that it had had in the past.

Furthermore, with the establishment of the Cameri theater and its public image as "the theater of the youth," the Habima, for the first time in its history, had a fierce competitor. The Cameri's popularity meant that the Habima became only one of Israel's theaters, and not always the best. The Cameri had a tremendous impact, both artistic and social, on the Habima, and the competition with this theater involved a total reassessment of the Habima's artistic policy and style of production. This reassessment resulted in a further adjustment to the surrounding reality, another step in the theater's secularization.

Secularization on the Organizational Level

The Habima's secularization also involved a structural differentiation of status and function. The theater's growth in size and complexity was accompanied by bureaucratization, increasing inner differentiation, and functional specificity.

In Moscow, the actors had participated actively in both the physical and symbolic creation of the theater. The Habima had been founded as a community-centered theater, an actors' cooperative. Collectivism, equality, and fraternity had been the theater's central values. Until 1948, the actors' collective was the ultimate authority in the theater; all issues (artistic, administrative, and financial) were discussed and resolved by majority vote at the general assembly of the collective. Thus, there was little structural differentiation of authority between the collective and the Board of Directors.

Following the 1948 crisis, the actors' collective no longer had ultimate power; the management was now in the hands of an elected board, and there was a clear line of demarcation between the authority of the collective and that of the Board of Directors. Indeed, the Habima's secularization on the organizational level was gradual but thorough; tasks and functions that formerly were shared equally by all members in a rather diffuse way were gradually transferred to specific and specialized organizational bodies.

In 1968, the actors' cooperative was dissolved. After half a century of active involvement in the direction of the theater, the actors' chief responsibility was now only to perform. With the recognition of the Habima as Israel's State Theater a further bureaucratization took place. The Habima became a public trusteeship, with a Board of Trustees, a General Director, an Artistic Director, and an Administrative Director, all appointed by the government.

The actors' collective had had both functions and dysfunctions. The collectivist discipline and asceticism that the cooperative had imposed on every individual member had definitely contributed to the theater's survival in the difficult economic and cultural conditions that had prevailed in Palestine. But the collective also had unintended disruptive consequences for the theater's operation. The cooperative, which had been established to administer the theater, came to acquire the dynamics of every bureaucracy; it brought about a situation in which the attention of many members shifted from the goals of the theater to the means that they themselves had developed. Adherence to the rules of the collective—especially to the principles of casting and selecting plays and to the rules of artistic and financial equality—had disruptive consequences for the theater's artistic development.[8]

In later years, when it became clear that the collective was no longer capable of directing the Habima, there were still many actors who opposed its dissolution. Again the Habima followed the dynamics of bureaucracies; the vested interests of many actors (especially the aged and the less able) increasingly diverted attention from the overall interests of the theater.

The dissolution of the Habima's collective after half a century of existence signified a crucial point in the theater's history because the collective had been one of the theater's distinctive features. There are no other theater groups in the world that have performed continuously and successfully for half a century without any kind of permanent support, private or public. Indeed, in spite of its inappropriateness for and incompatibility with the theater's size, complexity, and problems, it was this particular structure that saved the Habima from demise.

The greatest challenge of the Habima theater at present is to maintain its vitality and to adapt itself to a rapidly changing society. The theater has to assure its continuity and vitality in the face of new demands, new theaters, new audiences, and new artistic values.

Appendixes

Appendix 1
Members of the Habima Actors' Collective: 1917–1968

Name	*Year of Birth*	*Country of Origin*	*Admission into the Theater*	*Admission into the Collective*	*Year of Leaving*	*Year of Death*
Amitai, Chaim	1898	Lithuania	1932	1944		1973
Asherov, Misha	1924	Russia	1946	1956		
Avivit, Shoshana			1918	1918	1925	
Azikri, Nissim	1939	Bulgaria	1961	1966		
Banai, Yosef	1933	Israel	1954	1960	1962	
Baratz, Avraham	1894	Russia	1924	1924		1952
Bar-Shavit, Shlomo	1928	Israel	1947	1953		
Becker, Israel	1917	Poland	1948	1954		
Ben-Ari, Raikin		Russia	1921	1921	1927	1970
Ben-Chaim, Zvi	1898	Ukraine	1920	1920		1957
Ben-Zissi, Fordhaus	1896	Russia	1929	1946	1965	
Bertonov, Yehoshua	1879	Lithuania	1922	1922		1971
Binyamini, Menachem	1898	Poland	1927	1929		1959
Buchman, Nachum	1917	Russia	1940	1953		
Brook, Shlomo	1899	Ukraine	1920	1920		
Chechik, Efrati			1922	1922	1927	
Chemerinsky, Baruch	1892	Ukraine	1920	1920		1946
David, Baruch	1928	Bulgaria	1953	1966		
Duer, Shoshana	1912	Syria	1932	1947		
Edelmann, Chava			1920	1920	1927	
Efroni, Yehuda	1931	Israel	1951	1965		
Elias, Miriam			1918	1918	1924	
Factorovich, Elisheva						
Finkel, Bat-Ami	1906	Ukraine	1934	1947		
Finkel, Shimon	1905	Russia	1928	1929		

Appendix 1 (*continued*)

Name	*Year of Birth*	*Country of Origin*	*Admission into the Theater*	*Admission into the Collective*	*Year of Leaving*	*Year of Death*
Friedland, Daliah	1936	Israel	1954	1965		
Friedland, Zvi	1898	Ukraine	1920	1920	1966	1967
Friedman, Shraga	1924	Poland	1947	1953		1970
Gnessin, Menachem	1882	Poland	1917	1917, 1928	1923	1951
Goldina, Miriam (Zemach)		Russia	1920	1920	1927	
Golland, Yitzhak	1901		1922	1922	1927	
Govinskaia, Inna	1894	Russia	1920	1920		1957
Grober, Chayele		Russia	1917	1917	1927	
Halevi, Moshe	1895	Russia	1918	1918	1925	1974
Hendler, Channele	1901	Russia	1919	1919	1965	
Hiskiyahu, Avner	1926	Bulgaria	1953	1960	1962	
Itkin, David	1892		1919	1919	1927	
Kahn, Shlomo			1918	1918	1919	
Klutchkin, Raphael	1904	Russia	1928	1933		
Kutai, Ari	1900	Ukraine	1934	1946		
Lubich, Fanny	1903	Ukraine	1921	1921	1952	
Meskin, Aaron	1898	Russia	1919	1919		1974
Michaeli, Elisheva	1928	Israel	1955	1960	1965	
Ninio, Avraham	1918	Egypt	1939	1958		
Paduit, Aviva			1920	1920	1927	
Perach, Pnina	1922	Israel	1946	1953		
Persitz, Reuben			1918	1918	1925	
Prudkin, Alexander					1928	
Pudalowa, L.			1920	1920	1928	
Ravid, Shoshana	1925	Poland	1946	1953	1960	

Appendix 1 (*continued*)

Name	*Year of Birth*	*Country of Origin*	*Admission into the Theater*	*Admission into the Collective*	*Year of Leaving*	*Year of Death*
Raphael, Zvi	1898	Russia	1918	1918	1925	
Robintchik, Israel	1921	Poland	1957	1966		
Robins, Tamar	1898	Ukraine	1917, 1920	1920	1965	
Rodan, Yosef			1950	1960		
Rovina, Hanna	1888	Russia	1917	1917		
Rozen, Zvi	1911			1960		
Rubinstein, Yehuda	1890	Ukraine	1920	1920		1969
Rodensky, Shmuel	1902	Poland	1949	1953		
Schneider, Bath-Ami			1920	1920	1927	
Schneider, Benno					1927	
Segal, Shmuel	1924	Poland	1945	1953		
Shein, Niora	1902	Russia	1932	1946	1965	
Sherf, Asher	1932	Romania	1949	1962		
Tal, Ada	1921	Russia	1940	1953		
Vardi, Chava (Yoelit)			1919	1919	1923	
Vardi, David	1893	Ukraine	1917, 1938	1917, 1946	1923	1973
Viniar, Eliahu			1917	1917	1932	
Viniar, Nechama			1918	1918	1932	
Warshawer, Ari	1898	Russia	1920	1920		
Yudelevich, Tmima	1892	Poland	1918	1918	1965	1967
Zemach, Binyamin	1902	Russia	1919	1919	1927	
Zemach, Nachum	1887	Russia	1917	1917	1927	1939
Zemach, Shifra (Barakas)		Russia	1919	1919	1927	
Zohar, Miriam	1929	Romania	1951	1954		

Appendix 2
The Habima Repertoire: 1918–1978

Play	Playwright	Director	Date of Presentation	Number of Performances
1. *Neshef Bereshit* (Evening of Beginning)		E. Vakhtangov	Oct. 8, 1918	104
a. The Eldest Sister	S. Asch			
b. The Hot Sun	I. Katzenelson			
c. The Fire	I. L. Peretz			
d. The Bone	I. D. Berkowitz			
2. *The Eternal Jew*	D. Pinski	V. Mchedelov	Dec. 1919	
2a. *The Eternal Jew* (new production)	D. Pinski	V. Mchedelov	June 5, 1923	304
3. *The Dybbuk*	S. Anski	E. Vakhtangov	Jan. 31, 1922	1,000+
4. *The Golem*	H. Leivik	B. Vershilov	Mar. 15, 1925	340
5. *Jacob's Dream*	R. Beer-Hoffman	B. Suchkevitch	Nov. 1925	90
6. *The Flood*	H. Berger	B. Vershilov	Dec. 1925	45
7. *The Treasure*	S. Aleichem	A. Diki	Nov. 29, 1928	120
8. *David's Crown*	Calderón de la Barca	A. Diki	May 23, 1929	125
9. *Twelfth Night*	W. Shakespeare	M. Chekhov	Sept. 15, 1930	87
10. *Uriel Acosta*	K. Gutzkow	A. Granovsky	Sept. 24, 1930	182
11. *The Devil's Disciple*	G. B. Shaw	Z. Friedland	July 1, 1931	22
12. *The Sacred Flame*	S. Maugham	E. Viniar	July 2, 1931	112
13. *Chains*	H. Leivik	B. Chemerinsky	Dec. 16, 1931	126
14. *Tartuffe*	Molière	Y. Bertonov and A. Baratz	Feb. 27, 1932	37

NOTE: English translations of titles not italicized unless play was published in English.

Appendix 2 (*continued*)

Play	Playwright	Director	Date of Presentation	Number of Performances
15. *Periphery*	F. Langer	Z. Friedland	May 10, 1932	65
16. *Amcha*	S. Aleichem	Z. Friedland and B. Chemerinsky	Nov. 24, 1932	157
17. *Yom Shishi Hakatzar* (The Short Friday)	C. N. Bialik	B. Chemerinsky	Jan. 9, 1933	162
18. *Rahab*	H. Sackler	B. Chemerinsky	May 11, 1933	30
19. *The Jew Suess*	L. Feuchtwanger	Z. Friedland	July 26, 1933	88
20. *Three Thieves*	H. Notari	Z. Friedland	Dec. 16, 1933	29
21. *Oto Veet Bno* (Him and His Son)	I. D. Berkowitz	B. Chemerinsky	Jan. 30, 1934	32
22. *Witchcraft*	S. Aleichem	B. Chemerinsky	Apr. 30, 1934	85
23. *Wolves*	R. Rolland	Z. Friedland	May 16, 1934	30
24. *Professor Mannheim*	H. Wolf	L. Lindberg	July 25, 1934	68
25. *The Imaginary Invalid*	Molière	L. Lindberg	Aug. 11, 1934	31
26. *Igeret Uriah* (Uriah's Letter)	E. Bernhard	Z. Friedland	Jan. 13, 1935	23
27. *The Inspector-General*	N. Gogol	Z. Friedland	Mar. 23, 1935	41
28. Green Fields	P. Hirschbein	L. Lindberg	June 30, 1935	153
29. *The Golem's Dream*	H. Leivik	L. Lindberg	Aug. 1935	37
30. *Four Generations*	L. Cohen Van Delft	Z. Friedland	Nov. 25, 1935	42
31. *Upon a Fiddle*	S. Aleichem	B. Chemerinsky	Dec. 17, 1935	176
32. *Loyalties*	J. Galsworthy	Z. Friedland	Feb. 17, 1936	13
33. *Love on the Dole*	R. Gow and W. Greenwood	B. Chemerinsky	Mar. 23, 1936	16
34. *The Merchant of Venice*	W. Shakespeare	L. Jessner	May 14, 1936	42

NOTE: English translations of titles not italicized unless play was published in English.

Appendix 2 (*continued*)

Play	Playwright	Director	Date of Presentation	Number of Performances
35. *Belail Ze* (This Night)	N. Bistritzki	Z. Friedland	June 3, 1936	6
36. *Hacheshbon Haacharon* (The Last Account)	N. Sokolov	B. Chemerinsky	June 14, 1936	4
37. *Wilhelm Tell*	F. Schiller	L. Jessner	July 18, 1936	19
38. *It Is Hard to Be a Jew*	S. Aleichem	Z. Friedland	Dec. 12, 1936	113
39. *The Travels of Benjamin the Third*	Mendele mocher sforim	B. Chemerinsky and A. Baratz	Mar. 25, 1937	17
40. *Bury the Dead*	I. Shaw	Z. Friedland	May 4, 1937	56
41. *Shomrim* (Watchmen)	E. Hadani	Z. Friedland	Aug. 24, 1937	22
42. *The White Plague*	K. Čapek	B. Chemerinsky	Sept. 28, 1938	45
43. *Fathers and Sons*	W. Warner	Z. Friedland	Oct. 30, 1938	84
44. *The Marranos*	M. Zweig	Z. Friedland	Dec. 27, 1938	81
45. *The Cherry Orchard*	A. Chekhov	Z. Friedland	Mar. 28, 1939	22
46. *In Kasrilevka*	S. Aleichem	B. Chemerinsky	May 28, 1939	22
47. *Mirele Efros*	J. Gordin	Z. Friedland	July 19, 1939	228
48. *Who Is Who*	H. Leivik	B. Chemerinsky	Aug. 7, 1939	17
49. *The Mother*	K. Čapek	Z. Friedland	Dec. 3, 1939	107
50. *The Smith's Daughters*	P. Hirschbein	Y. Bertonov	Jan. 13, 1940	28
51. *Pillars of Society*	H. Ibsen	Z. Friedland	Oct. 3, 1940	20
52. *Reubeni, Prince of the Jews*	M. Brod	Z. Friedland	June 1, 1940	36
53. *Family Tangle*	W. Leon	A. Baratz	July 25, 1940	24
54. *My Son the Minister*	A. Birabeau	Z. Friedland	Aug. 26, 1940	50

NOTE: English translations of titles not italicized unless play was published in English.

Appendix 2 (*continued*)

Play	Playwright	Director	Date of Presentation	Number of Performances
55. *God, Man and the Devil*	J. Gordin	B. Chemerinsky	Oct. 15, 1940	33
56. *Glorius, the Miracle*	W. Warner	Z. Friedland	Dec. 14, 1940	27
57. *Michal Bat Saul* (Michal, Daughter of Saul)	A. Ashman	B. Chemerinsky	Jan. 11, 1941	142
58. *Jerusalem and Rome*	N. Bistritzki	Z. Friedland	Mar. 26, 1941	42
59. *The Guilty Innocent*	A. Ostrovsky	Y. Bertonov	Apr. 26, 1941	32
60. *Graduation*	L. Fodor	Z. Friedland	July 12, 1941	110
61. *The Merchant of Warsaw*	R. Branstaetter	B. Chemerinsky	Oct. 27, 1941	31
62. *The Rape of the Sabine Women*	P. von Schoenthan	Z. Friedland	Nov. 23, 1941	31
63. *Two Worlds*	M. Zweig	B. Chemerinsky	Jan. 18, 1942	27
64. *The Concert*	H. Bahr	Z. Friedland	Mar. 8, 1942	28
65. *Crime and Punishment*	F. Dostoevsky/Levinson	Z. Friedland	Apr. 25, 1942	91
66. *Haadama Hazot* (This Earth)	A. Ashman	B. Chemerinsky	Sept. 19, 1942	213
67. *Morning Star*	E. Williams	Z. Friedland	Nov. 28, 1942	48
68. *Men of Russia* (The Russian People)	K. Simonov	Z. Friedland	Apr. 3, 1943	80
69. *Jephtha's Daughter*	K. Boschvitz	B. Chemerinsky	June 26, 1943	42
70. *Tevye the Dairyman*	S. Aleichem	B. Chemerinsky	Dec. 25, 1943	277
71. *I Will Live*	D. Bergelson	Z. Friedland	May 6, 1944	59
72. *Banim Ligvulam* (The Return of the Sons)	A. Beilin	Z. Friedland	Dec. 24, 1944	69
73. *Phèdre*	J. Racine	Z. Friedland	Apr. 28, 1945	52
74. *Marriage*	N. Gogol	Y. Bertonov	July 15, 1945	27

NOTE: English translations of titles not italicized unless play was published in English.

Appendix 2 (*continued*)

Play	Playwright	Director	Date of Presentation	Number of Performances
75. *Warsaw*	S. Asch	Z. Friedland	Nov. 25, 1945	42
76. *Habsora* (The Annunciation)	A. Ashman	Y. Bertonov	Mar. 17, 1946	29
77. *Hamlet*	W. Shakespeare	Z. Friedland	May 26, 1946	55
78. *The Flood*	H. Berger	Z. Friedland	July 14, 1946	19
79. *The Dreyfus Affair*	H. J. Rehfisch and Z. Herzog	Z. Friedland	Dec. 1, 1946	24
80. *The Admirable Crichton*	J. M. Barrie	A. Baratz	Jan. 12, 1947	17
81. *Oedipus Rex*	Sophocles	T. Guthrie	Feb. 9, 1947	55
82. *The Heine Family*	S. Groneman	S. Finkel	Apr. 13, 1947	24
83. *Bamitbach* (Kitchen Folk)	S. Aleichem	Y. Bertonov	June 15, 1947	29
84. *Ahavat Zion* (The Love of Zion)	A. Mapu	Z. Friedland	July 15, 1947	101
85. *Ghosts*	H. Ibsen	S. Finkel	Sept. 16, 1947	55
86. *Kiddush Hashem* (Martyrdom)	S. Asch	Z. Friedland	Dec. 23, 1947	29
87. *Day and Night*	S. Anski	S. Finkel	Jan. 25, 1948	51
88. *Outward Bound*	S. Vane	Z. Friedland	Mar. 2, 1948	17
89. *Noah*	A. Obey	S. Finkel	Mar. 31, 1948	16
90. *Bearvot Hanegev* (In the Wastes of the Negev)	Y. Mossinson	S. Finkel	Feb. 10, 1949	227
91. *Saul*	M. Zweig	S. Finkel	May 7, 1949	9
92. *A Midsummer Night's Dream*	W. Shakespeare	J. Gellner	May 25, 1949	121
93. *Montserrat* (*Hostages*)	E. Robles	H. Clurman	July 4, 1949	90

NOTE: English translations of titles not italicized unless play was published in English.

Appendix 2 (*continued*)

Play	Playwright	Director	Date of Presentation	Number of Performances
94. *Ahavat Neurim* (Young Love)	A. Ashman	A. Baratz	Oct. 20, 1949	43
95. *Barbara Blumberg*	C. Zuckmayer	E. Shenlank	Dec. 11, 1949	21
96. *The Silver Whistle*	R. A. McEnroe	S. Finkel	Jan. 15, 1950	28
97. *Othello*	W. Shakespeare	J. Gellner	Mar. 5, 1950	100
98. *Our Town*	T. Wilder	E. Shenlank	Mar. 26, 1950	33
99. *Beketz Hayamim* (At the End of the Days)	C. Hazaz	S. Finkel	June 15, 1950	12
100. *I Rusteghi* (*The Obstinate*)	C. Goldoni	Z. Friedland	July 27, 1950	30
101. *Miss Mabel*	R. C. Sheriff	S. Finkel	Oct. 26, 1950	29
102. *Bet Hillel* (The House of Hillel)	M. Shamir	Z. Friedland	Dec. 3, 1950	64
103. *The Sheep Well*	Lope De Vega	M. Halevi	Jan. 22, 1951	25
104. *Death of a Salesman*	A. Miller	J. Gellner	Mar. 4, 1951	111
105. *The Marriage of Figaro*	Beaumarchais	J. Gellner	Apr. 1, 1951	55
106. *The Legend of the River* (*The Siren*)	A. Casona	A. Ninio	May 20, 1951	32
107. *Mother Courage*	B. Brecht	L. Lindberg	July 15, 1951	45
108. *The House of Bernarda Alba*	F. G. Lorca	L. Strasberg	Oct. 7, 1951	10
109. *The Little Foxes*	L. Hellman	Z. Friedland	Nov. 11, 1951	24
110. *Baderech Leeilat* (On the Way to Eilat)	A. Megged	S. Friedman	Dec. 5, 1951	39
111. *The Father*	A. Strindberg	S. Finkel	Jan. 6, 1952	40
112. *The Taming of the Shrew*	W. Shakespeare	J. Gellner	Mar. 6, 1952	35
113. *The Fortress*	E. Robles	Z. Friedland	May 14, 1952	22

NOTE: English translations of titles not italicized unless play was published in English.

Appendix 2 (*continued*)

Play	Playwright	Director	Date of Presentation	Number of Performances
114. *Peer Gynt*	H. Ibsen	S. Malmquist	June 1, 1952	85
115. *Mother Nature*	A. Birabeau	A. Ninio	July 9, 1952	43
116. *The Story of a Soldier*	C.-F. Ramuz	R. Mordo	Aug. 30, 1952	13
117. *The Blue Bird*	M. Maeterlinck	R. Mordo	Oct. 6, 1952	107
118. *Ani Rav Hovel* (I, the Captain)	Yosh	I. Becker	Nov. 13, 1952	72
119. *The Physician in Spite of Himself*	Molière	R. Klutchkin	Dec. 25, 1952	24
120. *The Story of a Prince (Kabzensohn and Hungerman)*	A. Goldfaden/Licht	D. Licht	Jan. 25, 1953	45
121. *John Gabriel Borkman*	H. Ibsen	S. Finkel	Feb. 15, 1953	7
122. *Liliom*	F. Molnar	J. Gellner	Mar. 25, 1953	19
123. *Lost in the Stars*	M. Anderson/K. Weill	J. Gellner	Apr. 30, 1953	218
124. *Shmo Olech Lefanav* (His Name Precedes Him)	E. Kishon	I. Becker	July 29, 1953	118
125. *Caesar and Cleopatra*	G. B. Shaw	H. Clurman	Sept. 24, 1953	17
126. *Achzar Mikol Melech* (Most Cruel of All—the King)	N. Aloni	S. Friedman	Dec. 19, 1953	57
127. *The Living Corpse*	L. Tolstoy	I. Becker	Jan. 9, 1954	33
128. *Escapade*	R. MacDougal	A. Asseo	Feb. 6, 1954	68
129. *Lel Sufa* (Stormy Night)	M. Shamir	Z. Friedland	Mar. 22, 1954	55
130. *Macbeth*	W. Shakespeare	S. Malmquist	Apr. 18, 1954	50
131. *The Crucible*	A. Miller	A. Asseo	July 3, 1954	42
132. *Hedva Veani* (Hedva and I)	A. Megged	I. Becker	Sept. 29, 1954	112

NOTE: English translations of titles not italicized unless play was published in English.

Appendix 2 (*continued*)

Play	Playwright	Director	Date of Presentation	Number of Performances
133. *The Caine Mutiny Court Martial*	H. Wouk	P. Frye	Oct. 23, 1954	114
134. *The Wild Duck*	H. Ibsen	S. Malmquist	Dec. 5, 1954	21
135. *Agadat Shlosha Vearbaa* (The Tale of Three and Four)	C. N. Bialik	S. Friedman	Feb. 12, 1955	41
136. *The Teahouse of the August Moon*	J. Patrick	J. Gellner	Mar. 5, 1955	133
137. *King Lear*	W. Shakespeare	J. Gellner	Apr. 21, 1955	94
138. *The Conquerors*	P. A. Breal	A. Ninio	July 2, 1955	21
139. *Henry IV*	L. Pirandello	Z. Friedland	Oct. 15, 1955	31
140. *Medea*	Euripides/Jeffers	P. Frye	Nov. 5, 1955	99
141. *Pandre the Hero*	Z. Schneur	S. Finkel	Dec. 3, 1955	51
142. *Maayanna* (To the Spring)	M. Politi	I. Becker	Jan. 21, 1956	19
143. *Faust*	J. W. Goethe	J. Gellner	Mar. 15, 1956	25
144. *A View from the Bridge*	A. Miller	H. Kalus	Apr. 14, 1956	119
145. *Jets*	J. Roy	S. Friedman	June 27, 1956	25
146. *I Like Mike*	A. Megged	I. Becker	Aug. 23, 1956	127
147. *The Brothers Karamazov*	F. Dostoevsky/Coupeau	Z. Friedland	Oct. 6, 1956	28
148. *Shahor Al Gabei Lavan* (Black on White)	E. Kishon	Y. Zilberg	Dec. 29, 1956	51
149. *The Diary of Anne Frank*	F. Goodrich and A. Hackett	I. Becker	Jan. 22, 1957	179
150. *Anna Christie*	E. O'Neill	H. Kalus	Feb. 23, 1957	100

NOTE: English translations of titles not italicized unless play was published in English.

Appendix 2 (*continued*)

Play	Playwright	Director	Date of Presentation	Number of Performances
151. *Snonit Behof Mayomba* (A Swallow on the Shore of Mayomba)	Yosh	S. Friedman	June 11, 1957	61
152. *The Slaughter of the Innocents*	W. Saroyan	P. Frye	Oct. 10, 1957	22
153. *Thieves' Carnival*	J. Anouilh	H. Kalus	Oct. 26, 1957	33
154. *The Egg*	F. Marceau	A. Barsac	Dec. 7, 1957	167
155. *Zrok Oto Laklavim* (Throw Him to the Dogs)	Y. Mossinson	P. Frye	Jan. 18, 1958	54
156. *The Visions of Simone Machard*	B. Brecht	I. Becker	Mar. 15, 1958	52
157. *Hanna Szenes*	A. Megged	A. Asseo	May 31, 1958	115
158. *Shesh Knafaim Laechad* (Each Had Six Wings)	H. Bartov	A. Ninio	June 28, 1958	78
159. *Rehov Hamdregot* (The Street of Stairs)	Y. Hendel	I. Becker	Oct. 21, 1958	38
160. *Lysistrata*	Aristophanes	M. Volanakis	Dec. 17, 1958	53
161. *A Touch of the Poet*	E. O'Neill	P. Frye	Jan. 28, 1959	41
162. *The Merchant of Venice*	W. Shakespeare	T. Guthrie	Feb. 24, 1959	37
163. *Look Back in Anger*	J. Osborne	H. Kalus	Apr. 23, 1959	54
164. *The Trees Die Standing*	A. Casona	J. Shen	May 23, 1959	130
165. *Herr Biedermann*	M. Frisch	S. Friedman	June 17, 1959	40
166. *The Visit*	F. Duerrenmatt	Y. Millo	Oct. 17, 1959	134

NOTE: English translations of titles not italicized unless play was published in English.

Appendix 2 (*continued*)

Play	Playwright	Director	Date of Presentation	Number of Performances
167. *Twelve Angry Men*	R. Rose	A. Ninio	Dec. 12, 1959	136
168. *Agadat Shlosha Vearbaa* (The Tale of Three and Four)	C. N. Bialik	S. Friedman	Mar. 24, 1960	12
169. *Uncle Vanya*	A. Chekhov	J. Shen	Apr. 3, 1960	13
170. *Mademoiselle*	G. Duval	I. Becker	June 11, 1960	54
171. *The Threepenny Opera*	B. Brecht	Y. Millo	July 13, 1960	48
172. *A Long Day's Journey into Night*	E. O'Neill	H. Kalus	Nov. 1, 1960	33
173. *The Miracle Worker*	W. Gibson	A. Ninio	Dec. 3, 1960	170
174. *The Marriage of Mr. Mississippi*	F. Duerrenmatt	Z. Friedland	Jan. 4, 1961	20
175. *The Long, the Short and the Tall*	W. Hall	M. Asherov	Mar. 26, 1961	23
176. *Julius Caesar*	W. Shakespeare	P. Coe	July 1, 1961	29
177. *Gigi*	Colette	A. Ninio	Sept. 25, 1961	121
178. *Mrs. Warren's Profession*	G. B. Shaw	J. Cristoff	Oct. 16, 1961	22
179. *Bigdei Hamelech* (The Emperor's Clothes)	N. Aloni	N. Aloni	Dec. 9, 1961	37
180. *Herr Puntila and His Servant Matti*	B. Brecht	S. Bunim	Jan. 14, 1962	14
181. *Inherit the Wind*	J. Lawrence and R. E. Lee	J. Gellner	Mar. 3, 1962	48
182. *Emil and the Detectives*	E. Kaestner/J. Gellner	J. Gellner and M. Sigley	Mar. 20, 1962	44

NOTE: English translations of titles not italicized unless play was published in English.

Appendix 2 (*continued*)

Play	Playwright	Director	Date of Presentation	Number of Performances
183. *The Queen and the Rebels*	U. Betti	M. Golan	Mar. 24, 1962	7
184. *The Age of the Innocent*	Z. Lenz	E. Moskovitz	May 2, 1962	18
185. *Isle of Aphrodite*	A. Parniss	A. Kabachnik	June 30, 1962	25
186. *Bereshit* (Genesis)	A. Megged	A. Kabachnik	July 11, 1962	233
187. *Dira Lehaskir* (A Flat to Let)	S. Bar-Shavit	I. Becker	Sept. 22, 1962	90
188. *Irma La Douce*	A. Breffort and M. Monnot	A. Ninio	Nov. 6, 1962	242
189. *Yaldei Hatzel* (Children of the Shadow)	B.-Z. Tomer	I. Becker	Nov. 28, 1962	206
190. *War and Peace*	L. Tolstoy/ E. Piscator	J. Gellner	Dec. 17, 1962	38
191. *The Physicists*	F. Duerrenmatt	A. Ninio	Mar. 23, 1963	77
192. *Right You Are if You Think You Are*	L. Pirandello	J. Gellner	May 18, 1963	120
193. *Exit the King*	E. Ionesco	E. Debel	Oct. 12, 1963	42
194. *Photo Finish*	P. Ustinov	A. Asseo	Oct. 19, 1963	180
195. *Billy Liar*	W. Hall and K. Waterhouse	L. Filer	Dec. 19, 1963	74
196. *Requiem for a Nun*	W. Faulkner/ A. Camus	A. Asseo	Apr. 25, 1964	52
197. *La Parisienne*	H. Becque	Y. Zilberg	June 13, 1964	76
198. *The Deputy*	R. Hochhuth	A. Ninio	June 16, 1964	126
199. *Masa Lenineveh* (A Journey to Nineveh)	Y. Amichai	J. Gellner	July 21, 1964	38

NOTE: English translations of titles not italicized unless play was published in English.

Appendix 2 (*continued*)

Play	Playwright	Director	Date of Presentation	Number of Performances
200. *The Mother*	K. Čapek	Z. Friedland	Sept. 21, 1964	112
201. *The Comedy of Errors*	W. Shakespeare	E. Debel	Oct. 10, 1964	97
202. *Miss Julie*	A. Strindberg	R. Morgan	Dec. 1, 1964	54
203. *The Lover*	H. Pinter	R. Morgan	Dec. 1, 1964	54
204. *Blues for Mister Charlie*	J. Baldwin	A. Ninio	Jan. 17, 1965	67
205. *Who's Afraid of Virginia Woolf?*	E. Albee	H. Kalus	Feb. 11, 1965	219
206. *The Sunset*	I. Babel	S. Friedman	Mar. 8, 1965	36
207. *A Sleep of Prisoners*	C. Fry	Y. Zilberg	May 16, 1965	18
208. *It Is Hard to Be a Jew*	S. Aleichem	A. Ninio	June 23, 1965	80
209. *Sunday in New York*	N. Krasna	Y. Zilberg	Aug. 8, 1965	80
210. *Mishpat Pythagoras* (The Tale of Pythagoras)	N. Alterman	S. Friedman	Aug. 24, 1965	14
211. *Le malentendu*	A. Camus	E. Debel	Oct. 25, 1965	38
212. *Hashchuna* (The Neighborhood)	Y. Bar-Nathan	Y. Rodan	Nov. 18, 1965	116
213. *Diary of a Madman*	N. Gogol/T. Atar	Z. Friedland	Nov. 20, 1965	10
214. *Oliver!*	L. Bart	P. Coe	Jan. 17, 1966	58
215. *Le mal court* (*Border Encounter*)	J. Audiberti	M. Almaz	Jan. 19, 1966	25
216. *The Subject Was Roses*	F. Gilroy	A. Ninio	May 4, 1966	39
217. *Itzik Wittenberg*	C. Rosenfarb	I. Becker	May 7, 1966	16
218. *Tonight Ionesco*	E. Ionesco	D. Bergman	May 22, 1966	23
a. *The New Tenant*				
b. *A Maid to Marry*				

NOTE: English translations of titles not italicized unless play was published in English.

Appendix 2 (*continued*)

Play	Playwright	Director	*Date of Presentation*	*Number of Performances*
c. *Improvisation*				
d. *Nightmare for Two*				
219. *Othello*	W. Shakespeare	P. Drumgol	Sept. 10, 1966	97
220. *Nathan the Wise*	G. E. Lessing	P. Frye	Oct. 8, 1966	27
221. *Enchanted Night* and *Death Sentence*	S. Mrozek J. Krasinsky	R. Morgan	Oct. 30, 1966	63
222. *The Maids*	J. Genet	M. Almaz	Nov. 26, 1966	25
223. *Haona Haboeret* (The High Season)	A. Megged	A. Kabachnik	Jan. 13, 1967	39
224. *Haadama Hazot* (This Earth)	A. Ashman	Y. Rodan	Jan. 16, 1967	46
225. *Tango*	S. Mrozek	A. Bardini	Mar. 7, 1967	96
226. *A Lilly of Little India*	D. Howarth	A. Ninio	Apr. 6, 1967	18
227. *A Flea in Her Ear*	G. Feydeau	P. Drumgol	Aug. 2, 1967	64
228. *The Promise*	A. Arbusov	R. Morgan	Aug. 15, 1967	130
229. *Becket*	J. Anouilh	H. Kalus	Nov. 1967	94
230. *Two by Two*	A. Leakum	R. Morgan	Dec. 1967	45
231. *Separate Tables*	T. Rattigan	J. Gellner	Jan. 1968	62
232. *Point H*	Y. Jamiaque	D. Levin	Mar. 1968	43
233. *Célimare the Beloved*	E. Labiche	N. Kessel	June 1968	43
234. *The Dance of Death*	A. Strindberg	M. Shfarver	June 1968	23
235. *Ot beeretz Haplaot* (Letters in Wonderland)	U. Offek	M. Sigley	Aug. 1968	110
236. *Little Murders*	J. Feiffer	A. David	Oct. 1968	35
237. *Waiting for Godot*	S. Beckett	Y. Yzraely	Dec. 1968	62

NOTE: English translations of titles not italicized unless play was published in English.

Appendix 2 (*continued*)

Play	Playwright	Director	Date of Presentation	Number of Performances
238. *Doda Liza* (Aunt Liza)	N. Aloni	N. Aloni	Jan. 1969	88
239. *Blithe Spirit*	N. Coward	D. Harper	Feb. 1969	20
240. *Shimshon*	Y. Mossinson	D. Levin	Mar. 1969	20
241. *Volpone*	B. Jonson	D. William	Apr. 1969	50
242. *Six Characters in Search of an Author*	L. Pirandello	Y. Yzraely	Aug. 1969	109
243. *The Fantasticks*	T. Jones	M. Sigley	Oct. 25, 1969	[a]
244. *The Summer*	R. Wingarten	T. Toma	Jan. 1970	[a]
245. *Haloch Hazor* (Roundtrip)	I. Eliraz	A. Tamir	Feb. 1970	[a]
246. *The Seagull*	A. Chekhov	J. Hirsch	Mar. 1970	[a]
247. *Arturo Ui*	B. Brecht	M. Blackmore	Mar. 1970	[a]
248. *The Shoemaker's Holiday*	T. Dekker	D. William	Mar. 1970	[a]
249. *A Delicate Balance*	E. Albee	M. Meacham	Apr. 1970	103
250. *Celebration*	D. Storey	M. Meacham	June 1970	47
251. *Jimi*	B.-Z. Tomer	R. Miron	Aug. 1970	[a]
252. *Amélie*	G. Feydeau	T. Toma	Aug. 22, 1970	[a]
253. *Jews of Silence*	E. Wiesel	P. Frye	Nov. 11, 1970	106
254. *The Liar*	C. Goldoni	R. Miron	Nov. 21, 1970	75
255. *Akedat Yosef* (The Sacrifice of Joseph)	Y. Keniuk	Y. Keniuk	Nov. 21, 1970	17
256. *The Chairs*	E. Ionesco	D. Levin	Dec. 9, 1970	111
257. *Peer Gynt*	H. Ibsen	Y. Yzraely	Feb. 13, 1971	45
258. *The Rose Tattoo*	T. Williams	M. Meacham	Mar. 4, 1971	84
259. *Meever Lagvulin* (Beyond the Border)	I. H. Brener	Y. Mundy	Mar. 24, 1971	19

NOTE: English translations of titles not italicized unless play was published in English.
[a] No data.

Appendix 2 (*continued*)

Play	Playwright	Director	Date of Presentation	Number of Performances
260. *Saint Joan*	G. B. Shaw	M. Meacham	May 1, 1971	46
261. *Colombe*	J. Anouilh	T. Toma	June 19, 1971	54
262. *Relatively Speaking*	A. Ayckbourn	T. Jones	July 10, 1971	165
263. *Caligula*	A. Camus	E. Debel	Aug. 21, 1971	22
264. *Hazoanim shel Yafo* (The Gypsies of Jaffa)	N. Aloni	N. Aloni	Oct. 4, 1971	107
265. *Theodore*	E. Schneider	N. Nitai	Oct. 26, 1971	24
266. *The Architect and the Emperor*	F. Arrabal	D. Levin	Nov. 27, 1971	9
267. *A Dream Play*	A. Strindberg	S. Malmquist	Dec. 11, 1971	13
268. *Herod and Miriam*	F. Hebbel	A. Szafianski	Jan. 15, 1972	13
269. *Lel Haazmaut shel Mar Sheffi* (Mr. Sheffi's Independence Eve)	A. Raz	M. Asherov	Jan. 15, 1972	113
270. *Home*	D. Storey	M. Meacham	Feb. 26, 1972	35
271. *Stempeniu*	S. Aleichem	S. Bunim	Mar. 8, 1972	46
272. *A Dog's Will* (*The Virgin's Game*)	A. Suassuna	Y. Millo	May 13, 1972	187
273. *The Rockefeller Family*	R. D. Obaldia	R. Miron	June 3, 1972	11
274. *Picnic for Two*	A. Nicolaj	Z. Stolper	July 1, 1972	47
275. *Hachnasat Kala* (A Bridal Canopy)	S. Y. Agnon/Y. Yzraely	Y. Yzraely	Aug. 9, 1972	159
276. *Beketz Hayamim* (At the End of the Days)	C. Hazaz	D. Levin	Sept. 7, 1972	22
277. *What the Butler Saw*	J. Orton	T. Jones	Nov. 4, 1972	15
278. *Mazal Betula* (Virgo)	A. Chen	S. Atzmon	Nov. 21, 1972	37
279. *Tfos et Haganav* (To Catch a Thief)	Y. Lapid	N. Nitai	Jan. 6, 1973	72

NOTE: English translations of titles not italicized unless play was published in English.

Appendix 2 (*continued*)

Play	Playwright	Director	Date of Presentation	Number of Performances
280. *The Aspern Papers*	M. Redgrave	T. Jones	Feb. 10, 1973	46
281. *Everything in the Garden*	E. Albee	M. Meacham	Mar. 10, 1973	49
282. *Doctor Faustus*	C. Marlowe	A. Sachs	May 2, 1973	15
283. *Old Times*	H. Pinter	L. Schach	May 12, 1973	23
284. *Cat on a Hot Tin Roof*	T. Williams	M. Meacham	May 30, 1973	54
285. *The Merry Wives of Windsor*	W. Shakespeare	A. Asseo	July 14, 1973	40
286. *The Eternal Husband*	F. Dostoevsky W. Lieblein	E. Shavit	Sept. 15, 1973	35
287. *Shalom* (Peace)	Y. Bar-Yosef	D. Gidron	Oct. 18, 1973	92
288. *How the Other Half Loves*	A. Ayckbourn	M. Sperber	Dec. 8, 1973	68
289. *Ho, Ho, Julia*	E. Kishon	E. Kishon	Dec. 29, 1973	251
290. *Like a Tear in the Ocean*	M. Sperber	M. Sperber	Jan. 19, 1974	11
291. *Slamming Doors*	M. Fermaud	N. Michoels	Mar. 20, 1974	45
292. *Danton's Death*	G. Büchner	Y. Millo	June 6, 1974	17
293. *Catsplay*	I. Orkeny	H. Kaut-Howson	Sept. 1, 1974	43
294. *Hatuna* (A Wedding)	Y. Bar-Yosef	T. Levy	Sept. 7, 1974	53
295. *Long Day's Journey into Night*	E. O'Neill	M. Meacham	Oct. 19, 1974	82
296. *Macbett*	E. Ionesco	D. Bergman	Nov. 30, 1974	37
297. *Al Kalut Daat Utzviut* (On Frivolity and Hypocrisy)	A. Wolfsohn	O. Nitzan	Dec. 28, 1974	319
298. *The Day They Kidnapped the Pope*	J. Bethencourt	P. Frye	Mar. 8, 1975	38
299. *Hostages*	E. Robles	M. Asherov	May 10, 1975	83
300. *Eddie King*	N. Aloni	N. Aloni	May 15, 1975	42

NOTE: English translations of titles not italicized unless play was published in English.

Appendix 2 (*continued*)

Play	Playwright	Director	Date of Presentation	Number of Performances
301. *Dreyfus*	J. C. Grumberg	L. Schach	Aug. 9, 1975	13
302. *The Treasure*	S. Aleichem	O. Nitzan	Oct. 15, 1975	88
303. *Mother Courage*	B. Brecht	D. Levin	Nov. 1, 1975	114
304. *The Castle*	F. Kafka/M. Brod	Y. Yzraely	Jan. 1, 1976	22
305. *King John*	F. Duerrenmatt	D. Levin	Jan. 31, 1976	21
306. *Hagag* (The Roof)	H. Mitelpunkt	O. Nitzan	Mar. 31, 1976	49
307. *Kaddish*	A. Ginsberg	H. Snir	Apr. 24, 1976	31
308. *An Enemy of the People*	H. Ibsen	Y. Yzraely	May 15, 1976	25
309. *The Italian Straw Hat*	E. Labiche	O. Nitzan	July 31, 1976	138
310. *Who's Afraid of Virginia Woolf?*	E. Albee	H. Kalus	Nov. 13, 1976	82
311. *Richard III*	W. Shakespeare	D. Levin	Nov. 27, 1976	33
312. *Mei Tehom* (Deep Waters)	H. Mitelpunkt	O. Nitzan	Mar. 27, 1977	[a]
313. *The Good Person of Szechuan*	B. Brecht	D. Levin	1977	[a]
314. *Saturday, Sunday, Monday*	E. De Filippo	I. Eldad	1977	[a]
315. *The Imaginary Invalid*	Molière	C. Regy	1977	[a]
316. *D'You Know the Milky Way?*	K. Wittlinger	E. Shavit	1977	[a]
317. *Four Women*	P. Gems	H. K. Howson	1977	[a]
318. *Shmo Olech Lefanav* (His Name Precedes Him)	E. Kishon	A. David	Oct. 24, 1977	[a]
319. *Oedipus the King*	Sophocles	E. Shavit	Dec. 17, 1977	[a]
320. *The Kitchen*	A. Wesker	O. Nitzan	Jan. 26, 1978	[a]
321. *Woyzeck*	G. Büchner	D. Levin	Apr. 6, 1978	[a]
322. *A Midsummer Night's Dream*	W. Shakespeare	O. Nitzan	1978	[a]

NOTE: English translations of titles not italicized unless play was published in English.

[a] No data.

Appendix 3
Size of the Habima Actors' Collective: 1918–1968

Year	*Moscow Members*	*Palestinian Members*	*Israeli Members*	*Total Number*
1918	12			12
1922	40			40
1926	34			34
1927	21			21
1928	18	2		20
1932	16	2		18
1933	16	3		19
1944	16	4		20
1946	15	7		22
1947	16	9		25
1951	15	9		24
1952	13	9		22
1953	13	10	7	30
1954	13	10	9	32
1956	13	10	10	33
1957	11	10	10	31
1958	11	10	11	32
1959	11	9	11	31
1960	11	10	14	35
1962	11	10	13	34
1965	3	8	14	25
1966	3	8	17	28
1968	2	8	17	27

Notes

THIS BOOK is based on my doctoral dissertation ("The Theater as an Expression of Cultural and Political Nationalism—the Habima Theater, 1917–1968," Columbia University, 1977). Printing costs and the reader's convenience have, however, necessitated a considerable reduction in its annotation and documentation. The dissertation copy may be consulted in the Columbia University Library or through Microfilm Services, Ann Arbor, Michigan.

PREFACE

1. It may be useful to explain three terms used in this study. The term *national theater* (without capitals) signifies any theatrical art which is connected with political or nationalist movements. In this sense, the Habima had always been a national theater. The term *National Theater* (with capitals) denotes a theater that is officially recognized as such by the state. The Habima became Israel's National Theater in 1958. The term *state theater* denotes a theater that is fully or substantially financed by the state. In this sense, the Habima became Israel's State Theater in 1968, although its official title remained the National Theater Habima.

2. In this work, the term Palestine is used to describe the prestatehood period (1918–1948).

3. See, for instance, Merton, *Social Theory and Social Structure*, and Ben-David, *The Scientist's Role in Society*. I particularly follow Merton and Ben-David's institutional approach to the study of science as it is exemplified in Merton's earlier work *Science, Technology and Society in Seventeenth-Century England*. In this study, I follow Ben-David's approach to and definition of institutionalization: (1) the acceptance in a society of a certain activity as an important social function for its own sake; (2) the existence of norms that regulate conduct in the given field of activity in a manner consistent with the realization of its aims and with autonomy from other activities; and finally (3) some adaptation of social norms in other fields of activity to the norms of the given activity. On the whole, the institutional approach maintains that the social structure and social conditions of society determine its various fields of activity, such as science, art, etc.

4. For a further discussion of the differences between the sociological approach and that of the literary critic, see Burns, *Theatricality*, and Laurenson and Swingewood, *The Sociology of Literature*.

5. Quoted in Burns, *Theatricality*, pp. 5–6.

6. Huntley Carter, for instance, observed that "the Habima developed a method of production, and a technique of action which for originality, expressiveness and general power are among the most powerful and effective features in the New Theatre today." See *Russian Theatre*, p. 17. Clark and Freedly, in their *History of Modern Drama* wrote that "the Habima has established the reputation as one of the world's finest theatre collectives" (p. 636).

7. These reviews were collected from three major daily newspapers representing different political lines: *Haaretz*, established in 1917, representing the political center; *Davar*, established in 1925 by the Histadrut (the Israeli General Federation of Labor Unions) and later the official organ of Israel's Labor Party, representing the left of center; and *Yediot Acharonot*, the first evening newspaper of Palestine, established in 1937 and representing the right of center.

ONE: THE FOUNDING GROUP

1. See Norman, *Habima* (in Hebrew).

2. Interview with Binyamin Zemach, Zemach's brother and a Habima actor.

3. Norman, *Habima*, p. 34.

4. Bertonoff, *Curtain* (in Hebrew), pp. 55–56. Bertonov later joined the Habima in Moscow and became one of its leading actors.

5. M. Ungfeld, "The Moscow Theater Habima in Vienna," *Haaretz*, June 11, 1926.

6. Y. Bukstein, "Commemoration of Nachum Zemach," Zemach's file, the Habima Archive.

7. Bertonoff, *Curtain*, pp. 69–72.

8. Gnessin, *My Way* (in Hebrew).

9. From the by-laws of the Lovers of the Dramatic Art, quoted in Kohansky, *Hebrew Theatre*, p. 12.

10. Hanoch, *Habima* (in Hebrew), pp. 93–107; Rovina's file, the Habima Archive.

11. Talila Ben-Zakai, "The Theater Is My Life-Giving Drug: An Interview with Hanna Rovina," *Maariv*, September 20, 1974.

12. Gnessin, *My Way*, pp. 103–106.

13. Dubnov, *History of the Jews* 2: 400, 424.

14. Frumkin, Aronson, and Goldenwiser, *Russian Jewry*, pp. 96–114.
15. *Ibid.*, pp. 116–17.
16. Kochan, *Jews in Soviet Russia*, p. 101.
17. Norman, *Habima*, p. 151; Gnessin, *My Way*, p. 112.
18. Gnessin, *My Way*, pp. 112–13; Vardi, *On My Path* (in Hebrew), pp. 156–57.
19. Gnessin, *My Way*, p. 110.
20. Vardi, "On the Evening of Yom Kippur the Fate of the Habima was Determined," *Davar*, September 23, 1958.
21. Gnessin, *My Way*, p. 116.
22. Freeman, Kunitz, and Lozowick, *Voices of October*, p. 188.
23. In 1911 Stanislavsky formed the First Studio and, in 1916, the Second Studio. In 1921, a third and a fourth studio, as well as an operatic studio, were added. Functioning as schools, the studios were organized with a view to providing their members with as broad as possible a foundation in the various crafts of the art of the theater. All studios were under the personal supervision of Stanislavsky, who worked through a corps of men from the staff of the theater. See Stanislavsky, *My Life in Art*, pp. 413–14; Gorchakov, *Theater in Soviet Russia*, pp. 243–44.
24. Norman, *Habima*, p. 244; Kohansky, *Hebrew Theatre*, p. 30.
25. Norman, *Habima*, p. 157, quoted in Kohansky, *Hebrew Theatre*, p. 29.
26. Grober, *Both Sides*, (in Hebrew), pp. 69–71, 90.
27. Norman, *Habima*, pp. 60–61.
28. Hanoch, *Habima*, p. 122.
29. *Ibid.*, pp. 127–36; Bertonoff, *Curtain*, pp. 67–68.
30. Elon, *The Israelis*, p. 78; Madison, *Yiddish Literature*, p. 503.
31. Norman, *Habima*, p. 54.
32. Raphael Bashan, "Interview with Hanna Rovina," *Maariv*, September 6, 1964.
33. Hanoch, *Habima*, p. 153; interview with Tamar Robins, Habima actress.
34. The Habima members displayed many characteristics in common with the Jewish youth involved in Zionist politics. Elon discusses these characteristics in his *The Israelis*, p. 113.
35. See the definition of generations in Karl Mannheim, "The Problem of Generations," in his *Essays*, pp. 303–304.
36. Howe, *World of Our Fathers*, p. 16.
37. Erikson, *Young Man Luther*, p. 42.
38. Elon, *The Israelis*, pp. 78–79.
39. Bertonoff, *Curtain*, p. 77.
40. Norman, *Habima*, p. 205.
41. Hanoch, *Habima*, p. 24.
42. Howe, *World of Our Fathers*, p. 116.

TWO: IDEOLOGY AND REPERTOIRE: 1917–1926

1. Howe, *World of Our Fathers*, pp. 18–19.
2. Ashkenazic Jews are descendants of the Jews from Italy and France who settled in the Rhineland about one thousand years ago, migrating thereafter throughout Germany and Eastern Europe. Sephardic Jews are descendants of the Jews who were expelled from Spain and Portugal in the fifteenth century. The pronunciation of Hebrew differed in the two communities.

3. Norman, *Habima* (in Hebrew), p. 36.
4. Ben-Ari, *Habima,* pp. 132–33.
5. Leah Goldberg, "Problems of the Hebrew Theater," *Bamot* (August 1951), p. 10.
6. Ben-Ari, *Habima,* p. 235.
7. Norman, *Habima,* p. 181.
8. *Ibid.*, pp. 244–46.
9. Norman, *Habima,* p. 193.
10. *Ibid.*, p. 192.
11. Ben-Ari, *Habima,* p. 231.
12. Norman, *Habima,* pp. 34–35.
13. Vardi, *On My Path* (in Hebrew), p. 126.
14. Norman, *Habima,* pp. 35, 92.
15. Gnessin, *My Way* (in Hebrew), p. 115.
16. Norman, *Habima,* p. 151.
17. Ben-Ari, *Habima,* pp. 18–19.
18. Ibid., p. 246.
19. Gorchakov, *Theater in Soviet Russia,* pp. 20–52.
20. Lifson, *Yiddish Theatre,* pp. 285–86, 296.
21. Ben-Ari, *Habima,* p. 180.
22. Merton, *Social Theory and Social Structure,* p. 354.
23. Ben-Ari, *Habima,* p. 30.
24. *Ibid.*, p. 31.
25. *Ibid.*, Appendix 1, "Maxim Gorky on the Habima," pp. 239–40.
26. Kohansky, *Hebrew Theatre,* p. 45.
27. Ben-Ari, *Habima,* p. 110.
28. The Habima began to rehearse *The Dybbuk* before the production of *The Eternal Jew,* but because of Vakhtangov's serious illness this production was postponed.
29. Landis, *Great Jewish Plays,* pp. 15–16; Lifson, *Yiddish Theatre,* p. 257.
30. Anski did not live to see his play performed. The Vilna Troupe premiered *The Dybbuk* on December 9, 1920, at the end of the thirty-day period of mourning following Anski's death.
31. In describing the content of *The Dybbuk,* I draw on Yosef I. Yzraely, "Vakhtangov Directing *The Dybbuk,*" pp. 16–17.
32. Vardi, *On My Path,* p. 122.
33. Norman, *Habima,* p. 235.
34. Yzraely, "Vakhtangov Directing," p. 27.
35. *Ibid.*, pp. 59–90.
36. Ben-Ari, *Habima,* p. 140; Kohansky, *Hebrew Theatre,* p. 36.
37. Norman, *Habima,* pp. 263–65, quoted in Kohansky, *Hebrew Theatre,* p. 43.
38. Norman, *Habima,* p. 268, quoted in Kohansky, *Hebrew Theatre,* p. 44.
39. Norman, *Habima,* p. 291, quoted in Kohansky, *Hebrew Theatre,* p. 45.
40. Norman, *Habima,* pp. 281–82, quoted in Kohansky, *Hebrew Theatre,* pp. 45–46.
41. Naturalism in art is fidelity to nature or real life, an adherence to fact. Stanislavsky upheld this form, particularly in the plays of Chekhov. As Vakhtangov described it: "Stanislavsky demanded . . . that the audience forget that it is in the theatre, that it come to feel itself living in the atmosphere and milieu in which the characters of the play live." Cole and Chinoy, *Directors on Directing,* p. 185. Vakhtangov developed a different theatrical doctrine, "Fantastic Realism": "The correct theatrical means, when discovered, gives

to the author's work a true reality on the stage. One can study these means, but the form must be created, must be the product of the artist's great imagination-fantasy. This is why I call it 'Fantastic Realism'." Simonov, *Stanislavsky's Protégé*, p. 146.

42. In Berlin, this group of actors founded a Hebrew theater, the TAI (Teatron Eretz Israeli-Palestinian Theater). The theater was headed by Gnessin, after he left the Habima in 1923, and operated in Palestine between 1924 and 1927. When the Habima first came to Palestine, in 1928, Gnessin rejoined the troupe and several other actors joined as well.

43. Bernstein-Cohen, *Drop in the Sea* (in Hebrew), pp. 126–28; Kutai, *Life and Stage* (in Hebrew), p. 89.

44. Landis, *Great Jewish Plays*, pp. 220–22.

45. Kohansky, *Hebrew Theatre*, pp. 50–51.

46. Ben-Ari, *Habima*, p. 156.

THREE: THE SOCIAL CONTEXT: JEWISH AND RUSSIAN

1. Kochan, *Jews in Soviet Russia*, p. 81.

2. *Ibid.*, p. 77.

3. *Ibid.*, p. 104.

4. *Ibid.*

5. The Yevkom itself was dissolved in 1924, together with the People's Commissariat for National Affairs of which it was a subdivision. Six years later, in 1930, the Yevsektsia was dissolved.

6. Kochan, *Jews in Soviet Russia*, p. 217.

7. *Ibid.*, pp. 232–68; Liptzin, *Yiddish Literature*.

8. Picon-Vallin, *Le théâtre juif*, p. 59.

9. Kochan, *Jews in Soviet Russia*, p. 77. The decrease between 1897 and 1926 in the percentage of Jews who identified Yiddish as their mother tongue (from 97 to 70 percent) is an indication of the assimilation of Russian Jewry during these years. Notwithstanding, the percentage of the Jews who identified Yiddish as their mother tongue was still considerable in 1926.

10. Halevi, *My Road upon Stages* (in Hebrew), p. 39. It is noteworthy that in its first five seasons, (1918–1923), the Habima gave only 320 performances (64 performances per season as an average), and that *The Dybbuk* was performed only 300 times in four years (from January 1922 to January 1926).

11. Ben-Ari, *Habima*, p. 141.

12. *Ibid.*, pp. 30, 36; Grober, *Both Sides* (in Hebrew), p. 99.

13. Halevi, *My Road upon Stages*, p. 39.

14. Until the October Revolution, only five theaters received subsidies from the Palace Department. These were the Alexandrinsky, the Maryinsky, and the Mikhailovsky in Petrograd, and the Bolshoi and the Maly in Moscow.

15. The following discussion draws on Fitzpatrick, *Commissariat of Enlightenment*, pp. 139–61.

16. *Ibid.*, p. 144.

17. *Braun, Meyerhold on Theatre*, pp. 17–22, 75–80, 159–67.

18. Gorchakov, *Theater in Soviet Russia*, pp. 115–20; Slonim, *Russian Theater*, pp. 240–42.

19. Gorchakov, *Theater in Soviet Russia*, p. 197.
20. Norman, *Habima* (in Hebrew), p. 393.
21. *Ibid.*, pp. 393–94.
22. *Ibid.*, pp. 396–97.
23. *Ibid.*, pp. 398–99.
24. *Ibid.*, p. 399.
25. Interview with Binyamin Zemach.
26. Ben-Ari, *Habima*, p. 139.
27. This is apparent from two certificates issued by the Department of Academic State Theaters on July 13, 1923 and October 24, 1925. Norman, *Habima*, p. 399.
28. Vardi, *On My Path* (in Hebrew), pp. 153–54.
29. Ben-Ari, *Habima*, p. 84.
30. Simonov, *Stanislavsky's Protégé*, pp. 149–50; Yzraely, "Vakhtangov Directing," p. 34.
31. Huntley Carter, the theater historian, classified the Russian theaters of this period into three groups representing different political and artistic lines: the Left (Meyerhold, the Proletcult, etc.); the Center (the state theaters; and the Right (the Moscow Art Theater). See, e.g., his *Russian Theatre*, pp. 30–32.
32. Magarshack, *Stanislavsky*, pp. 353–76; Nemirovitch-Dantchenko, *My Life*.
33. Braun, *Meyerhold on Theatre*, pp. 159–80.
34. *Ibid.*, p. 168.
35. Gorchakov, *Theater in Soviet Russia*, pp. 120–23, 197–98.
36. *Ibid.*, p. 197.
37. Ben-Ari, *Habima*, p. 241.
38. *Ibid.*, pp. 239–40.
39. It should be pointed out that in 1921 Gorky helped Bialik and several other Hebrew writers get permits to leave Russia for Palestine.
40. Ben-Ari, *Habima*, pp. 148–50.
41. *Ibid.*, pp. 53–54.
42. Kirstof, "Critic and Commissar," pp. 25–28.
43. Andrey Zhdanov, the Party spokesman in the Writers Congress in 1934, quoted in Slonim, *Russian Theater*, p. 332.
44. Stalin, quoted in Slonim, *Russian Theater*, p. 333.
45. Gorchakov, *Theater in Soviet Russia*, p. 364.

FOUR: THE SOCIAL STRUCTURE OF THE HABIMA

1. Ben-Ari, *Habima*, pp. 232–33.
2. Norman, *Habima* (in Hebrew), p. 61.
3. Grober, *Both Sides* (in Hebrew), pp. 84–85; Gnessin, *My Way* (in Hebrew), pp. 116–17.
4. Nahirny, "Ideological Groups," pp. 398, 400.
5. Kohansky, *Hebrew Theatre*, p. 20; Halevi, *My Road upon Stages* (in Hebrew), p. 36.
6. Ben-Ari, *Habima*, p. 27.
7. Quoted in Kohansky, *Hebrew Theatre*, p. 19.
8. Meyer, *Soviet Political System*, pp. 28, 233, 329.
9. Ben-Ari, *Habima*, p. 145.
10. *Ibid.*

11. *Ibid.*, p. 21.
12. *Ibid.*, pp. 21–22.
13. *Ibid.*, p. 106.
14. *Ibid.*, p. 145.
15. Fitzpatrick, *Commissariat of Enlightenment*, p. 271.
16. Gorchakov, *Theater in Soviet Russia*, pp. 244–45.
17. Slonim, *Russian Theater*, pp. 241–42.
18. Halevi, *My Road upon Stages*, p. 33; Grober, *Both Sides*, p. 135.
19. Bertonoff, *Curtain* (in Hebrew), p. 186.
20. Simonov, *Stanislavsky's Protégé*, p. 146.
21. Interview with Tamar Robins.
22. Bertonoff, *Curtain*, pp. 67, 186.
23. Ben-Ari, *Habima*, p. 136.
24. Halevi, *My Road upon Stages*, pp. 73–74; Simonov, *Stanislavsky's Protégé*, p. 14.
25. Tchemerinsky, *Tchemerinsky's Book*, (in Hebrew) 1: 60–74.
26. Ben-Ari, *Habima*, p. 41.
27. Carter, *Russian Theatre*, p. 182.
28. Interview with Channele Hendler.
29. Vardi, *On My Path* (in Hebrew), p. 135.
30. Halevi, *My Road upon Stages*, p. 75.
31. Interview with Shlomo Bar-Shavit.
32. Ben-Ari, *Habima*, p. 245.
33. *Ibid.*, p. 240.
34. Duverger, *Political Parties*, pp. 119–26.
35. Elon, *The Israelis*, p. 118; Spiro, *Kibbutz*, p. 283.
36. Klinov, "Conversations with Rovina," *Davar*, September 28, 1945.

FIVE: THE HABIMA IN EUROPE AND THE UNITED STATES

1. Ben-Ari, *Habima*, p. 241.
2. Interview with Tamar Robins.
3. Ben-Ari, *Habima*, p. 159.
4. Kochan, *Jews in Soviet Russia*, p. 111.
5. Ben-Ari, *Habima*, p. 163.
6. "The Soviet Government Forbids the Habima to Meet with Zionists," *Davar*, October 20, 1926.
7. Ben-Ari, *Habima*, p. 163.
8. Hanoch and Schwartz, *Habima* (in Hebrew), pp. 12–13.
9. Ben-Ari, *Habima*, pp. 161–68.
10. Kohansky, *Hebrew Theatre*, pp. 77–79.
11. M. Ungfeld, "The Moscow Theater Habima in Vienna," *Haaretz*, June 11, 1926.
12. Hanoch and Schwartz, *Habima*, p. 13.
13. Kohansky, *Hebrew Theatre*, p. 79.
14. Ben-Ari, *Habima*, p. 163.
15. *Ibid.*, p. 139.
16. *Ibid.*, p. 173.

17. Kohansky, *Hebrew Theatre*, p. 80.
18. Norman, *Habima* (in Hebrew), p. 188.
19. Brooks Atkinson, review of *The Dybbuk, New York Times,* December 14, 1926.
20. Kohansky, *Hebrew Theatre*, p. 82.
21. Review of *The Golem, New York Times,* February 5, 1927.
22. Brooks Atkinson, review of *The Eternal Jew, New York Times,* December 21, 1926.
23. Kohansky, *Hebrew Theatre*, p. 82.
24. Lifson, *Yiddish Theatre*, pp. 579–80.
25. *Ibid.*, pp. 179–80.
26. Howe, *World of Our Fathers*, p. 207.
27. Ben-Ari, *Habima*, pp. 194–95.
28. *Ibid.*, p. 192.
29. Burns Mantle, ed., *The Best Plays of 1926–1927* (New York: Arno, 1976).
30. Ben-Ari, *Habima*, p. 86.
31. Protocol, the Habima Council, June 10, 1926, the Habima Archive, Tel-Aviv, Israel.
32. *Ibid.*, September 19, 1926.
33. *Ibid.*, December 22, 1926.
34. The majority group included Rovina, Meskin, Chemerinsky, Bertonov, and others.
35. Grober, *Both Sides* (in Hebrew), pp. 135–37; Ezra Lahad, "On the Split of the Habima," *Al Hamishmar*, October 18, 1968.
36. Interview with Binyamin Zemach.
37. Most of the actors who participated in the original production of *Jacob's Dream* (in Moscow) happened to stay on with Zemach in New York; this was one of the major reasons for the choice of this play.
38. Ben-Ari, *Habima*, p. 202.
39. *Ibid.*, p. 203.

SIX: THE SEARCH FOR A PERMANENT HOME

1. Klausner, *Habima Diary* (in Hebrew), pp. 16–17.
2. Interview with Binyamin Zemach.
3. Finkel, *Stage* (in Hebrew), p. 132.
4. A. Z., "Welcome to Habima," *Haaretz*, March 27, 1928.
5. S. Yavnieli, "After *The Golem* and *The Dybbuk*," *Davar*, June 3, 1928. The history of Palestinian immigration since the beginnings of the Zionist movement is conventionally divided into *Aliyot*, a series of successive waves of immigration: the First *Aliya* (1882–1904), the Second *Aliya* (1904–1914), the Third *Aliya* (1919–1924), and the Fourth *Aliya* (1924–1928).
6. Eliezer Steinman, "To the Habima," *Ktuvim*, March 15, 1928.
7. The Lovers of the Hebrew Stage performed in Palestine from 1904 to 1914; the Hebrew Theater was founded in 1920; the Dramatic Theater in 1922; the TAI (Teatron Eretz Israeli-Palestinian Theater) was established in Berlin in 1923 and settled in Palestine in 1924; the Ohel Theater was founded in 1925.
8. Chaim Harari, "The Habima in Palestine," *Haaretz*, May 11, 1928.
9. Y. Lufban, "The Habima in Palestine," *Hapoel Hatzair*, June 30, 1928.
10. K., "With the Habima," *Haaretz*, March 27, 1928.
11. Harari, "Habima in Palestine."

12. K., review of *The Golem, Haaretz,* April 1, 1928.
13. B. Y., review of *Jacob's Dream, Haaretz,* April 15, 1928.
14. Y. Norman, review of *The Dybbuk, Davar,* May 3, 1928.
15. Arian, *Ideological Change,* p. 73; Shapiro, *Organization of Power* (in Hebrew), pp. 16, 21–22.
16. Finkel, *Stage,* p. 136.
17. Kohansky, *Hebrew Theatre,* pp. 116–17.
18. Review of *The Treasure, Davar,* November 30, 1928.
19. Shlomo Zemach, "A People's Theater," *Haaretz,* December 14, 1928.
20. Keshet-Kopilowitz, "On the Spirit of the Habima," *Hapoel Hatzair,* December 21, 1928.
21. Kohansky, *Hebrew Theatre,* pp. 117–18.
22. Y. Lufban, review of *David's Crown, Hapoel Hatzair,* May 31, 1929.
23. Elisheva, review of *David's Crown, Davar,* July 9, 1929.
24. Discussion of *David's Crown, Haaretz,* June 17, 1929.
25. Kohansky, *Hebrew Theatre,* p. 118.
26. *Ibid.*, p. 119.
27. A. Kabak, "My Opinion," *Ktuvim,* June 27, 1929.
28. Zemach, "A People's Theatre."
29. Y. Norman, review of *David's Crown, Ktuvim,* May 30, 1929. Kabak, "My Opinion."
30. Klausner, *Habima Diary,* pp. 37–38.
31. Bialik, "For the Habima," *Haaretz,* July 6, 1928.
32. "The Performances of the Habima in the Valley," *Davar,* May 13, 1928.
33. Tchemerinsky, *Tchemerinsky's Book* (in Hebrew), 2: 71.
34. Klausner, *Habima Diary,* p. 51.
35. Shapiro, *Organization of Power,* pp. 22, 159, 163.
36. Protocol, the Habima Collective, January 31, 1929.
37. *Ibid.*, February 18, 1929.
38. Y. Klinov, Discussion of the Hebrew Theater in Berlin, *Doar Hayom,* November 15, 1929.
39. "The Hebrew Theatre Habima," *Youth and Nation* 15 (March 1947): 15.
40. Kohansky, *Hebrew Theatre,* p. 120.
41. *Ibid.*, p. 121.
42. Gorbin H. Wood, the drama critic of *Time and Tide,* quoted in Kohansky, *Hebrew Theatre,* p. 123.
43. *Ibid.*, pp. 124–25.
44. *Ibid.*, p. 121.
45. *Bama* (November 1933), 2: 11.
46. Klausner, *Habima Diary,* pp. 57–60.

SEVEN: IDEOLOGY AND REPERTOIRE: 1931–1948

1. Log, review of *Michal, Daughter of Saul, Davar,* January 16, 1941, quoted in Kohansky, *Hebrew Theatre,* p. 143.
2. Gamzu, review of *The Love of Zion, Haaretz,* July 20, 1947.
3. Liptzin, *Yiddish Literature,* pp. 66–68.
4. "Bialik on *Amcha,*" *Bama* (May 1933), 1:7–12.

5. Fichman, review of *Amcha, Moznaim,* January 26, 1933.

6. Log, review of *It Is Hard to Be a Jew, Davar,* December 14, 1936.

7. Hanoch, review of *It Is Hard to Be a Jew, Davar,* December 10, 1936.

8. Zussman, review of *Tevye the Dairyman, Davar,* December 31, 1943; Gamzu, review of *Tevye the Dairyman,* December 30, 1943.

9. Gurelik, review of *Children of the Fields, Haaretz,* July 5, 1935.

10. Luvrani, review of *Children of the Fields, Davar,* July 3, 1935.

11. Log, review of *Mirele Efros, Davar,* July 26, 1939.

12. Kohansky, *Hebrew Theatre,* p. 137.

13. Gurelik, review of *God, Man and the Devil, Haaretz,* October 23, 1940.

14. Log, review of *God, Man and the Devil, Davar,* October 23, 1940.

15. "A Jew Like Suess," *Haaretz,* August 1, 1933.

16. Klinov, review of *Professor Mannheim, Haaretz,* July 27, 1934. Practically the same review was written by several other critics.

17. Log, review of *The Merchant of Venice, Davar,* May 15, 1936.

18. Klinov, review of *The Merchant of Venice, Haaretz,* May 22, 1936.

19. S., "The Trial of Shylock in Tel-Aviv," *Haaretz,* June 28, 1936; *Bama* (October 1936), 11–12: 23–41.

20. Shofman, review of *I Will Live, Davar,* May 19, 1944.

21. Zussman, review of *I Will Live, Davar,* May 19, 1944.

22. Gamzu, review of *I Will Live, Haaretz,* May 12, 1944.

23. Gamzu, review of *Kiddush Hashem, Haaretz,* January 2, 1948.

24. Gurelik, review of *Watchmen, Haaretz,* August 27, 1937.

25. Discussion of *Watchmen, Bama* 16 (December 1937): 21–25.

26. Krupnik, review of *This Earth, Haboker,* quoted in Kohansky, *Hebrew Theatre,* p. 145.

27. Log, review of *This Earth, Davar,* quoted in Kohansky, *Hebrew Theatre,* p. 145.

28. Uriel, review of *The Return of the Sons, Yediot Acharonot,* January 5, 1945.

29. Kohansky, *Hebrew Theatre,* p. 120.

EIGHT: THE HABIMA AND THE JEWISH COMMUNITY OF PALESTINE

1. These were the Ohel theater, which will be examined in this chapter, and the Mateh (the Broom), a theater of political and social satire, founded in 1928.

2. The term "classical play" is used in the broadest and most general sense, and refers to any drama which has retained critical as well as popular favor over an extended period of time. "Contemporary plays" refers to those plays that were presented by the Habima within five years after they had been written. "Modern plays" are those which are neither "classical" nor "contemporary."

3. Lifschitz, "On the Theater in Palestine," *Haaretz,* December 17, 1934.

4. Lifschitz, "The Hebrew Theater in 1939," *Haaretz,* September 17, 1939.

5. *Bama* (May 1936), 10: 34–39.

6. Leopold Jessner, "On the Palestinian Theater and Its Mission," *Bama* 10 (May 1936): 3–7.

7. *Bama* (August 1940), vol. 25; (October 1940), vol. 26.

8. *Ibid.*

9. The Habima's file on *The Imaginary Invalid,* the Habima Archive.
10. Kohansky, *Hebrew Theatre,* p. 137.
11. Gamzu, review of *Marriage, Haaretz,* July 20, 1945.
12. Gurelik, review of *Bury the Dead, Haaretz,* May 9, 1937.
13. In 1965 the Habima presented a new production of *The Mother* (with Rovina); this also had a wide appeal (with 112 performances).
14. See, for instance, Gamzu, review of *Men of Russia, Haaretz,* April 6, 1943; and Zussman, review of *Morning Star, Davar,* December 20, 1942.
15. Kohansky, *Hebrew Theatre,* p. 139.
16. For a detailed discussion of the Habima's 1948 tour, see chapter 10.
17. Gordon Craig in the London *Times,* November 14, 1937.
18. The Habima's File of Statistics of Performances, the Habima Archive.
19. Klausner, "Reflections on the Future of the Habima," *Haaretz,* November 10, 1932.
20. Uri, Baratz, and Lavie, "To All the Settlements," *Hapoel Hatzair,* May 27, 1932.
21. Klausner, *Habima Diary* (in Hebrew), pp. 158–61; "Chug Habima," *Haaretz,* December 9, 1932; *Bama* (April 1938), 17: 68.
22. Klausner, *Habima Diary,* pp. 199–201.
23. Halevi, *My Road upon Stages* (in Hebrew), pp. 96–97.
24. *Ibid.*, p. 98.
25. *Ibid.*, pp. 102–3.
26. *Ibid.*, pp. 110–12.
27. Kohansky, *Hebrew Theatre,* p. 104.
28. Halevi, *My Road upon Stages,* pp. 163–65.
29. Kohansky, *Hebrew Theatre,* p. 132.
30. Of the five productions that were presented abroad, three were biblical (*Jacob and Rachel, Jeremiah,* and *Queen Esther*). The other two were *Peretz Evenings* and *The Lower Depths.*
31. Klausner, *Habima Diary,* pp. 41–43.
32. Gershony, "The Hebrew Theater in Palestine," *Doar Hayom,* October 17, 1931.

NINE: ORGANIZATIONAL STRUCTURE: THE ACTORS' COLLECTIVE

1. Shapiro, *Organization of Power* (in Hebrew), p. 200.
2. Spiro, *Kibbutz,* p. 4.
3. *Ibid.*, pp. 29–30.
4. The Constitution of the Habima Theater-A Cooperative Ltd., the Habima Archive.
5. *Ibid.*, paragraph 5.
6. *Ibid.*, paragraph 14.
7. *Ibid.*, paragraph 17.
8. The Habima By-Laws: Regulations of Internal Order and Discipline of the Moscow Theater Habima, Chapter 1, paragraph 1a.
9. Constitution, paragraph 18a.
10. On ideological collectivism in the kibbutz, see Spiro, *Kibbutz,* pp. 6, 198.
11. Gnessin, Protocol, the Habima Collective, October 8, 1948.
12. Ben-Ari, *Habima,* p. 117.
13. *Ibid.*, p. 118.

14. *Ibid.*
15. *Ibid.*, p. 145.
16. *Ibid.*, p. 46. Vakhtangov worked with each of the twelve beggars in *The Dybbuk* on the individual characterizations of their roles—each had his own life story and a specific physical deformity—although they were part of a group.
17. Constitution, paragraph 34.
18. Finkel, *Stage* (in Hebrew), p. 135.
19. Klausner, *Habima Diary* (in Hebrew), pp. 58, 97.
20. Protocol, the Habima Collective, February 14–16, 1930.
21. *Ibid.*, June 5, 1930; Klausner, *Habima Diary*, pp. 97–99.
22. Protocol, the Habima Collective, June 12, 1930.
23. *Ibid.*, January 17, 1944.
24. By-Laws, Chapter B, paragraphs 4–5.
25. Protocol, the Habima Artistic Committee, September 30, 1930.
26. Protocol, the Habima Council, April 8, 1926.
27. Constitution, paragraph 17a.
28. Protocol, the Habima Collective, July 3, 1933.
29. *Ibid.*, August 1, 1933.
30. *Ibid.*
31. *Ibid.*, February 21, 1944.
32. Shapiro, *Organization of Power*, pp. 162–63.
33. Klausner, *Habima Diary*, pp. 143, 153.
34. Protocol, the Habima Council, February 4, 1926.
35. Ben-Ari, *Habima*, pp. 164–65.
36. This editorial is quoted in Kohansky, *Hebrew Theatre*, p. 84.
37. By-Laws, paragraphs 19, 23.
38. Finkel, *Stage*, p. 148.
39. Uri Kesari, "Some Observations on the Habima," *Doar Hayom*, November 6, 1932.
40. Interview with Ada Tal.
41. Interview with Batya Lancet.
42. Constitution, paragraph 5.
43. Protocol, the Habima Board of Directors, July 16, 1932.

TEN: ORGANIZATIONAL STRUCTURE: ARTISTIC AND ADMINISTRATIVE DIRECTION: 1931–1948

1. Klausner, *Habima Diary* (in Hebrew), pp. 146–49.
2. Protocol, the Habima Collective, January 24, 1933; November 28, 1934.
3. *Ibid.*, February 11, 1934.
4. By-Laws, Chapter A, paragraphs 1b, 1d, 1h.
5. Constitution, paragraphs 4, 17b.
6. Finkel, *Stage* (in Hebrew); Hanoch, *Habima* (in Hebrew), pp. 201–205.
7. Protocol, the Habima Collective, June 26, 1929.
8. Finkel, *Stage*, p. 141.
9. These were: Yaakov Avital in 1931; Chaim Amitai, Shoshana Duer, and Niura Shein in 1932; and Bat-Ami Finkel and Ari Kutai in 1934.
10. Protocol, the Habima Collective, November 30, 1934.

11. *Ibid.*, September 12, 1932.
12. Protocol, the Habima Board of Directors, July 28, 1932.
13. Protocol, the Habima Collective, December 30, 1933.
14. Protocol, the Habima Board of Directors, July 29, 1932.
15. Constitution, paragraph 31.
16. For a discussion of this issue, see Simmel, *The Sociology of Georg Simmel*, pp. 90–93.
17. Protocol, the Habima Collective, December 2, 1934.
18. See Merton, *Social Theory and Social Structure*, pp. 346–47.
19. Interview with Shimon Finkel.
20. Protocol, the Habima Collective, December 29, 1942.
21. Protocol, the Habima Collective, December 3–4, 1934.
22. Klausner, *Habima Diary*, p. 208; Finkel, *Stage*, p. 190.
23. Especially noteworthy among Friedland's students were Nachum Buchman, Ada Tal, and Avraham Ninio, who later became leading actors of the Habima, and Batya Lancet, Hanna Maron, Yitzhak Shilo, and Yosef Yadin, who joined the Cameri in the forties and distinguished themselves as actors.
24. Finkel, *Stage*, pp. 200–201.
25. Protocol, the Habima Collective, December 18, 1944.
26. *Ibid.*, October 1, 1946.
27. *Ibid.*, September 30, 1946.
28. *Ibid.*, May 26, 1941.
29. Novak, "The Theater Is My Life's Love—An Interview with Zvi Friedland," *Davar*, June 24, 1966.
30. For a discussion of the relationship between Israel's young generation and the Cameri theater, see chapter 12.
31. Gamzu, "Twenty-Five Years of the Habima's Existence," *Haaretz*, October 22, 1943.
32. Bar-Yosef, "On the Problem of Cooperatives in the Theater," *Davar*, July 13, 1945.
33. These actors were: Amitai in 1944; Kutai, Ben-Zissi, and Shein in 1946; and Bat-Ami Finkel and Duer in 1947.
34. Protocol, the Habima Collective, August 15, 1946.
35. Tyrone Guthrie, "Impressions of the Habima," *Theatre Arts Monthly* (August 1947); 31: 32.
36. Protocol, the Habima Collective, April 20–22, 1947.
37. Brooks Atkinson, "Palestine's Habima Players Revive *The Dybbuk* Here as Homeland Faces Crisis," *New York Times*, May 3, 1948.
38. *Ibid.*
39. Review of *The Golem*, *New York Times*, May 17, 1948.
40. Finkel, *Stage*, pp. 209–10.
41. Feurstein, "The Causes of the Internal Crisis at the Habima," *Yediot Acharonot*, October 8, 1948.
42. Neuman, "The Habima—Where To?", *Davar*, October 15, 1948.
43. "Details of the Arrangement at the Habima," *Haaretz*, August 29, 1948.
44. Protocol, the Habima Collective, September 19, 1948.
45. Finkel's group included Meskin and Klutchkin as well as other excellent actors.
46. Protocol, the Habima Collective, September 20, 28, 1948.
47. Chermoni, "The Habima Opens Its Curtains," *Haolam*, December 2, 1948.

48. Protocol, the Habima Collective, September 28, 1948.
49. *Ibid.*, October 8, 1948.
50. *Ibid.*, September 28, 1948.

ELEVEN: IDEOLOGY AND REPERTOIRE: 1949–1968

1. Samuel Levy, "Critical Study of Habima Plays" pp. 29–32.
2. Kohansky, *Hebrew Theatre*, p. 161.
3. On *In the Wastes of the Negev*," *Davar*, March 2, 1949.
4. Interviews with Ada Tal and Shmuel Segal.
5. *Al Hamishmar*, February 18, 1949.
6. Gamzu, review of *In the Wastes of the Negev*, *Haaretz*, February 18, 1949.
7. *Hamashkif*, February 14, 1949.
8. See, for instance, Gamzu, review of *Hedva and I*, *Haaretz*, October 6, 1954; and Zussman, review of *I Like Mike*, *Davar*, September 28, 1956.
9. Rapaport, review of *I Like Mike*, *Maariv*, September 29, 1956.
10. This analysis of the kibbutz plays draws on Levy, "Critical Study of Habima Plays," pp. 29–68, although he classifies these plays differently.
11. For a discussion of the pioneer image and ideology, see Eisenstadt, *Israeli Society*, pp. 17–18, 147–48.
12. Arian, *Ideological Change*, p. 73. In 1951, for instance, there were 213 kibbutzim with 67,618 people constituting only 4.7 percent of the total population.
13. Samuel *Structure of Society*, pp. 67–81.
14. *Anne Frank* won both the Pulitzer Prize for best play and the Drama Critics Award for the best Broadway production.
15. See, for instance, Zussman, review of *The Diary of Anne Frank*, *Davar*, February 1, 1957.
16. Nahor, review of *The Diary of Anne Frank*, *Yediot Acharonot*, January 23, 1957.
17. A review quoted in Levy, "Critical Study of Habima Plays," pp. 85–86.
18. Nahor, review of *Children of the Shadow*, *Yediot Acharonot*, December 4, 1962; Ben-Ami, review of *Children of the Shadow*, *Maariv*, December 5, 1962.
19. Zussman, review of *The Deputy*, *Davar*, June 26, 1964; Nahor, review of *The Deputy*, *Yediot Acharonot*, June 21, 1964.
20. Horowitz, review of *The Deputy*, *Haaretz*, June 26, 1964.
21. Hanoch Bartov's remarks in the theater's program for *Each Had Six Wings*, the Habima Archive.
22. See, for instance, Gamzu, review of *The Neighborhood*, *Haaretz*, December 13, 1965; Nahor, review of *The Street of Stairs*, *Yediot Acharonot*, October 22, 1959.
23. Gamzu, review of *Each Had Six Wings*, *Haaretz*, July 4, 1958.
24. Zussman, review of *The Neighborhood*, *Davar*, December 17, 1965.
25. This discussion of *Most Cruel of All—the King* draws on Kohansky, *Hebrew Theatre*, pp. 168–69.
26. *Ibid.*, p. 168.
27. Gamzu, review of *Most Cruel of All—the King*, *Haaretz*, December 25, 1953.
28. Rapaport, review of *Most Cruel of All—the King*, *Maariv*, December 22, 1953.
29. Bar-Akiva, review of *Genesis*, *Bama* 14 (Spring 1962): 74.
30. Evron, review of *Genesis*, *Haaretz*, July 20, 1962.

31. *The Israeli Theatre 1961/1962*, Ezra Zussman, ed. (Tel-Aviv: The Israeli Center of the International Theatre Institute, 1963), p. 25.

32. Goldberg, review of *At the End of the Days, Davar,* June 12, 1950; Zussman, review of *At the End of the Days, Davar,* June 23, 1950.

33. Gamzu, review of *The Story of a Prince, Haaretz,* January 30, 1953. Gamzu wrote that he could understand the Habima's wish to present a nostalgic view of life in the ghetto, but he disagreed with the choice of this particular play.

34. "Israeli Drama During 25 Years of Israel's Statehood," in *The Israeli Theatre 1971/1972*, ed. Matti Megged (Tel-Aviv: The Israeli Center of the International Theatre Institute, 1973).

TWELVE: THE HABIMA AND ISRAELI SOCIETY

1. To keep abreast of latest developments, important new plays by European dramatists were often produced in Israel at about the same time as in the capitals of Europe, and on occasion even before productions in Paris, London, or New York. In 1963, for instance, the Habima presented Duerrenmatt's *The Physicists,* only two years after it had been written and prior to productions in many other world theater centers.

2. Gamzu, review of *The Siren, Haaretz,* May 25, 1951.

3. Neuman, review of *Barbara Blumberg, Davar,* December 16, 1949.

4. The Habima was officially recognized as the National Theater of Israel in October 1958, on the occasion of its fortieth anniversary. See the discussion of this issue in chapter 13.

5. See, for instance, Nahor, review of *Irma La Douce, Yediot Acharonot,* November 12, 1962; Gamzu, review of *A Flat to Let, Haaretz,* October 1, 1962; and Zussman, review of *Irma La Douce, Davar,* November 16, 1962.

6. *Irma La Douce* ran for 242 performances, with a total audience of 224,095; *Gigi* ran for 121 performances, and *A Flat to Let* for 90.

7. In 1948, the Jewish population numbered 716,678, of which 54.8 percent was from Europe and America, 35.4 percent Israeli-born, and 9.8 percent from Asia and Africa. But in 1951 out of a Jewish population of 1,404,392, 47.2 percent came from Europe and America, 27.6 percent from Asia and Africa, and 25.2 percent was Israeli-born. Between 1919 and 1948, the vast majority (87.8 percent) of immigrants came from Europe, whereas between 1948 and 1960, 53.4 percent of the immigrants who came to Israel were from Asia and Africa. For further details, see Statistical Abstract of Israel (Jerusalem: Government Printer, 1961), pp. 43, 86.

8. *Omanut Laam* (Art for the People) is a governmental program, established in 1966, which brings productions from all theaters to small towns and settlements.

9. Protocol, the Habima Board of Directors, May 23, 1962.

10. Protocol, the Habima Collective, June 13, 1962.

11. The Habima'a File of Statistics of Performances, the Habima Archive.

12. Until July 1962, the Habima had one hall, the Big Hall, which had opened in 1945 and seated 1,100 people. In December 1967, the Big Hall was closed for renovation; it reopened in March 1970.

13. These were: Yemima Millo, Yosef's wife, Avraham Ben-Yosef, Rosa Lichtenstein, and Batya Lancet. The following discussion of the Cameri theater draws on Kohansky, *Hebrew Theatre*, pp. 146–58.

14. Interview with Batya Lancet, one of the Cameri's founders and leading actresses.

15. These were: Sholem Aleichem's *Wandering Stars* in 1950, Sammy Groneman's *Queen of Sheba* in 1951, and Clifford Odets's *Awake and Sing* in 1952.

16. Interview with Batya Lancet; Shakow, *Theatre in Israel*, pp. 63–64.

17. Peter Frye was a graduate of Piscator's school in New York. He began to direct at the Cameri in 1949. Hy Kalus, a student of Lee Strasberg, began staging at the Cameri in 1954. Both Frye and Kalus worked at the Habima.

18. For instance, Nissim Aloni, Nathan Alterman, Ephraim Kishon, Moshe Shamir, Yigal Mossinson and others wrote plays for both the Habima and the Cameri.

19. *In the Wastes of the Negev* was the Habima's most popular production during the entire period; it ran for 227 performances, with a total audience of 248,007. *He Walked through the Fields* was given 171 performances in 1948, and another 130 times in 1956. The two versions were seen by 249,013 people.

20. Kohansky, *Hebrew Theatre*, p. 153.

21. Shakow, *Theatre in Israel*, p. 83.

THIRTEEN: ORGANIZATIONAL STRUCTURE: ARTISTIC AND ADMINISTRATIVE DIRECTION: 1949–1968

1. For a definition and discussion of generation units, see Mannheim, "The Problem of Generations," in his *Essays*, pp. 303–304.

2. Gamzu, "On Repertoire, Direction, and the Young Generation," *Haaretz*, July 11, 1947.

3. Intervview with Misha Asherov.

4. Protocol, the Habima Collective, February 3, 1953.

5. *Ibid.*

6. See Appendix 3. Chemerinsky passed away in 1946, Gnessin in 1951, and Baratz in 1952.

7. These were Shlomo Bar-Shavit, Nachum Buchman, Shraga Friedman, Pnina Perach, Shoshana Ravid, Shmuel Rudensky, Shmuel Segal, and Ada Tal. For a description of these actors, see Appendix 1.

8. Protocol, the Habima Collective, June 3, 1958.

9. *Ibid.* April 17–19, 1956.

10. Protocol, the Habima Board of Directors, December 28, 1954.

11. *Yediot Acharonot,* October 23, 1955, the Habima's File on the National Theater, the Habima Archive.

12. *Lamerhav,* April 1, 1956, the Habima's File on the National Theater, the Habima Archive.

13. Shenkar, "On Behalf of the Habima," *Haaretz,* June 17, 1956.

14. Zussman, "A State Theater?", *Davar,* November 4, 1955.

15. Fachter, "A State Theater or a Good Theater," *Davar,* December 30, 1955.

16. Meskin, Protocol, the Habima Collective, April 17, 1956.

17. Vardi, "A State Status for the Habima," *Yediot Acharonot,* January 27, 1956.

18. Finkel, *Stage* (in Hebrew), p. 255.

19. Apart from Zvi Friedland, who had been the theater's chief director in the pre-

statehood period, the three other staff directors were: Shraga Friedman, Israel Becker, and Avraham Ninio, all younger actors.

20. Protocol, the Habima Collective, June 3, 19, 1958. The two members on the Board that directed the theater were Misha Asherov and Shlomo Bar-Shavit, both younger actors; the other members were very old and were men of compromise.

21. Protocol, the Habima Collective, December 25, 1959.

22. For example, Chekhov's *Uncle Vanya* was presented only 13 times, Duerrenmatt's *The Marriage of Mr. Mississippi*, 20, and Hall's *The Long, the Short and the Tall*, 23.

23. Protocol, the Habima Board of Directors, April 10, 1961.

24. Bar-Shavit, *ibid.*, March 17, 1961.

25. Protocol, the Habima Collective, April 14, 1961.

26. *Ibid.*

27. *Ibid.*, April 17, 1961.

28. Protocol, the Habima Collective, June 15, 1962.

29. *Ibid.*

30. The tour repertoire included three plays: *The Dybbuk*, of course, and two Israeli plays, Bartov's *Each Had Six Wings* and Tomer's *Children of the Shadow*.

31. Bat-Ami, Protocol, the Habima Board of Directors, October 20, 1965.

32. Protocol, the Habima Collective, October 30, 1965.

33. See Appendix 3. In addition to the eight actors admitted in 1953 (most of whom became distinguished actors), the Habima admitted other young actors during the fifties and sixties. Especially noteworthy were Israel Becker and Miriam Zohar (the Habima's best dramatic actress) in 1954, Misha Asherov in 1956, and Elisheva Michaeli in 1960.

34. Ohad, "Who Will Save the Habima?", *Haaretz*, June 17, 1966.

35. It should be pointed out that both Bardini and Kalus demanded full powers and refused to be appointed by the collective because they knew that the same collective could dismiss them. Both directors refused to work under the various interest groups of the collective and made it clear that unless radical organized changes were made they could not accept the position. Protocol, the Habima Board of Directors, February 5, March 19, and September 24, 1967, and January 14, 1968.

36. Jesaja Weinberg, "Structural Changes in the Israeli Theatre," in *The Israeli Theatre 1969/1970* (Tel-Aviv: The Israeli Center of the International Theatre Institute, 1971).

FOURTEEN: THE SEARCH FOR AN ARTISTIC IDENTITY: 1969–1977

1. Finkel, *Margin of the Bill* (in Hebrew), p. 46.

2. Interview with Shimon Finkel; Boshes, "Give Finkel a Chance," *Haaretz*, August 21, 1970.

3. Finkel was appointed for three years; in 1973, his term was extended for another two.

4. *Ibid.*

5. Finkel, *Margin of the Bill*, p. 74.

6. These were Yehuda Efroni, Misha Asherov, Shlomo Bar-Shavit, Lia Konig, Tova Pardo, and Miriam Zohar.

7. Finkel, *Margin of the Bill*, p. 127.

8. Ohad, "A Theater on a Hot Tin Roof," *Haaretz*, June 29, 1973.

9. Interviews with Misha Asherov and Shlomo Bar-Shavit.

10. Naaman, "The Hopes and Dreams of the National Theater," *Yediot Acharonot*, March 7, 1975.

11. Guthrie, *Life in the Theatre*, p. 273.

12. Francis Merrill, "French Stage: Symbol of an Old Culture," *Theatre Arts* (November 1955), 39: 27.

13. The Habima's File of Statistics, the Habima Archive.

14. The Big Hall, with a seating capacity of 1,000, the Small Hall, with a seating capacity of 300, and the Habimartef, with a seating capacity of 150.

15. The Habima's File of Statistics, the Habima Archive.

CONCLUSION

1. Berger, *Sacred Canopy*, pp. 105–25.

2. See, for instance, O'Dea, *Sociology of Religion*, p. 37. O'Dea suggests that the process of secularization takes place on three levels: the intellectual, the cultic, and the organizational.

3. Merton, *Science, Technology and Society*, p. xix.

4. Nahirny, "Ideological Groups."

5. This expression is borrowed from Max Weber, who distinguished between people who live for and people who live off politics. See Hans W. Gerth and C. Wright Mills, trs., *From Max Weber: Essays in Sociology* (New York: Oxford University Press, 1946), pp. 77–156.

6. I have greatly benefited from the discussion of routinization by Berger and Luckmann in their *Social Construction of Reality*.

7. This discussion is based on Weber's famous theory of "the routinization of charisma"; see *Theory*, pp. 358–73.

8. In this sense, too, the Habima theater followed the dynamics of many bureaucratic organizations. This transformation is described in the sociological literature as the "displacement of goals," whereby "an instrumental value becomes a terminal value." In other words, "adherence to the rules, originally conceived as a means, becomes transformed into an end-in-itself." For a discussion of this matter, see Merton, *Social Theory and Social Structure*, p. 253.

Selected Bibliography

UNPUBLISHED MATERIAL

Asherov, Misha. Interview. Tel-Aviv, June 30, 1975.
Bar-Shavit, Shlomo. Interview. Tel-Aviv, June 16, 1975.
Bertonov, Shlomo. Interview. Tel-Aviv, June 26, 1975.
Bertonov, Yehoshua. Collection of private papers. The Theater Archive. Tel-Aviv University, Israel.
File of the Habima's Actors. The Habima Archive, Tel-Aviv.
File of the Habima's Productions. The Habima Archive, Tel-Aviv.
Finkel, Shimon. Interview. Tel-Aviv, June 11, 1975.
Friedland, Zvi. Collection of private papers. The Theater Archive. Tel-Aviv University, Israel.
Hendler, Channele. Interview. Tel-Aviv, June 29, 1975.
Kirstof, Jane. "Critic and Commissar: A. V. Lunacharskii on Art." Ph.D. dissertation, Columbia University, 1972.
Klausner, Margot. Interview. Tel-Aviv, June 13, 1975.
Klutchkin, Raphael. Interview. Tel-Aviv, June 20, 1975.
Lancet, Batya. Interview. Tel-Aviv, July 4, 1975.
Levy, Samuel. "A Critical Study of Habima Plays as an Expression of

Israeli Nationalism from 1948–1968." Ph.D. dissertation, Bowling Green State University, 1972.

Lipsey, Alfred. "The History of the Habimah Theatre." Master's essay, University of Southern California, 1941.

Protocols, the Habima Board of Directors, 1926–1968. The Habima Archive, Tel-Aviv.

Protocols, the Habima Collective, 1928–1968. The Habima Archive, Tel-Aviv.

Robins, Tamar. Interview. Tel-Aviv, June 22, 1975.

Segal, Shmuel. Interview. Tel-Aviv, June 25, 1975.

Tal, Ada. Interview. Tel-Aviv, June 24, 1975.

Yzraely, Yosef I. "Vakhtangov Directing *The Dybbuk*." Ph.D. dissertation, Carnegie-Mellon University, 1971.

Zemach, Binyamin. Interview. Jerusalem, July 1, 1975.

PUBLISHED MATERIAL IN HEBREW

Almagor, Dan, and Amikam Gurevich, eds. *Masach Acharon al Shraga Friedman* [Last Curtain on Shraga Friedman]. Tel-Aviv: Amikam, 1973.

Bamah [Stage]. Magazine. 1933–1948; 1959–1977.

Bernstein-Cohen, Miriam. *Ketipa Bayam* [A Drop in the Sea]. Tel-Aviv: Massada, 1971.

Bertonoff, Joshua. *Orot Mibead Lamasach* [Light behind the Curtain]. Tel-Aviv: Reshafim, 1969.

Davar. Newspaper. 1925–1968.

Finkel, Shimon. *Bama Uklaim* [On Stage and Backstage]. Tel-Aviv: Am Oved, 1968.

——. *Bemavoch Tafkidai* [In the Labyrinth of My Roles]. Tel-Aviv: Mifalei Tarbut Vechinuch, 1971.

——. *Beshulei Sach Hakol* (Margin of the Bill). Tel-Aviv: Eked, 1976.

Gnessin, Menachem. *Darki im Hateatron Haivri: 1905–1926* [My Way with the Hebrew Theater: 1905–1926]. Tel-Aviv: Hakibbutz Hameuchad, 1946.

Grober, Chayele. *Mishnei Zidei Hamasach* [On Both Sides of the Curtain]. Haifa: Sifroni, 1973.

Gur, Israel. *Hateatron Haivri* [The Hebrew Theater]. Jerusalem: Kiryat Sefer, 1958.

——. *Maamad Tarbuti Lateatron Beisrael* [A Cultural Status to the Theater in Israel]. Jerusalem: Bama, 1968.

Haaretz. Newspaper. 1918–1968.

Halevi, Moshe. *Darki Alei Bamot* [My Road upon Stages]. Tel-Aviv: Massada, 1954.

Hanoch Gershon. *Habima Bat Kaf He* [The Habima is Twenty-Five Years Old]. Tel-Aviv: Albom, 1946.

Hanoch, Gershon, and Shulamit Schwartz, eds. *Habima—Teatron Ivri Beeretz Israel* [Habima—Hebrew Theater in Palestine]. Tel-Aviv: Bama, 1937.

Hapoel Hatzair. Newspaper. 1928–1948.

Klausner, Margot. *Yoman Habima* [The Habima Diary]. Tel-Aviv: Moadim, 1971.

Klinger, Ruth, ed. *Sefer Haomanut Vehaomanim Beeretz Israel* [The Book of Art and Artists in Palestine]. Tel-Aviv: Yavneh, 1946.

Kutai, Ari. *Chaim Ubama* [Life and Stage]. Tel-Aviv: Yavneh, 1972.

Maariv. Newspaper. 1949–1968.

Norman, Yitzhak, ed. *Bereshit Habima* [The Birth of the Habima]. Jerusalem: The Zionist Library, 1966.

Shoam, Chaim. *Chazon Umetziut Badrama Haisraelit* [Challenge and Dream in the Israeli Drama]. Ramat-Gan, Israel: Bar-Ilan University Press, 1975.

Tamuz, Binyamin, ed. *Hateatron Hakameri* [The Chamber Theater]. Tel-Aviv: Haaretz Print, 1955.

Tavarski, Yohanan, and Shlomo Even-Shoshan, eds., *Avraham Baratz*. Tel-Aviv: Hakibbutz Hameuchad, 1955.

Tchemerinsky, Baruch. *Derech Hayezira shel Bamai Ivri* [Tchemerinsky's Book: vol. 1, The Path of Creation of a Hebrew Director]. Tel-Aviv: Laam, 1947.

——. *Peiluto shel Ish Habima* [Tchemerinsky's Book: vol. 2, The Activities of a Man from Habima] Tel-Aviv: Hamenorah, 1967.

Vardi David. *Bederech Hiluchi* [On My Path]. Tel-Aviv: Massada, 1950.

Vast Binyamin, and Ezra Lahad, eds. *Menachem Binyamini*. Tel-Aviv: The Habima Theater, 1962.

Yediot Acharonot. Newspaper. 1937–1948.

PUBLISHED MATERIAL IN ENGLISH

Abramovitz, Raphael. *The Soviet Revolution 1917–1939*. New York: International Universities Press, 1962.

Adams, Arthur E., ed. *The Russian Revolution and Bolshevik Victory*. Boston: D. C. Heath, 1966.

Albrecht, Milton. "Does Literature Reflect Common Values?" *American Sociological Review* (December 1956), 21: 722–29.

Albrecht, Milton, James Barnett, and Mason Griff, eds. *The Sociology of Art and Literature.* New York: Praeger, 1970.

Apter, David, ed. *Ideology and Discontent.* New York: Free Press, 1964.

Arian, Alan. *Ideological Change in Israel.* Cleveland: Case Western University Press, 1970.

Becker, Howard S. "Notes on the Concept of Commitment." *American Journal of Sociology* (July 1960), 66: 32–40.

Ben-Ari, Raikin. *Habima.* A. H. Gross and I. Soref, trs. New York: Thomas Yoseloff, 1957.

Ben-David, Joseph. *The Scientist's Role in Society.* Englewood Cliffs, N.J.: Prentice-Hall, 1971.

Bendix, Reinhard. "Industrialization, Ideologies, and Social Structure." *American Sociological Review* 24 (October 1959), 24: 616–23.

Berger, Peter L. *The Sacred Canopy.* Garden City, N.Y.: Doubleday, 1969.

Berger, Peter L. and Thomas Luckmann. *The Social Construction of Reality.* Garden City, N.Y.: Doubleday, 1966.

Billington, James. *The Arts of Russia.* New York: Horizon Press, 1970.

Braun, Edward, ed. *Meyerhold on Theatre.* New York: Hill and Wang, 1969.

Burns, Elizabeth. *Theatricality.* New York: Harper and Row, 1972.

Carr, Edward H. *The Bolshevik Revolution 1917–1923.* New York: Macmillan, 1952.

Carter, Huntley. *The New Spirit in the Russian Theatre.* London: Brentano's, 1929.

Clark, Barrett H. and George Freely, eds. *A History of Modern Drama.* New York: Appleton-Century Crofts, 1947.

Cole, Toby and Helen K. Chinoy, eds. *Directors on Directing.* New York: Bobbs-Merrill, 1963.

Coser, Lewis. *Men of Ideas.* New York: Free Press, 1965.

Dubnov, Shimon M. *History of the Jews in Russia and Poland.* 3 vols. I. Friedlander, tr. Philadelphia: Jewish Publication Society of America, 1946.

Duncan, Hugh D. *Language and Literature in Society.* Chicago: University of Chicago Press, 1953.

——. *Symbols in Society.* New York: Oxford University Press, 1968.

Duverger, Maurice. *Political Parties: Their Organization and Activity in the Modern State.* B. North and R. North, trs. London: Methuen, 1954.

Duvignaud, Jean. *The Sociology of Art.* Timothy Wilson, tr. New York: Harper and Row, 1972.

Eisenstadt, Shmuel N. *Essays on Comparative Institutions.* New York: Wiley, 1965.

——. *Israeli Society.* London: Weidenfeld and Nicolson, 1966.

Elon, Amos. *The Israelis.* New York: Holt, Rinehart, and Winston, 1971.

Erikson, Erik H. *Young Man Luther.* New York: Norton, 1958.

Etzioni, Amitai. *Complex Organizations.* New York: Free Press, 1971.

Feuer, Lewis S. *The Conflict of Generations.* New York: Basic Books, 1969.

Fitzpatrick, Sheila. *The Commissariat of Enlightenment.* Cambridge: Harvard University Press, 1970.

Freeman, Joseph, Joshua Kunitz, and Louis Lozowick. *Voices of October: Art and Literature in Soviet Russia.* New York: Vanguard Press, 1930.

Frumkin, Jacob, Gregor Aronson, and Alex Goldenwiser, eds. *Russian Jewry (1860–1917).* Mirra Ginsburg, tr. New York: Thomas Yoseloff, 1966.

Gans, Herbert. *Popular Culture and High Culture.* New York: Basic Books, 1974.

Gershoni, Gershon K. *The Hebrew Theatre.* Jerusalem: Israel Digest, 1963.

Gilboa, Yehoshua A. *The Black Years of Soviet Jewry, 1939–1953.* Y. Shachter and D. Ben-Abba, trs. Boston: Little, Brown, 1971.

Goodlad, J. S. *A Sociology of Popular Drama.* London: Heinemann Educational Books, 1971.

Gorchakov, Nikolai A. *The Theater in Soviet Russia.* E. Lehrman, tr. New York: Columbia University Press, 1957.

Gorchakov, Nikolai M. *The Vakhtangov School of Stage Art.* G. Ivanov-Mumjiev, tr. Moscow: Foreign Languages Publishing House, 1959.

Greenberg, Louis. *The Jews in Russia.* 2 vols. New Haven: Yale University Press, 1944.

Gross, Feiliks, ed. *European Ideologies: A Survey of Twentieth-Century Political Ideas.* New York: Philosophical Library, 1948.

Guthrie, Tyrone. *A Life in the Theatre.* New York: McGraw-Hill, 1959.

Halpern, Benjamin. *The Idea of a Jewish State.* Cambridge: Harvard University Press, 1961.

Howe, Irving. *World of Our Fathers.* New York: Harcourt Brace Jovanovich, 1976.

Huaco, George A. *The Sociology of Film Art.* New York: Basic Books, 1965.

Kochan, Lionel, ed. *The Jews in Soviet Russia since 1917.* London: Oxford University Press, 1970.

Kohansky, Mendel. *The Hebrew Theatre: Its First Fifty Years.* Jerusalem: Israel Universities Press, 1969.

Landis, Joseph, ed. *The Great Jewish Plays.* New York: Horizon Press, 1966.

Laqueur, Walter. *A History of Zionism.* London: Weidenfeld and Nicolson, 1972.

Laurenson, Diana and Alan Swingewood, *The Sociology of Literature.* London: MacGibbon and Kee, 1972.

Lifson, David S. *The Yiddish Theatre in America.* New York: Thomas Yoseloff, 1965.

Liptzin, Solomon. *The Flowering of Yiddish Literature.* New York: Thomas Yoseloff, 1963.

——. *A History of Yiddish Literature.* New York: Jonathan David, 1972.

Lounatcharsky, Anatoli V. *Théâtre et révolution.* Paris: François Maspero, 1971.

Lowenthal, Leo. *Literature and the Image of Man.* Boston: Beacon Press, 1957.

——. *Literature, Popular Culture, and Society.* Englewood Cliffs, N.J.: Prentice-Hall, 1961.

Lukacs, Georg. "The Sociology of Drama." In Eric Bentley, ed., *The Theory of the Modern Stage*, pp. 425–50. London: Penguin Books, 1968.

Madison, Charles A. *Yiddish Literature.* New York: Fredrick Ungar, 1968.

Magarshack, David. *Stanislavsky: A Life.* New York: Chanticleer Press, 1951.

Mannheim, Karl. *Ideology and Utopia.* New York: Harcourt Brace and World, 1936.

——. *Essays on the Sociology of Knowledge.* Paul Keckemeti, ed. London: Routledge and Kegan Paul, 1952.

Marx, Karl. *Selected Writings in Sociology and Social Philosophy.* T. B. Bottomore, tr. London: McGraw-Hill, 1964.

Marx, Karl and Friedrich Engels. *The German Ideology.* New York: International Publishers, 1946.

Mead, George H. *Mind, Self, and Society.* Charles Morris, ed. Chicago: University of Chicago Press, 1934.

Merrill, Francis E. "Stendhal and the Self: A Study in the Sociology of Literature." *American Journal of Sociology* (March 1961), 66: 446–53.

Merton, Robert K. *Social Theory and Social Structure.* Enlarged edition. New York: Free Press, 1968.

——. *Science, Technology, and Society in Seventeenth-Century England.* New York: Harper and Row, 1970.

Meyer, Alfred G. *The Soviet Political System.* New York: Random House, 1965.

Monaco, Paul. *Cinema and Society: France and Germany during the Twenties.* New York: Elsevier, 1976.

Munk, Erika, ed. *Stanislavski and America.* New York: Hill and Wang, 1966.

Nahirny, Vladimir C. "Some Observations on Ideological Groups." *American Journal of Sociology* (January 1962), 67: 397–405.

Nemirovitch-Dantchenko, V. *My Life in the Russian Theatre.* John Cournos, tr. New York: Theatre Arts Books, 1968.

O'Dea, Thomas F. *The Sociology of Religion.* Englewood Cliffs, N.J.: Prentice-Hall, 1966.

——. *Sociology and the Study of Religion.* New York: Basic Books, 1970.

Parsons, Talcott. "The Role of Ideas in Social Action." *American Sociological Review* (October 1938), 3: 652–64.

——. *The Social System.* Glencoe, Ill.: Free Press, 1951.

Picon-Vallin, Béatrice. *Le théâtre juif soviétique pendant les années vingt.* Lausanne: La Cité–L'Age d'Homme, 1973.

Samuel, Edwin. *The Structure of Society in Israel.* New York: Random House, 1969.

Samuel Maurice. *The World of Sholem Aleichem.* New York: Knopf, 1943.

Sandrow, Nahma. *Vagabond Stars: A World History of Yiddish Theater.* New York: Harper and Row, 1977.

Sayler, Oliver M. *The Russian Theatre under the Revolution.* Boston: Little, Brown, 1920.

——. *The Russian Theatre.* New York: Brentano's, 1922.

Shakow, Zara. *The Theatre in Israel.* New York: Herzl Press, 1963.

Shapiro, Yonathan. *The Organization of Power.* Tel-Aviv: Am Oved, 1975.

Shils, Edward A. "Centre and Periphery." In *The Logic Of Personal Knowledge: Essays Presented to Michael Polanyi,* pp. 117–30. London: Routledge and Kegan Paul, 1961.

Simmel, Georg. *The Sociology of George Simmel.* Kurt H. Wolff, tr. and ed. New York: Free Press, 1950.

Simonov, Ruben. *Stanislavsky's Protégé: Eugene Vakhtangov.* Miriam Goldina, tr. New York: Drama Book Specialists, 1969.

Slonim, Marc. *Russian Theater: From the Empire to the Soviets.* New York: World, 1961.

Spiegel, Shalom. *Hebrew Reborn.* Philadelphia: Jewish Publication Society of America, 1962.

Spiro, Melford E. *Kibbutz.* New York: Schocken Books, 1972.

Stanislavsky, Konstantin. *My Life in Art.* G. Ivanov-Mumjiev, tr. Moscow: Foreign Languages Publishing House, 1925.

Starkoff, Bernard J. *250 Selected Plays of Jewish Interest.* Ohio: Union of American Hebrew Congregations, 1945.

Toumanova, Nina A. *Anton Chekhov.* New York: Columbia University Press, 1960.

Walzer, Michael. *The Revolution of the Saints.* New York: Atheneum, 1972.

Weber, Max. *The Protestant Ethic and the Spirit of Capitalism.* New York: Scribner's, 1958.

——. *The Theory of Social and Economic Organization.* A. M. Henderson and Talcott Parsons, trs. New York: Free Press, 1964.

White, Harrison C. and Cynthia White. *Canvases and Careers: Institutional Changes in the French Painting World.* New York: Wiley, 1965.

Zborowski, Mark and Elizabeth Herzog. *Life Is with People.* New York: Schocken Books, 1962.

Znaniecki, Florian. *The Social Role of the Man of Knowledge.* New York: Harper and Row, 1968.

Index

Levy, Emanuel, 1946-
The Habima: Israel's national theater, 1917-1977 : a study of cultural nationalism / Emanuel Levy. -- New York : Columbia University Press, 1979.

xix, 346 p. : ill. ; 24 cm.
Based on the author's thesis, Columbia University, 1977.
Bibliography: p. [329]-336.
Includes index.

1. Habimah. 2. Jews--Intellectual life. 3. Israel--Intellectual life. I. Title

PJo JOCCxc 79-12486